The Use of the Jewish Scriptures in the Johannine Passion Narrative

INTERPRETING JOHANNINE LITERATURE

The Interpreting Johannine Literature series is born from the desire of a group of Johannine scholars to bring rigorous study and explicit methodology into the teaching of these New Testament texts and their contexts. This series explores critical and perspectival approaches to the Gospel and Epistles of John. Historical- and literary-critical concerns are often augmented by current interpretive questions. Therefore, both a variety of approaches and critical self-awareness characterize titles in the series. Hermeneutical diversity and precision will continue to shed new light on the multi-faceted content and discourse of the Johannine Literature.

Titles in the Series

The Use of the Jewish Scriptures in the Johannine Passion Narrative: That the Scripture May Be Perfected (2024) by David M. Allen

Reading John through Johannine Lenses (2021) by Stan Harstine

Follow Me: The Benefits of Discipleship in the Gospel of John (2020) by Mark Zhakevich

What John Knew and What John Wrote: A Study in John and the Synoptics (2020) by Wendy E. S. North

Come and Read: Interpretive Approaches to the Gospel of John (2019) by Alicia D. Myers and Lindsey S. Jodrey, eds.

The Use of the Jewish Scriptures in the Johannine Passion Narrative

That the Scripture May Be Perfected

David M. Allen

LEXINGTON BOOKS/FORTRESS ACADEMIC
Lanham • Boulder • New York • London

Published by Lexington Books/Fortress Academic
Lexington Books is an imprint of The Rowman & Littlefield Publishing Group, Inc.
4501 Forbes Boulevard, Suite 200, Lanham, Maryland 20706
www.rowman.com

86-90 Paul Street, London EC2A 4NE, United Kingdom

Copyright © 2024 by The Rowman & Littlefield Publishing Group, Inc.

All rights reserved. No part of this book may be reproduced in any form or by any electronic or mechanical means, including information storage and retrieval systems, without written permission from the publisher, except by a reviewer who may quote passages in a review.

British Library Cataloguing in Publication Information Available

Library of Congress Cataloging-in-Publication Data

Names: Allen, David M., 1972– author.
Title: The use of the Jewish scriptures in the Johannine Passion narrative : that the scripture may be perfected / David M. Allen.
Description: Lanham : Lexington Books/Fortress Academic, [2024] | Series: Interpreting Johannine literature | Includes bibliographical references and index. | Summary: "This book examines the use of Israel's Scriptures in the Fourth Gospel's account of Jesus' death. It pays particular attention to John's concept of scriptural fulfilment, and particularly the accompanying 'perfection' of Scripture in this regard; for John, the status of the Jewish Scriptures is enhanced by Christ's Passion"— Provided by publisher.
Identifiers: LCCN 2024006442 (print) | LCCN 2024006443 (ebook) | ISBN 9781978715608 (cloth) | ISBN 9781978715615 (epub)
Subjects: LCSH: Bible. John—Criticism, interpretation, etc. | Jesus Christ—Passion. | Bible. Old Testament—Quotations in the New Testament. | Bible. John—Relation to the Old Testament.
Classification: LCC BS2615.52 .A445 2024 (print) | LCC BS2615.52 (ebook) | DDC 226.5/06—dc23/eng/20240503
LC record available at https://lccn.loc.gov/2024006442
LC ebook record available at https://lccn.loc.gov/2024006443

∞™ The paper used in this publication meets the minimum requirements of American National Standard for Information Sciences—Permanence of Paper for Printed Library Materials, ANSI/NISO Z39.48-1992.

Contents

Acknowledgments	vii
Introduction	1
Chapter 1: Mapping the Territory	11
Chapter 2: Quotation Usage in John's Passion Narrative	37
Chapter 3: Allusion Usage in John's Passion Narrative	107
Chapter 4: The Implications of Scriptural Usage in John's Passion Narrative (1): For Israel's Scriptures	145
Chapter 5: The Implications of Scriptural Usage in John's Passion Narrative (2): For the Fourth Gospel	171
Conclusion	197
Bibliography	203
Index	219
About the Author	227

Acknowledgments

The bulk of this book was written whilst on study leave from my role at the Queen's Foundation, and I am grateful to the Principal and colleagues at Queen's both for enabling the period of leave, and also for ensuring that my responsibilities were covered during it. I am also grateful to students at Queen's who have been privy to the content of the work (consciously or otherwise!), and who have therefore contributed to its argument and overall shape.

My thanks go to colleagues within the Jewish Scriptures in Early Christianity (JSEC) Seminar, which provides a regular locus for stimulating, collegial engagement with the kind of matters this volume seeks to address. In particular, I would like to thank Professor Susan Docherty and Professor Catrin Williams for their suggestion to undertake the work in the first place.

Introduction

SCRIPTURE AND THE FOURTH GOSPEL

Writing toward the end of the twentieth century, New Testament commentator Martin Hengel wistfully opined: "It is strange that the question of John's interpretation of Scripture has been left fully in the shadows of research interests."[1] Despite the abundance of scholarship devoted to the Gospel of John and to its manifold presenting questions, Hengel perceived a comparative lacuna in respect of commentary on its engagement with Israel's Scriptures.[2] His anxiety has been somewhat addressed in recent years, however, with a veritable explosion of interest in the ways in which the Fourth Evangelist utilized Jewish scriptural texts.[3] Whether through addressing the form(s) or source(s) of a cited quotation,[4] whether through considering the function of the scriptural appeal,[5] whether considering its use of a particular text or theme,[6] whether through comparison with other gospel or Second Temple usage,[7] or whether focused on the very particularity and distinctiveness of the Johannine handling,[8] or, indeed, some or all of the above,[9] the evangelist's treatment of Israel's Scriptures is now foregrounded as an established theme within Johannine scholarship.[10]

Such a rise in scholarly interest is surely warranted. As with other early Christian texts, the Gospel of John engages extensively in scriptural interpretation, reflecting pre-existing traditions and techniques while also manifesting its own distinctive exegetical approaches. In terms of the various processes it employs—direct scriptural citation, use of more allusive echoes, or drawing on familiar characters, themes, and narratives from within Israel's Scriptures—John participates in an existing practice of contemporary scriptural engagement.[11] Scriptural usage stretches across the entire landscape of the Gospel, from its opening appeal to Gen 1.1 (John 1.1) through to its climactic claims for scriptural fulfillment in response to Jesus's death (John 19.36–37), and even to the reminder, albeit in more ambiguous terms, of the scriptural warrant for Jesus's resurrection (John 20.9). Along the way, the reader frequently encounters other points of scriptural reference, whether through formal citation (the appeal to Isa 54.13 in John 6.45, for instance) or via invocation of wider narratival and thematic parallels (for example, the correspondences between the respective heavenly feedings of Exodus 16 and John 6.1–14). More broadly, the evangelist avers that the Scriptures testify to Jesus (1.45; 5.39); John's Jesus himself claims to be the one about whom Moses wrote (5.46) and whose day Abraham rejoiced to see (8.56). On encountering Jesus, Philip likewise declares him to be the focus of the Mosaic and prophetic writings (1.45). When quoting Isa 6.10 (John 12.40) and building on the prophet's visual encounter with enthroned Lord (Isa 6.1–3), the Gospel concludes that Isaiah saw and testified to the glory of *Jesus* (12.41). Within the vision, Jesus becomes the enthroned one and, from the Fourth Evangelist's perspective, when Isaiah uttered the prophecy, he was avowedly speaking about the pre-existent Jesus.

Scripture therefore ends up effectively functioning as a "speaking character" within the Johannine narrative, a distinctive, maybe even the ultimate, testimony to Jesus's identity.[12] The gospel is composed to inculcate belief in Jesus (20.31), either for the first time or in ongoing fashion.[13] John's primary scriptural hermeneutic is therefore avowedly christological,[14] with both its purpose statement (20.31) and its Prologue determinative in this regard (cf. 1.1–4). Just as Scripture traditionally testified to the divine will, in the Fourth Gospel it also testifies to the will *of Jesus*, who is openly "one" with the Father (10.30; cf. also 17.21). Just as Scripture is used to evidence or justify the non-response to Jesus (especially 12.37–41; cp. Isa 53.1, 6.9–10), so it will—must, even—be used to articulate the *correct* response to him and specifically to the implications of his death. As Maarten Menken summarily observed: "[t]o John, the Scriptures, both their text and the history recorded in them, legitimate Jesus."[15]

Of course, Scripture is not the *only* testimonial agent within the Gospel of John—or even the only one within its Passion narration (cf. 19.35 and the witness of the Beloved Disciple). But it is surely the primary one, the only one to which the evangelist specifically ascribes fulfillment designation (19.28). Scripture is central to the Johannine evangelistic enterprise, it "forms the foundational narrative on which the Fourth Gospel is built,"[16] and presents an "indispensable reference point and scaffolding" for its argumentation.[17] It provides "the background, both structural and theological, for the development of the narratives of the new revelation of God in the Jesus of John's Gospel."[18] To put it another way, "a meaningful reading of the Gospel of John is impossible apart from the Hebrew Bible."[19] Schnackenburg sums up John's fundamental dependence on Scripture, opining: "This Gospel would be unthinkable without the O.T. basis which supports it."[20]

We note, though, one important caveat in this regard. Particularly when compared to its Synoptic counterparts, the Fourth Gospel contains less unambiguous, explicit use of the Scriptures in Jesus's *public* ministry. In chapters

1–12, scriptural quotation is occasionally invoked for testimonial support, along with a parade of other witnesses, and there is still frequent scriptural appeal undergirding the discussion (*inter alia* 1.23; 2.17; 6.31, 45; 10.34, 12.13–15). The Fourth Gospel also makes various appeals to Mosaic authority (3.14; 5.45–46; 7:22–23)—Scripture remains far from *absent* in chapters 1–12. But its usage there is more subtle, less foregrounded, and the reader encounters proportionately less direct, explicit appeal to scriptural warrant.

This changes in the Gospel's second half, however. If the scriptural underpinning for Jesus's ministry in the first part of the Fourth Gospel is more implicit, it becomes far more prominent in part two, reaching its pinnacle within John's account of Jesus's death.[21] The change of introductory formula from 12.38 onward to include various forms of πληρόω particularly demarks this shift,[22] presenting the first instance of a number of Johannine claims to the explicit *fulfillment* of Scripture.[23] Drawing on 12.38–41, Johannes Beutler rightly contends that "in all instances [from 12.38 onward], 'scripture' gives witness to details of the passion and death of Jesus,"[24] underlining the way in which the second half of the Gospel explicitly associates Jesus's death and direct scriptural fulfillment. But even with the shift 12.38 initiates, the volume of fulfillment claims still anticipates its greatest intensity; it is the Gospel's formal narration of Jesus's death, what is customarily termed the Johannine Passion Narrative (John 18–19), where the scriptural dimension is found at its most developed. The Gospel's appeal to scriptural fulfillment punctuates the Passion account with increased frequency, and reaches its crescendo moment at the very point of Jesus's death. His climactic τετέλεσται utterance (19.30) encapsulates, as we shall see, the ultimate fulfillment, or teleiosis, of Scripture (19.28).

Here, then, is the focus of this volume—the interrelatedness of these two themes: the death of the Johannine Jesus and the contribution of Israel's Scriptures. Although much has been written about the different aspects of how John portrays Jesus's death, bringing forth many laudable studies,[25] and while, as noted above, the nature of John's *biblisch* usage has generated significant recent attention, it remains the case that both streams have not been brought together into one overall assessment of the subject.[26] The task of this volume is to address that lacuna, and to bring together both interconnected themes. We are seeking to offer a coherent assessment of the use of Israel's Scriptures in John's Passion Narrative, and to the interpretative implications that so arise. How specifically are Israel's Scriptures used to speak of Jesus's death, and what is distinctive about John's approach in so doing? We will suggest that these two foci are mutually intertwined and reinforcing, two sides of the same coin even. Scripture is fundamental to the Fourth Gospel's portrayal of Jesus's Passion, and attending to the full contours of John's use of the Old

Testament is necessary to tease out the overall significance of Jesus's death. Scripture provides the authentic heartbeat for John's Passion Narrative.

As such, we will consider the various ways in which John evokes the Jewish Scriptures within its Passion retelling, drawing particular attention to the fulfillment characterization with which John invests them. This is integral to the thesis we are outlining in respect of John's scriptural usage, and we will be considering the various "micro" fulfillment claims raised by the respective individual texts the Fourth Gospel cites (particularly, but not limited to, 19.24, 19.28 and 19.36–37). Alongside this, we will also consider the "macro" implications of the Johannine approach. Scripture is the central ingredient for John's retelling of Jesus's death, but in so doing, Scripture—and the very notion of what Scripture *is*—is impacted by its participation in John's cruciform discourse. That is, rather than being limited merely to those specific texts explicitly cited, Scripture *as a whole* is fulfilled. Particularly in 19.28–30, rather than merely discrete, individual texts, the Fourth Gospel addresses a wider curvature of scriptural discourse.[27] Taking the fulfillment claim set in motion by 12.38 to its climax, we will argue that John's Passion account narrates the culminative key to the *whole* of Scripture. When Jesus says "it is finished," he speaks not just of his own work, but also that of Scripture itself—his death impacts the very essence of what Scripture is and claims to be.

We will therefore want to explore the nature of that fulfillment (both micro and macro) and what it so entails. The Fourth Gospel, we will argue, claims Jesus's death enacts the completion, the perfection even, of Scripture, what we might term its formal teleiosis. Rather than bringing an end to Scripture's function, the converse is true; Jesus's death effects a new stage of its completeness. It is "elevated" to a shared status with Jesus's own words, and in addressing itself to Jesus's death, Scripture reaches its telos, its goal, its ultimate purpose. Albeit in its own particular fashion, and albeit manifesting numerous modes of scriptural association, the Fourth Gospel provides an exemplary articulation of both how Christ's death was understood κατὰ τὰς γραφὰς (1 Cor 15.3), and, in the light of his death, what that then means for the status of those Scriptures.

So thus far, we have two core, interrelated facets to the thesis this volume is setting forth: i) Scripture is fundamental to John's portrayal of Jesus's death, and ii) Scripture's ultimate function and status are changed by its participation in John's Passion retelling. But there is also more to be said, a third element to our discourse. Because of the deep interrelatedness of Israel's Scriptures and the Johannine Jesus, we will also want to explore the implications of the evangelist's scriptural usage, not just for Israel's Scriptures, but for the status of the Fourth Gospel too. That is, John itself is also impacted by its scriptural engagement—it is not left unaffected by its capacity for pronouncing the teleiosis of Scripture. John's use of Israel's Scriptures, and particularly its claim to pronounce the perfection of Scripture, is inextricably linked to the articulation of its *own* scriptural credentials. As we shall seek to explore, the Fourth Gospel places Jesus's words on the same footing as Scripture. As his disciples recall Jesus's citation of scriptural testimony in John 2.17 (Ps. 69.9), their subsequent, post-resurrection "belief" is equated with their remembrance of Jesus's words (2.22). Jesus's testimony and prophetic utterance thus assume similar authority to that of Scripture in terms of fulfillment expectation (cf. 18.9, 32).[28] The testimony of Jesus found within the Fourth Gospel thereby assumes quasi-scriptural status, and, as we shall argue in the later chapters, John presents its account avowedly *as Scripture*.

In sum, we propose that the Fourth Gospel itself is vindicated by its appeal to the Jewish Scriptures, particularly in its narration of Jesus's death, and specifically that its own scriptural credentials are evidenced by the overall appeal to Scripture. The full *telos*, and thus the whole question of what comprises Scripture, is encapsulated within the Passion retelling. John's Passion doesn't merely affirm Scripture; it fulfills it, elevates it, perfects it, and in so doing, it self-avowedly, self-consciously articulates its own scriptural credentials. Here, then, is our threefold thesis which the rest of the volume will seek to unpack:

1. More than any other element, Scripture is core to John's making sense of Jesus's death—it is the *sine qua non* ingredient of John's evangelistic initiative.
2. Scripture is impacted by its usage in John's Passion retelling—it is completed, fulfilled, and ultimately perfected, through the death of the Johannine Jesus.
3. And in this way, John's own Scriptural credentials are attested. John thinks of itself as Scripture, and this is particularly manifest in terms of its claim to perfect Israel's Scriptures.

MOVING FORWARD

How then will we proceed? In chapter 1, we begin by mapping the territory around which our argument will develop, considering the methodological issues raised therein. We will consider the concept and scope of the pre-existing Passion narrative, and its form within the Fourth Gospel. We will propose that John's Passion account is chapters 18–19, hence scoping out the resurrection narrative from our enquiry. This then leads onto some further consideration of the wider relationship between Jesus's death and Israel's scriptures, and particularly the notion that Christ died *according to* those Scriptures. How does John's account speak to such matters? Finally, chapter 1 turns to consider the intertextual approach we will invoke, and the role of the reader with that. How do we go about assessing John's Scriptural usage? How is John evoking intertextual links and with what effect?

The subsequent chapters turn to the Johannine text itself. John's use of scriptural citation and reference is something of a "matrix,"[29] and chapters 2 and 3 seek to map that matrix from a variety of angles and perspectives. Within discourse on early Christianity's appeal to the Jewish Scriptures, the use of quotations has tended to be the starting point for discussion as they are the overtly signalled or explicit points of connection. The prominence of quotations in John's account of Jesus's death is commensurate with this, and chapter 2 is devoted to consideration of these signalled quotations. Their emphasis on fulfillment—and the bizarre nature of the texts for which fulfillment is sought—warrant consideration in and of themselves, and in some detail. The differing text forms that John utilizes, and the *Vorlage* questions so raised, are also significant. As such, the quotations may be said to give a framework to the Passion account, a skeleton upon which John can pattern its paschal narration.

But at the same time, the quotations do not exhaust John's engagement with scriptural warrant or with its patterning of the Scriptures. John's web of intertextual connections extends to include more allusive forms of engagement, echoes—of different levels of volume, perhaps—that draw on John's scriptural heritage. To such matters we turn in chapter three. Here we tease out particular scriptural themes or motifs on which the Fourth Gospel draws—images such as creation, Adam and Eve, Israel's Passover, or the Suffering Servant.

This leads onto the next two chapters, in which we consider the significance of the Fourth Gospel's use of Scripture in its Passion Narrative. What are the implications, for both the Fourth Gospel and Scripture itself, of the intertextual encounter John's Passion retelling instigates? In chapter 4, we focus on how their Passion usage impacts upon Israel's Scriptures, how their status and authority are enhanced by the experience. We will suggest that the very concept of Scripture changes—it is not just fulfilled, it is brought to *perfection* through the agency of Jesus's death. In the following chapter, we extend the discussion to the third part of our thesis, and to the Fourth Gospel's own Scripture/γραφή status manifestation, occasioned by its Passion fulfillment of Scripture. We consider how the Passion Narrative evinces this scriptural claim, and then move to explore the ramifications for reading other parts of the Fourth Gospel in this light, inviting an intratextual as well as an intertextual perspective.

Our final chapter brings the discussion to a conclusion. It draws together the three elements of our core thesis and offers some final reflections on

John's Passion Narrative's scriptural usage, and what it entails for the concept of Scripture as a whole.

NOTES

1. Martin Hengel, "The Old Testament in the Fourth Gospel," *HBT* 12 (1990): 24.

2. Some terminological clarification is in order. Within this book, we use the term "s/Scripture" for mediating the Fourth Gospel's use of γραφή terminology and the implied authority invested therein. However, such terminology implies neither theological inspiration nor canonical authority. See the discussion of the scope of γραφή within chapter 4.

3. For helpful reviews/summaries of recent work in this area, see Alicia D. Myers, "Abiding Words: An Introduction to Perspectives on John's Use of Scripture," in *Abiding Words: The Use of Scripture in the Gospel of John,* ed. Alicia D. Myers and Bruce G. Schuchard, SBLRBS 81 (Atlanta: SBL, 2015), 1–20, who identifies three strands of scholarly approach—sources/methods/function; Ruth Sheridan, *Retelling Scripture: 'The Jews' and the Scriptural Citations in John 1:19–12:15*, BibInt 110 (Leiden: Brill, 2012); Bruce G. Schuchard, "Temple, Festivals and Scripture in the Gospel of John," in *The Oxford Handbook of Johannine Studies,* ed. Judith Lieu and Martinus C. de Boer (Oxford: Oxford University Press, 2018), 381–95, who offers an overall review of recent scholarship on the theme; Michael A. Daise, *Quotations in John: Studies on Jewish Scripture in the Fourth Gospel*, LNTS 610 (London: T&T Clark, 2020), 1–28; Kyle R. L. Parsons, "Search the Scriptures: A Survey of Approaches to the Use of Scripture in the Fourth Gospel," in *Biblical Interpretation in Early Christian Gospels. Volume 4: The Gospel of John*, ed. Thomas R. Hatina, LNTS 613 (London: T&T Clark, 2020), 1–28 separates his discussion into the categories of "historical," "literary," and "media."

4. Bruce G. Schuchard, *Scripture within Scripture: The Interrelationship of Form and Function in the Explicit Old Testament Citations in the Gospel of John,* SBLDS 133 (Atlanta: Scholars Press, 1992); Martinus J. J. Menken, *Old Testament Quotations in the Fourth Gospel: Studies in Textual Form* (Kampen, Netherlands: Kok Pharos, 1996); Daise, *Quotations in John.*

5. Andreas Obermann, *Die Christologische Erfüllung der Schrift im Johannesevangelium: Eine Untersuchung zur Johanneischen Hermeneutik Anhand der Schriftzitate*, WUNT 2/83 (Tübingen: Mohr Siebeck, 1996); Judith Lieu, "Narrative Analysis and Scripture in John," in *Old Testament in the New Testament: Essays in Honour of J.L. North,* ed. Steve Moyise (Sheffield: Sheffield Academic Press, 2000), 144–63; Jaime Clark-Soles, *Scripture Cannot Be Broken: The Social Function of the Use of Scripture in the Fourth Gospel* (Leiden: Brill, 2003); Alicia D. Myers, *Characterizing Jesus: A Rhetorical Analysis on the Fourth Gospel's Use of Scripture in its Presentation of Jesus*, LNTS 458 (London: T&T Clark, 2012); Sheridan, *Retelling*; Ruth Sheridan, *The Figure of Abraham in John 8: Text and Intertext*, LNTS 619 (London: T&T Clark, 2020).

6. Maarten J. J. Menken, "The Minor Prophets in John's Gospel," in *The Minor Prophets in the New Testament* ed. M. J. J. Menken and Steve Moyise, LNTS 377 (London: T&T Clark, 2009), 79–96; Maarten J. J. Menken, "Genesis in John's Gospel and 1 John," in *Genesis in the New Testament*, ed. Steve Moyise and Maarten Menken, LNTS 466 (London: T&T Clark, 2012), 83–98; Wiliam Randulph Bynum, "Quotations of Zechariah in the Fourth Gospel," in *Abiding Words: The Use of Scripture in the Gospel of John*, ed. Alicia D. Myers and Bruce G. Schuchard, SBLRBS 81 (Atlanta: SBL, 2015), 47–74.

7. Richard B. Hays, *Reading Backwards: Figural Christology and the Fourfold Gospel Witness* (London: SPCK, 2015); Richard B. Hays, *Echoes of Scripture in the Gospels* (Waco, TX: Baylor University Press, 2016).

8. Alicia D. Myers and Bruce G. Schuchard, *Abiding Words: The Use of Scripture in the Gospel of John* (SBLRBS 81; Atlanta: SBL, 2015); Rekha M. Chennattu, "Scripture," in *How John Works: Storytelling in the Fourth Gospel* ed. Douglas Estes and Ruth Sheridan, RBS 86 (Atlanta: SBL Press, 2016), 171–86; Schuchard, "Temple," 381–95; Karen H. Jobes, *John: Through Old Testament Eyes* (Grand Rapids, MI: Kregel Academic, 2021).

9. As we shall suggest, such differentiation/categorization of lenses and approaches has heuristic and explanatory value, but equally they can/do blend into each other, and an approach may end up being more composite in terms of character. Attention to the textual form of a cited quotation, for example, inevitably impacts upon its function within the Gospel text. Likewise, historical-critical study of form and redaction can also be helpfully juxtaposed alongside more reader-orientated assessments of John's approach. See for example Bruce G. Schuchard, "Form Versus Function: Citation Technique and Authorial Intention in the Gospel of John," in *Abiding Words: The Use of Scripture in the Gospel of John*, ed. Alicia D. Myers and Bruce G. Schuchard SBLRBS 81 (Atlanta: SBL, 2015), 23–45.

10. Cf. its inclusion as a distinct entry within the recent Judith Lieu and Martinus C. de Boer, *The Oxford Handbook of Johannine Studies* (Oxford: Oxford University Press, 2018).

11. Jörg Frey, *Theology and History in the Fourth Gospel: Tradition and Narration* (Waco, TX: Baylor University Press, 2018), 162.

12. Michael Labahn, "Scripture Talks Because Jesus Talks: The Narrative Rhetoric of Persuading and Creativity in John's Use of Scripture," in *The Fourth Gospel in First-Century Media Culture*, ed. Anthony Le Donne and Tom Thatcher, LNTS 426 (London: T&T Clark, 2011), 133–54. On the particular rhetorical ways in which John uses Scripture to characterize Jesus, see Myers, *Characterizing Jesus*. So also Hays, *Reading Backwards*, 82: "the identity of Jesus is deeply embedded in Israel's texts and traditions."

13. The textual variation in 20.31—whether the present or aorist form of πιστεύω— keeps both options open, and significantly so, one suggests.

14. And this ties in with the prevailing character and purpose of the Fourth Gospel—cf. Jean Zumstein, "The Purpose of the Ministry and Death of Jesus in the Gospel of John," in *The Oxford Handbook of Johannine Studies*, ed. Judith Lieu and Martinus C. de Boer (Oxford: Oxford University Press, 2018), 332: "John's story is

basically a Christological story: the person of Jesus, his history and meaning, are the focus of the Gospel."

15. Martinus J. J. Menken, "Observations on the Significance of the Old Testament in the Fourth Gospel," *Neot* 33 (1999): 140.

16. Myers, *Characterizing Jesus*, 1.

17. Lieu, "Narrative," 143. She continues: "it is Scripture that makes the Gospel 'work'" (143).

18. Chennattu, "Scripture," 173.

19. Jean Zumstein, "Intratextuality and Intertextuality in the Gospel of John," in *Anatomies of Narrative Criticism: The Past, Present, and Futures of the Fourth Gospel as Literature*, ed. Tom Thatcher and Stephen D. Moore (Atlanta: Society of Biblical Literature, 2008), 128. Zumstein uses the nomenclature of "Hebrew Bible" rather than "Old Testament" for well-established, appropriate reasons, but as we shall see, it is the Old Greek or LXX textual form that seems to be the most significant one for the Fourth Gospel's purposes.

20. Rudolf Schnackenburg, *The Gospel According to St John*, vol. 1 (Tunbridge Wells, UK: Burns & Oates, 1968), 1.124.

21. Susanne Luther, "The Authentication of the Narrative: The Function of Scripture Quotations in John 19," in *Biblical Interpretation in Early Christian Gospels. Volume 4: The Gospel of John*, ed. Thomas R. Hatina, LNTS 613 (London: T&T Clark, 2020), 161: "The climax of the Johannine narrative, namely the account of the crucifixion and death of Jesus (John 19:17–37), is interrupted repeatedly by Scripture quotations."

22. See Craig A. Evans, "On the Quotation Formulas in the Fourth Gospel," *BZ* 26 (1982): 79–83.

23. So also John 12.40, 13.18, 15.25, 19.24, 19.28, 19.36, 19.37.

24. Johannes Beutler, "The Use of 'Scripture' in the Gospel of John," in *Exploring the Gospel of John: In Honor of D. Moody Smith*, ed. R. Alan Culpepper and C. Clifton Black (Louisville, KY: Westminster John Knox, 1996), 158.

25. Most notably perhaps Gilbert van Belle, *The Death of Jesus in the Fourth Gospel* (Leuven: Leuven University Press, 2007).

26. Ruth Sheridan, "They Shall Look Upon the One They Have Pierced: Intertextuality, Intra-Textuality and Anti-Judaism in John 19.37," in *Searching the Scriptures: Studies in Context and Intertextuality*, ed. Craig A. Evans and Jeremiah Johnston, LNTS 543 (London: T&T Clark, 2015), 192n3, rightly points out that, however surprisingly, no monograph currently exists on the use of the Jewish Scriptures in the Fourth Gospel's Passion Narrative.

27. Beutler, "Use," 148 lists several leading Johannine commentators who concur with him on this point.

28. Wendy E. S. North, *A Journey Round John: Tradition, Interpretation and Context in the Fourth Gospel*, LNTS 534 (London: T&T Clark, 2015), 54–55.

29. Andreas J. Köstenberger, "The Use of the Old Testament in the Gospel of John and the Johannine Epistles," *SwJT* 64 (2021): 54.

Chapter 1

Mapping the Territory

Before we turn to the Johannine text and begin to explore the threefold thesis we have proposed, some initial mapping and contextual orientation will be beneficial to our enquiry. Three matters warrant further clarification. First, we will want to give a broad overview or map of John's Passion Narrative, the raw material with which we are working. What is the scope of that account—what are we including within it, and what are we excluding from our inquiry? As part of this, we will want to establish some further boundary markers, such as how/whether we will address the other (Synoptic) accounts of Jesus's death and assess their similarity to and difference from John's testimony. Second, we will want to situate—if only briefly—how John's scriptural usage in respect of Jesus's death fits within the broader New Testament (NT) construal. That is, if Scripture is indeed the heartbeat of John's Passion account, how does that relate to the wider NT perception of Jesus's death being according to the Scriptures (1 Cor 15.3—κατὰ τὰς γραφὰς)? To what extent does John's distinctive appeal to Scriptural *fulfillment*, for example, distinguish it from say Paul or Hebrews? And/or are there aspects of the NT's understanding of Jesus's death being κατὰ τὰς γραφὰς to which we will want to be attentive as we consider the Johannine portrayal? And third, we will also need to set down some methodological principles for our subsequent analysis. Our approach will be essentially intertextual, but the latter can be a somewhat ambiguous, multi-layered term, so some precision and clarity will be necessary in that regard.

THE JOHANNINE PASSION NARRATIVE

It barely warrants any justification to say that Jesus's death is the focal point of the Fourth Gospel, exhibiting its very culmination and climax.[1] The cross lingers across the Johannine account, from the Baptist's programmatic proclamation of 1.29, through several "lifting up" references dotted across the

Signs discourse (3.14, 8.28), and with its outcome formally and conclusively confirmed to the audience in 12.32–33. For the Gospel of John, the death of Jesus is the ultimate revelation of Jesus's divine glory, his crucifixion on a Roman cross ironically enacting the completion of Jesus's God-given task (cf. 19.28–30).[2] Alan Culpepper, attuned as anyone to the narrative shaping of Fourth Gospel, contends that the Passion Narrative is the "heart of the Gospel of John,"[3] its focal window, the place where John's evangelistic purposes are at their most foregrounded. Likewise, Robert Fortna ventures that the Fourth Gospel could be conceived of as "one extended passion narrative"; Jesus's death "stands at the heart of its message," and its essence is what makes the Friday "Good."[4] It is the fitting and anticipated climax to the entire Johannine account, to the extent that "the Passion in John encompasses nearly the whole of the Gospel."[5] With some justification, Jörg Frey contends that Martin Kähler's famous characterization of Mark as a "Passion Narrative with an extended introduction" more fittingly extends instead to John's evangelistic portrayal.[6]

Although Jesus's death is thematic for the whole of the Fourth Gospel, our concern is the specific narration of his death, what is customarily termed the Passion Narrative, and the particular scriptural usage found therein. However, whatever gospel account one uses, determining the precise contours of the Passion Narrative remains something of a subjective assessment. A primary question is simply where it might be said to begin, and John potentially sends different messages in this regard. For example, it has become commonplace to label the second block of the Fourth Gospel (chapters 13–20) as the "Book of the Passion" rather than the "Book of Glory,"[7] and such nomenclature should not be overlooked. As we shall see, consideration of the Johannine Passion Narrative's engagement with the Jewish Scriptures bleeds over into chapters 13–17 (and vice versa), and the resurrection account, even if absent of formal citation, likewise carries some element of the Passion's scriptural baggage.[8] Equally, the moment when Jesus issues the invitation to depart the upper room (14.31) might also be seen as initiating the "Passion" encounter, and/or heralding the moment from which Jesus heads to his death.[9] The fact that the group do not then leave until 18.1 complicates matters, and reinforces the way in which the boundaries of the Passion Narrative, however defined, will always remain somewhat blurred.[10]

But some formal definition of its parameters is still required, however. We shall consider John's Passion Narrative as comprising chapters 18–19, and there are good reasons for so doing. On the one hand, it marks the point when the Upper Room is departed, and this makes it—generally speaking—the unit that most other Johannine scholars point to when specifying the Passion Narrative's boundaries.[11] On the other hand, chapters 18–19 evince a discrete "narrative" of Jesus's death, one that might be said to exist independently *within* the Book of Glory or Book of the Passion. The unit presents, as Stibbe avers, a story in its own right;[12] it stands on its own two feet and exhibits structural markers in that way. For example, the narrative both begins and ends in a garden location (John 18.1, 19.41–42). Gardens, albeit different ones, bookend the discourse, a feature which, as we shall suggest in chapter 3, generates significant scriptural evocation.

There are admittedly other ways of calibrating the structure of the events surrounding Jesus's death. An *inclusio* of sorts, for example, functions between 12.38–40 and 19.36–37 in terms of them being the first and last use of fulfillment introductory formulae, and that could function to bind 12.38–19.37 together as a discrete unit.[13] Or such unity might equally be found between 12.13–15 and 19.36–37; both texts have paired scriptural quotations, with the second one in each instance derived from Zechariah.[14] These literary links are helpful insights and their significance should not be overlooked; we will want to draw on them in our subsequent analysis. However, they function less as explicit narrative markers, whereas the account boundaried within chapters 18–19 presents itself as a discrete narrative, particularly when compared to the similar retelling found in the other gospel Passion accounts.

If John's Passion Narrative is chapters 18–19, it follows, then, that such scoping discounts the evangelist's narration of the resurrection and subsequent gift of the Paraclete.[15] This is primarily because such matters are outside the self-standing narrative chapters 18–19 posit, but it also ensures our lens remains focused on Jesus's *death* rather than on his ensuing resurrection. Moreover, the resurrection account is notable for its *lack* of scriptural engagement when compared to the Passion account—explicitly so, at least. That the fulfillment quotation of 19.37 effectively closes the Johannine Passion and is thus the last of the string of such citations, without further need for scripturally sourced resurrection "fulfillment," presents something quite telling both for the functional role and purpose of 19.37, as well as for the Fourth Gospel's overall scriptural hermeneutic.

That is not to ignore the way in which the death and resurrection accounts are interrelated in John, nor to completely remove the resurrection from our discussion. Indeed, it is notable that the Fourth Gospel—unlike its synoptic counterparts—locates the passion and resurrection events in the same location (i.e., a garden) and such equivalence would seem to have explanatory significance. As we shall suggest, the case for John's Passion retelling alluding to Genesis creation imagery becomes stronger on this basis, extending the Genesis reference(s) into the Easter Sunday narrative. And the resurrection account still draws on Israel's Scriptures,[16] even if less demonstrably so, and invites the notion that the full understanding of scriptural fulfillment was a post-resurrection experience rather than one formed in the midst of

Jesus's ministry.[17] On the Sunday morning, Peter (and perhaps the Beloved Disciple) are said not yet to understand the scripture anticipating Jesus rising from the dead (20.9). The γραφή of 20.9 may be both a specific text such as Ps 16.10 (Ps 15.10 LXX) and a reference to the wider avowal of Scripture as demonstrative of Jesus's vocation.[18] And it is only in the aftermath of the resurrection that the disciples "believe" the scripture in respect of the fall of the Temple (2.22). But such important details notwithstanding, our focus will remain the Passion account and its particular usage of the Jewish Scriptures.

MAPPING JOHN'S PASSION

Generally speaking, John's Passion Narrative contains three constituent scenes, each of broadly the same length:[19]

John 18.1–27: Jesus's arrest and subsequent interrogation by the High Priest, along with interspersed accounts of Peter's response and denial (18.15–18, 25–27).

John 18:28–19.16a: Seven mini-scenes of Jesus's trial ensue before Pilate,[20] with the governor both reluctant to pass judgement on Jesus, and articulating a threefold declaration of his innocence (18.38, 19.4, 19.6).

John 19.16b–42: The crucifixion itself, and the subsequent burial of Jesus by Nicodemus and Joseph of Arimathea (19.38–42).

Stibbe classifies John 18–19 as a "triptych" of narrative christology,[21] and this is a helpful evocation of the feel or development of the Passion account. He further suggests that each aspect personifies Jesus in terms of a narrative theme (18.1–27 (good shepherd), 18.28–19.16a (king), and 19.16–42 (paschal lamb)), and such categorization also has heuristic value, particularly if/as we seek to tease out how far the respective themes derive from scriptural imagery (something which we will address particularly in chapter 3). However, as we shall see, these motifs are not the only ones John uses to portray Jesus in his death, and they are not limited merely to the specified scene. For example, we shall argue that, although it reaches its zenith in the crucifixion account, the Paschal lamb imagery is established from the gospel's beginnings. And similarly, the themes can blur over from one scene to another; particularly when scriptural imagery is invoked, Jesus's kingship is as prominent in his crucifixion as it is in his trial before Pilate.

In each element or scene, we will want to consider the (relative) function of scriptural imagery and whether one aspect of the triptych is more prominent or vocal in this regard. But at the outset of our discussion, some initial observations are worth noting. The trial scene contains no explicit scriptural quotation. And at least implicitly, the problems of 19.16 notwithstanding, Jewish responsibility for Jesus's death is not premised on scriptural fulfillment or approval. By contrast, at first glance, and before we engage in the detailed analysis to come, the weight of scriptural reference is found in the third element, the crucifixion scene, once more reaffirming John's inherent association of Israel's scriptures and Jesus's physical death. The crucifixion scene is replete with direct quotation (19.24, 19.28, 19.36–37), and chapter 2 will therefore be very much focused on that portion of the Passion account. Bearing in mind the significance of Jesus's death within the Gospel, the brevity of John's crucifixion account is also notable. But as we shall see, such brevity serves to sharpen the prominence of the scriptural imagery within it and underscores John's indebtedness to Scripture for narrating the death of Jesus.

Having established the parameters of the Johannine Passion Narrative, it is worth stressing what this volume is *not* seeking to do, particularly in relation to source-critical matters. Four related points may be made, the first of which concerns the mooted existence of an independent, pre-Markan Passion Narrative. We recognize that there remains debate within biblical scholarship as to whether such a self-standing Passion Narrative existed prior to the Gospels' formulation,[22] and some caution is certainly requisite in this regard, particularly if desiring specificity in terms of its content. But equally, there remains significant common testimony or key features of a pre-existing Passion Narrative across the biblical record; early Christian texts testify to *some* form of established tradition in respect of Jesus's death, to which was ascribed scriptural testimony or warrant (cf. 1 Cor 15.3ff).[23] Dibelius can thus conclude: "The Passion story is narrated by all four evangelists with a striking agreement never attained elsewhere,"[24] and the varying evangelistic presentations notwithstanding, the pre-existence of a Passion Narrative *tradition* makes sense in view of such "striking agreement." Dale Allison has composed a putative Passion account drawn from the Pauline epistles, again, suggestive of a contained batch of Jesus tradition that had been passed on to the apostle, conceivably with some form of scriptural connection.[25] The presence of such tradition within the Pauline corpus—particularly when compared with Paul's relative unfamiliarity with Historical Jesus matters—suggests his awareness of this established content, and that it may have formed part of earlier liturgical function. So although we might remain agnostic as to the precise content of an early Passion Narrative, there is surely sufficient evidence of "something"[26]; that is, "its existence seems to be plausible, probable even, and a contributory factor to making sense of what appears within the Passion accounts."[27]

That said, however, as with the Fourth Gospel itself, the *specific* outline of the pre-existent Passion Narrative content and/or its provenance is difficult to draw (and it is not clear how one would demonstrably prove it either way). The variation within the evangelistic Passion Narratives points to a variety of sources and/or cautions against specifying an over-fixedness, a further reason why some scholars have queried its pre-existence, at least in formal terms.[28] One must also give due attention to the importance John gives to eyewitness testimony (cf. 19.35, for example, also 21.24–25),[29] and to the evidential role this manifests. This seems particularly apposite bearing in mind the similar testimonial function Scripture itself offers in the first half of John and which forms, at least in part, one element of the overall trial motif that underpins the Fourth Gospel.[30]

For our consideration, then, a *via media* is suitable. On the one hand, it seems likely that John has inherited and used tradition derived from external sources, pre-Markan or otherwise; but on the other, we are not seeking to distinguish between what is Johannine and what is inherited, between what is "novel" in the Fourth Gospel and that which is "received." Our lens is synchronic rather than diachronic, and we likewise do not expect to distinguish between different versions or iterations of the Johannine Gospel. It equally excludes wider consideration of the implications for inter-Gospel relationships and developments, or broader questions of Historical Jesus and reading communities. Our concerns are not source-critical, and we rule out isolating and adjudicating on the Johannine evangelist's use (or non-use) of existing sources. Our interest is essentially Johannine and narratival.

Second, and related to this, is the relationship of John's Passion Narrative to that of its Synoptic counterparts. John's dependence—or otherwise—on Synoptic material is a longstanding question within biblical scholarship and it is not our intention to revisit it here in depth.[31] There will, of course, by necessity, be some comparison with the Synoptic Passion accounts, their (dis)similarity to John, and the degree to which the Fourth Gospel may be reworking the Synoptic presentation. Elements familiar from other accounts are absent in the Fourth Gospel—there is no Jewish trial (Mk 14.53–65) nor abandonment by his disciples, for example (cf. Mk 14.51–52). John 17 functions as an equivalent to the Gethsemane prayers, but relocated to the Upper Room. Hence the respective evangelistic accounts of Jesus's death offer a discrete example of the canonical gospels' interrelationships, and the interpretative insights gleaned from such comparisons can, of course, be significant in discerning the distinctiveness of John's scriptural hermeneutic.[32] Moreover, although, as we suggest below, we are giving particular priority to Israel's Scriptures in terms of the intertextual associations John's Passion Narrative generates, the Synoptic witness also forms—in some sense—part of the intertextual choir, thereby amplifying or extending the scope of John's intertextual engagement.³³ It is perfectly plausible that the evangelist has used features of the Synoptic tradition, affirmatively or otherwise, and hence comparison with their portrayal of the event, particularly in terms of scriptural usage, is generally warranted.

Third, one must recognize that the term "Passion Narrative" is something of a misnomer in terms of its Johannine manifestation. Where, in the Synoptic tradition, Jesus's distress and agony is foregrounded, John's account limits, removes even, such (negative?) emotional portrayal, and particularly in the crucifixion element of the triptych. Some may query whether "Passion" is even an appropriate term for John, as its evocation of any suffering theme is so watered down, absent even, with John's crucifixion scene instead exhibiting "a pervading calm, like an Italian primitive painting."³⁴ In several ways, John has cleansed the Passion account, removed from it the problematic matters of cruciform pain and mockery (though note, still, the soldiers' jeering—19.2–3) or the cry of abandonment (Mk 15.34); the suffering of the cross is muted, perhaps even to the point of absence. As we shall see, such removal is consistent with—necessary even—for John's christological assessment of the Passion, but its silence on such matters remains a significant departure from the parallel synoptic accounts. The crucifixion itself, the "climax" of the Johannine account, is "mentioned only very tersely."³⁵ To put it another way, perhaps with characteristic Johannine irony, "passion" (or pathos) is redefined as a moment of exaltation and glorification, a veritable enthronement of the king.³⁶

Fourth, this volume is not—at least in fundamental terms—a discussion of the atoning impact or implications of Jesus's death within the Fourth Gospel. Such studies exist,³⁷ and they testify in and of themselves to the significant task such discussion necessitates. This means that references to Jesus's death outside of the Passion Narrative—particularly when not mediated through or in terms of the Scriptures—are also generally outside our scope too.

THE DEATH OF CHRIST AND THE JEWISH SCRIPTURES

The task of the subsequent chapters will be to demonstrate the various ways in which Israel's Scriptures provide the heartbeat for John's Passion Narrative. But in making such an argument, we must first acknowledge its essential paradox, namely the tradition that Christ dies κατὰ τὰς γραφὰς (1 Cor 15.3—to which John seems to attest), and the lack of explicit scriptural testimony to that effect.³⁸ The witness of Scripture appears, at least on initial review, to run precisely counter to that notion. Paul himself, in the same epistle, concedes that the concept of the cross was a stumbling block to Jews (1 Cor

1.23). Similarly, in Justin's dialogue with Trypho, he reports his conversation partner as pointing to the scriptural testimony that underscores the essential cursedness (rather than triumph) of the one who is crucified: "your so-called Christ is without honour and glory, so that he has even fallen into the uttermost curse that is in the Law of God, for he was crucified" (31–32).[39] Bearing in mind Scripture's declaration of the curse the crucified one bears (cf. Deut 21.22–23; Gal 3.10–13),[40] the task of addressing the apparent contradiction of a "crucified Messiah," and especially its espoused scriptural warrant, runs across the full gamut of the NT witness. On what basis can Jesus's cruciform death, in Johannine terms or otherwise, be properly conceived of as "according to the Scriptures"?

Some of the earliest scholarly discourse considered this a relatively straightforward process, or at least one whereby the Scriptures could be mined to sustain the apologetic motivation. C. H. Dodd, for example, argued for an essential scriptural premise for the emerging kerygma or gospel, with Israel's Scriptures effectively functioning as the "substructure" of New Testament Theology.[41] Dodd identified several scriptural texts as salient in this regard, terming them *testimonia*, namely key, foundational texts so used by the early Church as integral to their christological reflection. He also surmised that the wider context of these testimonia were carried over when the NT writer cited one part of a source text or one specific verse; the whole of Psalm 22, for example, is invoked, even if only one verse is cited—for example, Ps 22.18 (cf. John 19.24).[42] Barnabas Lindars subsequently built on Dodd's work but emphasized the *apologetic* dimension more explicitly.[43] For Lindars, the Scriptures were mined for their endorsement of the kerygma, and for their consistency with, and testimony to, Jesus's cruciform suffering and death, even if this generated some "discontinuity" in terms of the scriptural text and its re-formulation in the NT milieu.[44]

A different line (and one particularly important for Johannine purposes bearing in mind the extent of scriptural fulfillment language John's Passion apportions to Jesus's death) was subsequently undertaken by Donald Juel. Although still attentive to the significance of early Christian scriptural usage, Juel underlined the veritable *absence* of scriptural testimony for a crucified messiah.[45] Although a righteous sufferer is well attested in the psalmic corpus, its explicit extension to a *messianic* figure remained, for Juel at least, a fundamental lacuna and hence the critical interpretative question that required addressing.[46] He argued that the early Church thus undertook the task of "messianic exegesis," a process whereby Scripture was interrogated to discern how, in spite of the contrary evidence, the Scriptures might be shown to demonstrate that Jesus was the Christ. In Juel's perspective, messianic exegesis "had to explain the scandal of the cross and the reality of the resurrection as events unanticipated by Israel's scriptures."[47] Or to put it another way, the NT authors necessarily engaged in constructive exegetical work that could explain how texts such as Psalm 22 or Psalm 69 could be conceived of in messianic terms.[48]

With its significant Passion/scripture association, the Fourth Gospel presents an exemplary case for assessing how the κατὰ τὰς γραφὰς formulation is outworked, and we might draw attention to three particular features to orientate our analysis in this regard:

1. *Fulfilment:* John explicitly associates Jesus's death not just with scriptural testimony, but with its veritable *fulfillment* (cf. 19.24, 19.28, 36–37). This fulfillment dimension accredited to Scripture is not unique to the Passion Narrative, of course, (cf. 12.28; 13:18; 15.25; 17:12), but it reaches its focus therein.[49] The evangelist's strategy likely has some apologetic function derived from the particular Johannine situation (i.e., rebutting his opponents' suggestion that this could not happen—12.34; cf. also 3.11–15, 8.28), that evidences a wider manifestation of the problem across the NT corpus (even if John's portrayal is perhaps louder than its evangelistic peers). As Evans surmises: "What the Johannine community needed was more than an explanation of the passion, but an explanation that established the *very grounds* for rejection, for Israel's rejection of the Messiah was unthinkable."[50]

2. *Function:* We might press this even further, and to consideration of what the evangelist's purpose statement intends by "believe" (20.31). That is, the scriptural warrant for the events narrated in John—and particularly its account of Jesus's death—are present both for outsiders/opponents (the apologetic) dimension, but also serve to reinforce the scriptural perspectives of the Fourth Gospel's insiders (recognizing the essential counter-intuitive dimension of Christ's death being κατὰ τὰς γραφὰς). The Fourth Gospel's appeal to scriptural fulfillment responds to its *own* (scripturally sourced) question proffered by the crowd in respect of the messiah and the lifting up of the Son of Man (12.34), in effect reflecting the inherent tension of the crucified messiah concept. It is therefore no coincidence that within several verses of 12.34, John introduces the quotational introductory formula announcing scriptural fulfillment and locates Jerusalem's disbelief and rejection of Jesus as itself quintessentially demonstrative of this principle (12.37–41).[51] John thus uses Scripture to critique and qualify prior scriptural perception. Or rather, John deploys Scripture *against* Scripture to demonstrate the ultimate *fulfillment* of Scripture.

3. *Perspective:* There is, of course, a diachronic, forward-facing narrative flow to John's account. But in line with the later reflection κατὰ τὰς γραφὰς occasioned, in terms of its scriptural appropriation, the Fourth

Gospel avowedly evidences a retrospective lens. That is, "the full meaning of the Jesus event only becomes perceptible *from its end*, that is Jesus's death and resurrection."[52] By "end," we mean the chronological sense, the post-Easter hermeneutic that the evangelist lays on the text, such that the significance of an event, and the scriptural basis for it, only comes forth *after* that event, in the "remembrance" occasioned by the resurrection. As noted above, the disciples do not understand the Scripture that Jesus would rise from the dead (20.9), and it is only *after* the resurrection that the disciples "remember" Jesus's words and the citation of Ps 69.9 (John 2.17–22) and so come to understand and believe them (2.22). That Jesus's death was κατὰ τὰς γραφὰς was a belated realization; the disciples only remember the things written (γράφω) about Jesus after his glorification (12.16).[53] But at the same time, as we will see, the telic or climactic dimension to "end" is also a contributory factor to its scriptural warrant. What Jesus's death achieved, its goal or end, is integral to its capacity to be κατὰ τὰς γραφὰς, and we find that outworked in the second aspect of our core thesis, how John's scriptural usage impacts the status of Scripture.

Hence we make no apology for focusing on scriptural usage within John's Passion Narrative and on its overall impact within the Fourth Gospel's evangelistic strategy. The prevailing κατὰ τὰς γραφὰς demands require it. As per our first core thesis element, Scripture is embedded in the very essence of the John's Passion, and it is necessarily so. One simply cannot talk about the Johannine Passion without extensive interaction with the Jewish Scriptures.

METHODOLOGY—INTERTEXTUAL READING AND THE JOHANNINE READER

Having established our focal "text" as John 18–19, and having set our presenting topic within its wider NT/κατὰ τὰς γραφὰς context, a third and final preparatory task remains, namely to establish the methodology we will use to consider our threefold thesis.[54] Our approach will be an essentially *intertextual* enterprise; we seek to adopt an intertextual posture in respect of the reading of the Johannine text. What does that entail?

Watson et al. offer a broad definition of intertextuality, namely "a text's representation of, reference to and use of phenomena in the world outside the text being interpreted."[55] For our purposes, the "phenomena" under consideration will be Israel's Scriptures, and the various ways John draws on them to pursue its evangelistic purposes. And at one level, such a posture requires no justification. As Stefan Alkier affirms: "Through the intertextual connection of the canon, it is hermeneutically justifiable to read and interpret every biblical writing in the light of every other biblical writing."⁵⁶ Likewise, Richard Hays, one of the most prominent advocates of intertextual reading within biblical studies, ventures that the lens is particularly apposite for interpreting the Fourth Gospel's christological purposes: "John reads the entirety of the Old Testament as a web of symbols that must be understood as figural signifiers for Jesus and the life that he offers."⁵⁷ John therefore avowedly invites this intertextual play; it is not something "imposed" on the text, particularly in the Passion Narrative which so explicitly invites connections to the Jewish Scriptures. The volume of potential connections, its frequent usage of γραφή forms, and the strong pointer to scriptural fulfillment demands the reader explore references and connections beyond the Fourth Gospel parameters.

But three points of qualification may be made at the outset. First, we recognize that intertextuality is not the only means by which the function of Israel's Scriptures in the Fourth Gospel might be assessed, and one can explore John's use of the Scriptures in a number of ways without necessarily adopting an intertextual stance.⁵⁸ An approach might be motivated by Historical-Critical interests, for example, focusing on the *Vorlage* or source of John's citations.⁵⁹ Or it might be informed by wider methodological concerns seeking after the function of the scriptural usage.⁶⁰ And likewise, intertextual engagement is not limited merely to attending to John's use of Israel's Scriptures; we have already acknowledged, for example, that the Synoptics are in some fashion intertextually related to the Johannine account. Some might equally observe that John's own sources, and the history of the text's diachronic composition, present an intertextual journey, at least up to the point of its final received form. And within our own iteration of intertextual engagement, historical-critical insights remain interpretatively fruitful. As Moyise opines: "In their extreme form, neither historical criticism nor theories of intertextuality are suited to the task of studying the use of Scripture in the New Testament. But used *together* they are able to complement one another."⁶¹ So although historical-critical insights do not drive our approach, they are equally not absent from our methodological toolkit.

Second, we recognize that intertextuality is technically not a method, but rather a theory, a perspective on how texts interrelate with one another.⁶² It takes multiple forms, therefore, and manifests a diversity of interpretative agendas or postures;⁶³ it is not a neutral discourse or approach. But that surely serves to commend its application to the Fourth Gospel. The latter can hardly be said to be "neutral" in its kerygmatic formulation (20.31), its christological hermeneutic infusing and shaping its scriptural engagement. Where historical criticism has tended to detach itself from such theological or ideological matters, intertextuality celebrates them, and hence an intertextual standpoint seems warranted bearing in mind the Fourth Gospel's self-avowed christological perspective. As Puskas and Robbins contend in respect of the intertextual approach: "How confounding would be our reading of FG *without* an intertextual engagement with the Scripture of Israel."[64] Similarly, as Jean Zumstein avers, for the modern reader we are ascribing to its interpretation, the Gospel of John has always been part of a larger literary collection. It doesn't exist in isolation—it is itself an intertext.[65] It assumes—*requires* even—the existence of other texts in order for its christological purposes to be manifest. Both the volume of scriptural links John makes and the christological perspective it adopts encourage the use of an intertextual lens for reading its Passion Narrative. And at the same time, Zumstein recognizes the way in which the Fourth Gospel's character is both *inter*textual and *intra*textual.[66] That is, John exhibits numerous internal features—irony, plot, characters—that contribute to textual meaning, which render it a "self-interpreting narrative" and which work with the intertextual/scriptural connections the evangelist draws. We will therefore be attentive to the intratextual implications of the Fourth Gospel's intertextual engagement. As our subsequent analysis will demonstrate, John's intratextuality and intertextuality are dialogical, mutually informing features.

Third, in the light of the second and third elements of our thesis (the relationship of the respective γραφή identities of both Scripture and the Fourth Gospel), our lens might be described as "interscriptural" as much as "intertextual." As Obermann's seminal work on John's use of the Old Testament rightly underscores, the Fourth Gospel is an exercise in *Schriftverständnisses*.[67] That is, the texts with which the evangelist engages are more than mere *texts*—they carry authority and weighting in respect of their scriptural status, and as we shall see in chapter five, this has implications for the Fourth Gospel's own identity too. John considers itself to be "scriptural" and thus initiates a wider conversation discussion as to what ultimately constitutes Scripture and how different scriptural texts interrelate to and inform each other.

Recent scholarship has also drawn attention to intertextuality's multiple iterations or forms.[68] Hence some further specification as the nature of our intertextual method is required, some further clarification as to how we will employ it. Broadly speaking, our approach sits closest to what Moyise terms "dialogical intertextuality,"[69] the way(s) in which "the alluded text adds a 'voice' to the alluding text, so that the reader is forced to configure multiple 'voices.'"[70] When the evangelist invokes a prior scriptural text, its juxtaposition alongside the Johannine testimony evokes an intertextual conversation, with both texts interpreting and re-interpreting each other. Something new or different results from the intertextual exchange. Again, as with the second and third elements of core thesis, John's definition of Scripture and what comprises it are changed; Scripture is perfected, and the Fourth Gospel's self-identification as Scripture is articulated.

We will therefore examine the various links (or intertexts) John evokes between its narration of Jesus's Passion and the corpus of Israel's Scriptures, and consider the interplay so evoked. These links include:

- *Quotations:* These are citations from Israel's Scripture, found in broadly the same lexical form to their original source, and signaled by some preceding introductory formula. This has generally been the most common means by which John's scriptural usage was previously assessed, as the introductory formula initiates the intertextual interest—it is explicitly signalled. We shall say more about the grounds for determining a quotation's existence, and the issues this raises, in chapter 2. In dealing with quotations, we will also draw on another intertextual feature, metalepsis, namely the effect of using the quotation, and the impact of/on its former context in its new situation.[71] How much baggage does a Johannine quotation bear in its new context? When John's Passion makes the quotation, how much of the original source accompanies the citation? Such questions are significant as they pertain to the particularity of the individual texts to which John attributes fulfillment. It may be, as Beutler opines, that the specific source of the scripture is negligible for the evangelist, and that all that matters is the text's scriptural credentials; John is essentially concerned just with the *overall* fulfillment of Scripture (of whatever texts it is comprised).[72] But applying a metaleptic lens considers the degree to which John's usage *does* have ramifications for the specific texts involved, whether it does indeed matter which individual Psalm or which part of Zechariah is said to be being fulfilled (and how/why so). Such metaleptic concerns will form a key part of our analysis for all John's cited quotations.
- *Composite quotations:* Recent scholarship on intertextuality in the NT has also drawn attention to the phenomenon of composite questions, an amalgam of constituent scriptural texts presented as one overall citation.[73] In this way, John *qua*-author extends its intertextual quest, participating in further textual interplay, combining texts to breed new ones, and presenting them as composite quotations.[74] We will be attentive to their presence within the Johannine Passion Narrative, and the degree to which the evangelist is metaleptically evoking the context of all elements of the composite question, thereby enabling a much wider intertextual discourse.
- *Allusions:* These intertexts share some similar language to the preceding scriptural texts but lack the directive signalling of the quotation form. They may be lexical allusions (i.e., links to a particular phrase or words), or may be thematic/situational ones that draw on common motifs or concepts. We shall suggest that the latter are more prominent as far as John

18–19 is concerned, and they evoke a series of more storied intertexts across John's Passion account.
- *Echoes:* Defining echoes is a more complex task, as the grounds for their existence may be merely one common word. And their identification only raises further interpretative questions. As Judith Lieu rightly opines: "discernment of apparent echoes of the Hebrew Scriptures is easier than their interpretation."[75] Generally speaking, we shall consider echoes as less obvious (though not necessarily less potent) allusions, and hence will avoid formulaically trying to distinguish one form from the other, instead treating them as relatively interchangeable terms and focusing on the intertextual effect(s) so generated.

The challenge with discerning allusions and echoes, of course, is the inherent subjectivity to their recognition, and this can lead to significant debate as to the grounds for an echo's existence and/or criticism for excessive enthusiasm in their identification.[76] Who generates them? The author? The implied reader? The real reader? The modern reader? Some will want to pursue more definiteness in this regard, and/or desire criteria or grounds for justifying the grounds for the mooted echo. However such approaches, though laudable, still remain inherently subjective, and demonstrating certainty as to the genuineness of an allusion will always be difficult. Richard Hays, for example, drew out seven criteria for recognizing the presence of an echo, and helpfully so, but his subsequent consideration of mooted echoes—whether in Paul or in the Gospels—does not actually use the criteria to assess the legitimacy of the echo.[77] Working with intertexts remains an art rather than a science.

This does not mean a completely open-ended or untested analysis, however. We will be attentive to the degree to which the mooted allusion or echo manifests at least some of the following elements: "common vocabulary, common word order, common theme(s), similar imagery, similar structure, (and) similar circumstance(s)"[78]; the perceived volume of the echo is integral to its function and efficacy. Likewise we will prioritize Hays' satisfaction criterion—does the mooted allusion yield interpretative insight, does it ultimately "work"? We still want to read the text "well" and with integrity.[79] We will also have in mind another feature of intertextuality—relevance theory[80]—and its capacity for assessing the validity of a perceived allusion, and how it entails what Steve Smith terms "a framework for understanding how readers approach texts," particularly modern readers.[81] Relevance theory assesses the relevance of the alleged intertext, and the effect it has on the reader concerned. Pursuing the relevance concept further, Smith speaks of "enriching references" (as opposed to "essential" ones), namely those intertexts that some readers will notice, thereby adding interpretive depth, but which other readers can miss without causing detriment to the central message of the text.⁸² We will want to be attentive to an allusion's potential enrichment capacity, the way in which it might add extra flavor and understanding to the evangelist's discourse.

But we will not apply this formulaically or slavishly. We wish to keep options open and remain cautious as to adjudicating on the relative plausibility or otherwise of the echo's existence, and begin instead from the premise that it is at least *possible*. We will initiate the dialogue Moyise proposes and see what interpretative benefit is so outworked. After all, an open-ended dimension to this is entirely appropriate for the multi-layered Johannine text. And just because an allusion may only work for a minority of readers, that does not exclude its existence or efficacy; rather, it testifies to deepening the engagement in a very Johannine way. John has incorporated Israel's sacred texts and stories into its own story, and in such a way that connections are multivalent, multidirectional, and multitemporal. Hence there will be a resulting open-endedness to our discussion, and readers of this volume will likely come to different assessments of the efficacy of links made. Our hope is to open up space for exploration of possible interfaces between the given texts; we wish to allow for the possibility of multiple references and not seek to restrict them, not rush to adjudicate on their legitimacy. Quite simply, some will be more likely than others, but we leave it to the contemporary reader to adjudicate for themselves.

This then has implications for the identity of our perceived reader, and particularly their assumed interpretative competency. As Alkier succinctly states: "Texts have no meaning but rather enable the production of meaning in the act of reading." Although we may dissent from Alkier's suggestion that texts have *no* meaning in and of themselves (i.e., they do preserve at least some purpose, meaning or intent from their production), the reader's involvement is surely integral to the interpretative process. Addressing the function of symbols of within the Fourth Gospel, the kind of which scriptural allusions represent, Ruben Zimmermann similarly contends: "The discovery of the meaning of the symbolic requires the active involvement of the reader from the beginning. It is only through symbolic communication between John or the text of the Gospel and a reader that meaning can be discovered through subtle and implicit clues."⁸³ Such is the way of intertextual reading, in that the reader assumes particular (co?-)responsibility for generating meaning and significance.⁸⁴ A text's meaning is a joint operation between reader and author—and that is particularly invited by the Fourth Gospel.⁸⁵ The reader is addressed directly by the text—cf. "you" of 20.31; they are asked to participate, to partake, to engage in the process of meaning-generation and to respond, at least in John's terms, with belief.

To put it another way, John's *modus operandi*—including but not limited to its use of the Jewish Scriptures—tends toward the suggestive or ambiguous, and resists absolute assessments of authorial intent. The intertextual reader—contemporary or modern, implied or real, competent or ignorant—is always integrally involved in the act of generating meaning, but it is especially so within John and its Passion retelling. Textual meaning becomes more indeterminate—or at least more determined by the reader's interaction and, as a result, there is more space for semantic creativity. This likewise leaves (invited?) space for wider exploration of intertextual and interscriptural association, and/or for a plurality of intertexts to be brought to the interpretative table, rather than it being reduced to merely one or two specific options. The loaded Johannine image of the Lamb of God, for example, has been resolved in numerous forms, each of which would/could be defended by their respective proponent(s).[86]

Hence as we begin our intertextual analysis, clarity as to type of reader we anticipate is necessary. We wish to attend to real readers—not idealized ones—and particularly those who read today, the contemporary or modern reader. Modern readers will be invested in the reception of texts from both Testaments, and in that sense are more competent (or competent in different ways) than the first readers of John's gospel. The particular scriptural self-conception—whether that of John or of Israel's sacred texts—has chronologically-subsequent interpretative implications, as Moyise so recognizes: "the very nature of Scripture is that it speaks to new generations." And such characterization invites the modern reader into the enterprise of sacred meaning-making the Fourth Gospel generates.

The modern reader will also be a competent one, competent enough to make the intertextual/interscriptural connections the Passion Narrative evokes. It probably goes without saying that some knowledge or awareness of Israel's Scriptures is a prerequisite for the reader—intertextual or otherwise; the Scriptures are foundational to John's christological hermeneutic and offer "the familiar literary stock from which the Gospel grows. Readers who come to the Fourth Gospel without a knowledge of this Scripture will be very much more perplexed than those whose reading of Scripture has determined their outlook and expectations."[87] A competent reader—contemporary, modern, or otherwise—will have at least some knowledge and awareness of the wider context of John's intertexts.

At the same time, reader competency will be a variable phenomenon. And the Fourth Gospel is exactly the sort of text for which there is potential for multi-layered intertextual connections to be made. As noted earlier, we will want to speak of interpretative *possibilities* rather than definite ones, as that seems entirely in keeping with Johannine scriptural usage and symbolism, always inviting that further layer of engagement. This does not mean an infinite number of readings, and a wise, intertextual reader will be attentive to the legitimacy and appropriateness of the readings they generate, or the textual echoes at which they arrive. But at the very least, our approach will be to allow for the possibility of such readings to arise or be considered, and/or resist notions of certainty or absoluteness.[88] The intertextual mindset adopts a more imaginative rather than cautious perspective, it invites that assessment and wider appreciation, and has the potential for opening up new points of connection and scriptural intertext. The Fourth Gospel invites many intertextual views to the interpretive table.

This has ramifications, of course, for those readers who are not persuaded by the writer's argument, and who do not come to believe (20.31). If the recognition of scriptural intertexts and John's kerygmatic purposes are so intertwined, what happens in respect of an uninformed or insufficiently competent reader—to what extent does their limited ability to make intertextual connections limit the Fourth Gospel's evangelistic character? For that reason, we will want to be attentive to *how* much intertextual awareness or competency is required by the reader, and the degree to which limited awareness impacts upon John's persuasiveness.

Related to this is the perception that allusions are only allusions if they are "intended" by the author, and thereby consciously made.[89] We would want to contend the reverse, as above, that intertextual allusions may be reader-driven or reader-generated, and in some sense "freed" from authorial responsibility or generation. Those that are in tandem with the Johaninne step, and/or appearing to be author-generated are still important, of course, and are likely more relevant or potent as a result. But for a scripturally astute audience—and there is good reason to believe that at least some of John's audience may be so described—the very plurality and multi-dimensionality of the Hebrew Scriptures at least opens the possibility of their generating connections within/across the Scriptures that the evangelist themselves would not have recognized or noticed. That is the true for the modern reader, we suggest, who has been shaped by ongoing reception tradition. Moreover, if "the mind behind the Gospel is one steeped in scriptural language and metaphors,"[90] then it is plausible, very likely even, that scriptural images and motifs will unconsciously "leak" into the Passion discourse even if not technically intended or deliberately signalled (and of course, one wonders how one ever demonstrates that something is "intended" anyway).

In short, the intertextual reader is assumed be sufficiently competent to make at least some of the invited intertextual connections John's Passion Narrative sets forth. And this seems entirely consistent with the way in which scriptural understanding is portrayed within the Fourth Gospel itself. That is, by their participation in/with the text, the reader is expected to make connections between Scripture and the words/actions of Jesus. What "happens" when the reader's intertextual radar is actively switched on, when they accept the text's invitation to leave its boundaries and explore external points of association and connection? John's approach is not monochrome but rather plural, and, at times, somewhat creatively so, and this gives the reader further interpretative permission to make connections for themselves.

* * *

Having established the Passion Narrative parameters for our enquiry, having set the question within the wider context of how the NT authors conceived of Jesus's death as κατὰ τὰς γραφὰς, and having mapped the intertextual approach that will undergird our enquiry, we now turn to the Fourth Gospel itself, and to consideration of the scriptural intertexts it attests.

NOTES

1. Cp. the extensive treatment of a variety of related themes in Belle, *Death*. The very existence of such a large volume testifies to the centrality of Jesus's death within the Fourth Gospel.

2. Beth M. Stovell, *Mapping Metaphorical Discourse in the Fourth Gospel: John's Eternal King*, Linguistic Biblical Studies 5 (Leiden: Brill, 2012), 296 considers the Passion Narrative to be the "metonymic core" of the Fourth Gospel, "a concrete event that the rest of John's Gospel interprets through metaphor."

3. R. Alan Culpepper, "The Theology of the Johannine Passion Narrative: John 19:16b-30," *Neot* 31 (1997): 21.

4. Robert T. Fortna, *The Fourth Gospel and its Predecessor: From Narrative Source to Present Gospel* (Edinburgh: T&T Clark, 1988), 283. Cf. likewise Zumstein, "Purpose," 339: "The death of Jesus is not a marginal element in the Fourth Gospel. It is the constant horizon of the story."

5. John T. Carroll and Joel B. Green, *The Death of Jesus in Early Christianity* (Peabody, MA: Hendrickson, 1995), 82–89.

6. Frey, *Theology*, 188.

7. So Hays, *Echoes-Gospels*, 285; Marianne Meye Thompson, "'They Bear Witness to Me': The Psalms in the Passion Narrative in the Gospel of John," in *The Word Leaps the Gap: Essays on Scripture and Theology in Honor of Richard B. Hays*, ed. J. Ross Wagner, et al. (Grand Rapids, MI: Eerdmans, 2008), 268.

8. For example, the relationship between 19.34 and 20.22, or the κῆπος imagery inaugurated in 18.1 carrying over into 19.41 and/or to Mary Magdalene's mistaking of Jesus for a gardener (20.15).

9. So Margaret Daly-Denton, *John: An Earth Bible Commentary: Supposing Him to Be the Gardener* (London: T&T Clark, 2017), 201; though in effect for Daly-Denton, 14.31 triggers 18.1ff.

10. Cf. Kari Syreeni, *Becoming John: The Making of a Passion Gospel*, LNTS 590 (London: T&T Clark, 2019). Syreeni avers that the Passion Narrative was a later addition or redaction to the Fourth Gospel, which was originally more or less the present form of chapters 1–12. Irrespective of one's assessment of Syreeni's arguments, it

still, albeit for other reasons, raises questions as to where one locates the boundaries of what is subsequently termed the Johannine Passion Narrative. At the same time, Syreeni's work also attests—again from a different perspective to many other commentators—the foundational aspect of the Passion for John, and in the form in which we have it: "The *passion-orientated redaction* is so extensive and vital to the present form of the Gospel that I call it the *becoming of John*" (emphasis original—2).

11. *Inter alia*, Jo-Ann A. Brant, *John*, PCNT (Grand Rapids, MI: Baker Academic, 2011), 231; Craig S. Keener, *The Gospel of John: A Commentary*, 2 vols. (Peabody, MA: Hendrickson, 2003), 1067.

12. Mark W. G. Stibbe, *John as Storyteller: Narrative Criticism and the Fourth Gospel*, SNTSMS 73 (Cambridge, UK: Cambridge University Press, 1992). On the genre of the Passion, see Stibbe, *John as Storyteller*, 121–47, who characterizes it as tragedy.

13. Lieu, "Narrative," 150–51. She believes this is more probable than 19.24 and 19.37 forming their own *inclusio*.

14. Bynum, "Quotations," 47–74. See also Wm. Randolph Bynum, *The Fourth Gospel and the Scriptures: Illuminating the Form and Meaning of Scriptural Citation in John 19:37*, NovTSupp 144 (Leiden: Brill, 2012).

15. C. H. Dodd, *The Interpretation of the Fourth Gospel* (Cambridge, UK: Cambridge University Press, 1953), 423–43, for example, retains the resurrection events within his scoping of the Passion Narrative. Note, though, that we shall argue (in chapter 4) that the Paraclete is in some sense given at the point of Jesus's death, with 19.30 anticipating 20.21–23.

16. See for example Lidija Novakovic, *Raised from the Dead According to Scripture: The Role of Israel's Scripture in the Early Christian Interpretations of Jesus' Resurrection*, T&T Clark Jewish and Christian Texts 12 (London: Bloomsbury T&T Clark, 2012).

17. Cf. Larry W. Hurtado, "Remembering and Revelation the Historic and Glorified Jesus in the Gospel of John," in *Israel's God and Rebecca's Children: Christology and Community in Early Judaism and Christianity*, ed. David B. Capes, et al. (Waco, TX: Baylor University Press, 2007), 197: "John actually makes an explicit and emphatic distinction between the understanding of Jesus's significance in the pre-resurrection and the post-resurrection situations." Hurtado cites Painter's assessment in support: "Of the four Gospels, only John explicitly makes clear the epistemological distance/difference between the time of Jesus's ministry and the post-resurrection period in which the Gospel was self-consciously written (see 2:22; 7:39; 12:16; 16:7, 13–16)."

18. See Brendan Byrne, "A Step Too Far: A Critique of Francis Moloney's Understanding of 'the Scripture' in John 20:9," *ITQ* 80 (2015): 152–53; for a different perspective, particularly in terms of the Beloved Disciple's scriptural awareness, see Francis J. Moloney, "'For as yet they did not know the Scripture' (John 20:9): A Study in Narrative Time," *ITQ* 79 (2014): 97–111. We discuss Moloney's position further in chapter 5.

19. Donald Senior, *The Passion of Jesus in the Gospel of John*, The Passion Series 4 (Collegeville, MN: Liturgical Press, 1991), 45 divides John's Passion into four

scenes—that is., he splits the arrest and subsequent interrogations. Bearing in mind John's subsequent appeal to threefold happenings (cf. 18.27 (13.38), 21.14, 21.17; cf. also 2.19–20), we prefer the rhetorical three episodes.

20. So Andrew T. Lincoln, *The Gospel According to Saint John* (Peabody, MA: Hendrickson, 2005), 458.

21. Stibbe, *John as Storyteller*, 179.

22. For example, see Helen K. Bond, "The Triumph of the King: John's Transformation of Mark's Account of the Passion," in *John's Transformation of Mark,* ed. Eve-Marie Becker, et al. (London: T&T Clark, 2021), 251–53; also Arthur J. Dewey, "The Locus for Death: Social Memory and the Passion Narratives," in *Memory, Tradition, and Text: Uses of the Past in Early Christianity*, ed. Alan Kirk and Tom Thatcher, Semeia Studies 52 (Atlanta: Society of Biblical Literature, 2005), 119–28.

23. So Marten J. J. Menken, "Old Testament Quotations in the Gospel of John," in *New Testament Writers and the Old Testament: An Introduction*, ed. John Court (London: SPCK, 2002), 29: 1 Cor 15.3–4 testifies that, "even before Paul . . . 'accordance with the Scriptures' was from the very beginning an essential part of Christian preaching and doctrine."

24. Martin Dibelius, *From Tradition to Gospel* (New York: Charles Scribner, 1934), 179.

25. See Dale C. Allison, *Constructing Jesus: Memory, Imagination, and History* (London: SPCK, 2010), 392–403.

26. This is effectively the argument of Joel B. Green, *The Death of Jesus: Tradition and Interpretation in the Passion Narrative*, WUNT 2/33 (Tübingen: Mohr, 1988), *passim*, which espouses a strong argument for the existence of some form pre-canonical Passion Narrative.

27. David Allen, *According to the Scriptures: The Death of Christ in the Old Testament and the New* (London: SCM, 2018), 9.

28. Cf. the discussion in Bond, "Triumph," 251–53.

29. See Richard Bauckham, *Jesus and the Eyewitnesses: The Gospels as Eyewitness Testimony* (Grand Rapids, MI: Eerdmans, 2006).

30. On the trial/lawsuit motif in the Fourth Gospel, see Lincoln, *Gospel*, 37–38; also Andrew T. Lincoln, *Truth on Trial: The Lawsuit Motif in the Fourth Gospel* (Peabody, MA: Hendrickson, 2000).

31. On such matters, cf. Raymond E. Brown, *The Death of the Messiah: From Gethsemane to the Grave a Commentary on the Passion Narratives in the Four Gospels*, 2 vols. (New Haven, CT: Yale University Press, 2008), 75–92. See also Wendy E. S. North, *What John Knew and What John Wrote: A Study in John and the Synoptics* (Lanham, MD: Fortress Academic, 2020), particularly as the Fourth Gospel's scriptural usage forms part of North's evaluation. We remain agnostic as to John's purposes in relation to the Synoptics—whether, for example, its composition is complementary to them or whether it offers some of corrective or differentiation. A plausible account may be made for either position, but neither particularly affects the outcome of our analysis.

32. See for example Bond, "Triumph," 251–67 and her comparison of the Markan and Johannine Passion accounts. She opines: "The Johannine passion narrative offers

a particularly rich example of the way in which an early Christian biographer has creatively refashioned an older source and infused it with new life" (267). See also Green, *Death of Jesus*, 105–34.

33. David Ford, "Reading Backwards, Reading Forwards, and Abiding: Reading John in the Spirit Now," *JTI* 11 (2017): 69–84.

34. Barnabas Lindars, *The Gospel of John* (London: Marshall, Morgan & Scott, 1972), 543.

35. Jörg Frey, *The Glory of the Crucified One: Christology and Theology in the Gospel of John* (Waco, TX: Baylor University Press, 2018), 211.

36. See further Paul D. Duke, *Irony in the Fourth Gospel* (Atlanta: John Knox, 1985). He notes: "The dominant irony concerning Jesus's destiny is that his death is in fact an exaltation."

37. See *inter alia* Belle, *Death*.

38. On this question more widely, see Allen, *According*, 1–25.

39. David E. Garland, "The fulfillment Quotations in John's Account of the Crucifixion," in *Perspectives on John: Method and Interpretation in the Fourth Gospel*, ed. Robert C. Sloan and Mikeal C. Parsons (Lampeter, UK: Edwin Mellen, 1993), 229.

40. Cf. Craig R. Koester, "Why Was the Messiah Crucified? A Study of God, Jesus, Satan and Human Agency in Johannine Theology," in *The Death of Jesus in the Fourth Gospel*, ed. Gilbert van Belle (Leuven: Leuven University Press, 2007), 163: "The crucifixion of Jesus the Messiah was a theological problem for early Christians. If the term *messiah* was associated with Israel's hopes for a strong and righteous ruler, crucifixion was a punishment given to rebels, slaves and violent criminals. If the Messiah was expected to reign with honour, death on the cross meant defeat and disgrace."

41. C. H. Dodd, *According to the Scriptures: The Sub-Structure of New Testament Theology* (London: Nisbet, 1952). This "substructure" element became the subtitle of Dodd's work.

42. Through this volume, we use the Hebrew/English numbering of the Psalms, rather than that of the Greek tradition, even if/as the Greek form was the one the evangelist utilized.

43. Barnabas Lindars, *New Testament Apologetic* (London: SCM, 1961). He describes Psalm 22 as "a quarry for pictorial details in writing the story of the Passion" (90).

44. Steve Moyise, *The Old Testament in the New: An Introduction* (London: Bloomsbury, 2015), 211–12.

45. Donald Juel, *Messianic Exegesis: Christological Interpretation of the Old Testament in Early Christianity* (Philadelphia: Fortress, 1988), 26: "Christian interpretation of the Scriptures arose from the recognition that Jesus was the expected Messiah and that he did not fit the picture." Cf. Jocelyn McWhirter, "Messianic Exegesis in the Fourth Gospel," in *Reading the Gospel of John's Christology as Jewish Messianism: Royal, Prophetic, and Divine Messiahs*, ed. Benjamin Reynolds and Gabriele Boccaccini, Ancient Judaism and Early Christianity 106 (Leiden: Brill, 2018), 124–48, which builds on Juel's approach and applies it specifically to the Fourth Gospel. She avers: "Jesus's first followers, who did believe in a crucified messiah, had to clear

an important hurdle as they searched the scriptures for relevant prophecies. They had to argue that passages about rejected sufferers actually refer to God's anointed one, the prophesied offspring of David" (125–26).

46. The exception was perhaps Psalm 89, especially vv50–51, which potentially yielded an association between messiahship and humiliation, but the text does not seem to have been explicitly used by the NT writers in terms of the Passion retelling (though John 12.34 possibly has Ps 89.36 in mind).

47. Myers, "Introduction," 3. See also pp. 2–4.

48. So Juel, *Messianic*, 103; Martin Hengel, *The Atonement: A Study of the Origins of the Doctrine in the New Testament* (London: SCM, 1981), 40–41. On the application of this to the Fourth Gospel, see McWhirter, "Messianic," 124–48.

49. Bynum, "Quotations," 53, for example, notes how the Passion citations "begin to take previously written scriptural material to a level of fulfillment that is beyond parallel."

50. Evans, "Quotation," 82, emphasis added.

51. Garland, "fulfillment," 229–50 reviews this scholarly debate. He suggests that John's scriptural use has more than an apologetic function, and instead begins to explore the wider soteriological implications of the appeal to Scripture.

52. Maarten J. J. Menken, "What Authority Does the Fourth Evangelist Claim for His Book?," in *Paul, John, and Apocalyptic Eschatology: Studies in Honour of Martinus C. de Boer*, ed. Jan Krans, et al. (Leiden: Brill, 2013), 190, emphasis added.

53. Cf. Byrne, "Step," 153: "The reference in 12:16 to 'glorification' rather than 'resurrection' is significant since 'glorification' comprises the passion and death of Jesus, as well as his resurrection and ascension, within the one overall movement of his return to the Father."

54. On recent methodological developments within the study of the NT writers' use of Israel's Scriptures, see David Allen and Steve Smith (ed.), *Methodology in the Use of the Old Testament in the New: Context and Criteria*, LNTS 597 (London: T&T Clark, 2019).

55. Duane Frederick Watson, *The Intertexture of Apocalyptic Discourse in the New Testament* (Atlanta: Society of Biblical Literature, 2002), 2.

56. Stefan Alkier, "Intertextuality and the Semiotics of Biblical Texts," in *Reading the Bible Intertextually*, ed. Richard B. Hays, et al. (Waco: Baylor University Press, 2009), 12.

57. Hays, *Echoes-Gospels*, 344.

58. One notes the objection of Florian Wilk, "Paul as User, Interpreter, and Reader of the Book of Isaiah," in *Reading the Bible Intertextually*, ed. Richard B. Hays, et al. (Waco: Baylor University Press, 2009), 99: "With respect to Paul . . . one should not study and describe the relationship of the Testaments of the Christian Bible exclusively in terms of the concept of intertextuality." The voice of the Hebrew Bible text must also be heard on its own terms.

59. One thinks of Menken, *Quotations in the Fourth Gospel* as a primary instance of this, or similarly Günter Reim, *Studien zum alttestamentlichen Hintergrund des Johannesevangeliums*, SNTSMS 22 (Cambridge, UK: Cambridge University Press,

1974); Edwin D. Freed, *Old Testament Quotations in the Gospel of John*, NovTSupp vol. XI (Leiden: Brill, 1965).

60. The work of Sheridan, *Retelling* and Myers, *Characterizing Jesus* is commonly cited in this regard.

61. Steve Moyise, "Intertextuality and Historical Approaches to the Use of Scripture in the New Testament," in *Reading the Bible Intertextually*, ed. Richard B. Hays, et al. (Waco, TX: Baylor University Press, 2009), 32, emphasis added.

62. Moyise, "Intertextuality and Historical Approaches," 23.

63. Hays, *Echoes-Gospels*, 344 proposes using the language of "*sensibility* rather than strategy."

64. Charles B. Puskas and C. Michael Robbins, *The Conceptual Worlds of the Fourth Gospel: Intertextuality and Early Reception* (Eugene, OR: Cascade Books, 2021), 44, emphasis added.

65. Zumstein, "Intratextuality," 121–22. He helpfully underscores how the Fourth Gospel is a "networked text"—it "presumes the existence of other writings."

66. Zumstein, "Intratextuality," 121–35.

67. Obermann, *Erfüllung*.

68. See, for example, the various forms in B. J. Oropeza and Steve Moyise, *Exploring Intertextuality: Diverse Strategies for New Testament Interpretation of Texts* (Eugene, OR: Cascade, 2016). Even though we don't embrace its precise contours, Sheridan, *Figure*, 47–87 offers an excellent discussion of the issues that arise when applying an intertextual lens to the Fourth Gospel.

69. Steve Moyise, "Dialogical Intertextuality," in B. J. Oropeza and Steve Moyise (eds.), *Exploring Intertextuality: Diverse Strategies for New Testament Interpretation of Texts* (Eugene, OR: Cascade, 2016), 3–15.

70. Moyise, "Dialogical Intertextuality," 14.

71. See further Jeannine K. Brown, "Metalepsis," in *Exploring Intertextuality: Diverse Strategies for New Testament Interpretation of Texts*, ed. B. J. Oropeza and Steve Moyise (Eugene, OR: Cascade, 2016), 29–41.

72. Beutler, "Use," 148. He lists several leading Johannine commentators who concur with him on this point.

73. See particularly Sean A. Adams and Seth Ehorn (ed.), *Composite Citations in Antiquity. Volume 1, Jewish, Graeco-Roman, and Early Christian Uses*, LNTS 525 (London: T&T Clark, 2016), 1–16; Sean A. Adams and Seth Ehorn (eds), *Composite Citations in Antiquity. Volume 2, New Testament Uses*, LNTS 593 (London: Bloomsbury, 2017), 1–15.

74. John is not alone in so doing, it represents standard Second Temple practice. See Christopher D. Stanley, "Composite Citations: Retrospect and Prospect," in *Composite Citations in Antiquity. Volume One, Jewish, Graeco-Roman, and Early Christian Uses*, ed. Sean A. Adams and Seth Ehorn, LNTS 525 (London: T&T Clark, 2016), 204: "The practice of 'composite citation' . . . appears often enough in the literature of Greco-Roman antiquity to qualify as an established literary technique."

75. Judith Lieu, "Scripture and Feminine in John," in *Feminist Companion to the Hebrew Bible in the New Testament*, ed. Athalya Brenner (London: Bloomsbury, 1996), 237.

76. Cf. for example the caution of Paul Foster, "Echoes without Resonance: Critiquing Certain Aspects of Recent Scholarly Trends in the Study of the Jewish Scriptures in the New Testament," *JSNT* 38 (2015): 96–111, and his critique of an excessive appropriation of mooted echoes.

77. Richard Hays, *Echoes of Scripture in the Letters of Paul* (New Haven, CT: Yale University Press, 1989), 29–32. See the related discussion in David Allen, "The Use of Criteria: The State of the Question," in *Methodology in the Use of the Old Testament in the New: Context and Criteria*, ed. David Allen and Steve Smith, LNTS 597 (London: T&T Clark, 2019), 129–41.

78. Dale C. Allison, *The Intertextual Jesus: Scripture in Q* (Harrisburg, PA: Trinity Press International, 2000), 11.

79. The role of community approval comes out in Richard B. Hays, "Continuing to Read Scripture with the Evangelists: A Response," *JTI* 11 (2017): 88: "the chief 'methodological' control must always remain participation in a community of critical readers formed by the character of the God attested in the very canonical Scriptures that we seek to interpret."

80. For an introduction to relevance theory's insights on intertextuality, see Peter S. Perry, "Relevance Theory and Intertextuality," in *Exploring Intertextuality: Diverse Strategies for New Testament Interpretation of Texts*, ed. B. J. Oropeza and Steve Moyise (Eugene, OR: Cascade, 2016), 207–21.

81. Steve Smith, "The Use of Criteria: A Proposal from Relevance Theory," in *Methodology in the Use of the Old Testament in the New: Context and Criteria*, ed. David Allen and Steve Smith, LNTS 597 (London: T&T Clark, 2019), 143.

82. Smith, "The Use of Criteria," 150. Smith identifies five categories of allusion: essential references (required for the text's communicative effect to be achieved); enriching references; compositional references (those not related to the text's communicative purpose); unintentional references (those not intended by the author, but which could be appropriated by the reader, even if unrelated to the text's purpose); post-authorial references (those discovered by later readers).

83. Ruben Zimmermann, "Symbolic Communication between John and His Reader: The Garden Symbolism in John 19–20," in *Anatomies of Narrative Criticism: The Past, Present, and Futures of the Fourth Gospel as Literature*, ed. Tom Thatcher and Stephen D. Moore (Atlanta: Society of Biblical Literature, 2008), 234.

84. Following Iser, R. Alan Culpepper, *Anatomy of the Fourth Gospel: A Study in Literary Design* (Philadelphia: Fortress, 1983), 209 likewise reminds us: "the meaning of a text . . . is not inherent in it but must be produced or actualized by the reader."

85. Cf. Zumstein, "Intratextuality," 135: "reading a text as an intertext puts a premium on the competence of readers." This is in continuity with a general shift in hermeneutics to recognize the role of the reader (rather than just the author) in meaning generation.

86. See for example Jesper Tang Nielsen, "The Lamb of God: The Cognitive Structure of a Johannine Metaphor," in *Imagery in the Gospel of John: Terms, Forms, Themes, and Theology of Johannine Figurative Language*, ed. Jörg Frey, et al., WUNT 200 (Tubingen: Mohr Siebeck, 2006), and the various options listed there

(225–26). Nielsen conceives of the image as a blended space or metaphor upon which Passover Lamb and Suffering Servant (Isaiah 53) images are combined together.

87. Margaret Davies, *Rhetoric and Reference in the Fourth Gospel*, JSNTSupp 69 (London: Bloomsbury, 1992), 355.

88. In a survey of recent work on intertextuality and biblical studies, Geoffrey D. Miller, "Intertextuality in Old Testament Research," *CBR* 9 (2010): 283–309 distinguishes between author-related and reader-related approaches, contending that only the latter is properly described as "intertextual." The former is better conceived of as "inner-biblical exegesis." Whether or not one is persuaded by his conclusion and nomenclature, Miller at least (rightly) advocates for the reader's perspective to be included in discourse on the NT's use of Israel's Scriptures.

89. On such matters, see the discussion in Zimmermann, "Symbolic," 221–35; he advocates for plausibility (conventional and textual) to be the defining factor for authenticating an allusion or symbol.

90. Marion L. Soards, "The Psalter in the Text and Thought of the Fourth Gospel," in *Perspectives on John: Method and Interpretation in the Fourth Gospel*, ed. Robert C. Sloan and Mikeal C. Parsons (Lampeter, UK: Edwin Mellen, 1993), 261.

Chapter 2

Quotation Usage in John's Passion Narrative

Having completed the various mapping exercises of the previous chapter, we now turn to the Fourth Gospel itself, and to the pluriform scriptural interaction it undertakes. As observed above, the nature of the Passion Narrative's scriptural usage is something of a multi-dimensional matrix and it must therefore be assessed from several angles or perspectives. These include John's use of unsignaled or more loose allusions and echoes, along with the wider thematic scriptural connections its Passion account makes, and such matters will be reviewed in chapter 3. In this chapter, partly for heuristic reasons, but more because of the perceived significance of quotational usage, we begin the exercise by considering the explicit scriptural quotations the Fourth Evangelist cites.

Bearing in mind the Passion Narrative's focus on the direct fulfillment of these scriptural quotations, they seem an appropriate starting point for our own inquiry. John's quotational usage offers a window onto the first two aspects of our thesis—the quotations give the framework for both how Scripture functions as the heartbeat of John's Passion account and articulate how Scripture is thereby impacted. (We will focus more on the former than the latter in this chapter, though not exclusively so.) We begin with some methodological discussion on the identification and function of quotations, particularly in the Fourth Gospel context, and set out the parameters for their subsequent investigation. We then turn to consideration of each of the quartet of quotations—19.24, 19.28, 19.36 and 19.37—and explore how they function within the overall Passion Narrative retelling.

THE FOURTH GOSPEL'S USE OF QUOTATIONS

It is fair to say that research on John's use of the Jewish Scriptures has tended to prioritize its usage of explicit scriptural quotations. The latter is now a well-researched phenomenon within Johannine scholarship, and excellent reviews of the question may be found *inter alia* in recent monographs by Myers, Sheridan, or Daise,[1] and perhaps most significantly in Menken's rigorous enquiry into each of the Fourth Gospel quotation's textual *Vorlage*.[2] Our task is not to rehearse or restate their work. However, their respective contributions demonstrate several aspects of John's intertextual strategy to which any consideration of the Fourth Gospel's use of quotations must be necessarily attentive. Our discussion will interact in detail with such matters, so some mapping of the lie of the land is helpful.

Scholarly prioritization of John's use of quotations is for good reason, one suggests. As Michael Daise rightly observes, across the Fourth Gospel, its cited quotations "furnish a gateway in to the Fourth Gospel itself,"[3] providing a structure or framework for its evangelistic argumentation.[4] Likewise, Freed opines that "in no other writer are the O.T. quotations so carefully woven into the context and the whole plan of composition as in Jn."[5] This heuristic structuring is even more the case within John's Passion discourse, with its increase in both volume and concentration of explicit scriptural citation, particularly in the portrayal of crucifixion scene itself.[6]

And explicit quotations are, of course, more than just structural devices, more than merely marker points in the Fourth Gospel's overall argumentation. They also provide a primary focus on *how* the Gospel utilizes Scripture to build its case and, particularly for our purposes, a lens by which to assess how Jesus's Passion has *scriptural* warrant or basis. For example, using the terminology of 1 Cor 15.3 to which we drew attention in the previous chapter, Menken correctly opines that the Fourth Gospel's "quotations constitute the most explicit way to convey the idea that Jesus's ministry, death and resurrection were 'according to the Scriptures.'"[7] They are far from the sole way in which John's scriptural usage is outworked, of course, and we do not seek to claim that they are even the most potent feature of John's intertextual play. Indeed, there are ways in which the quotation mode is more limiting than that achievable through allusions, an aspect we shall consider further in chapter 3. However, quotations remain the most overt or foregrounded mode of intertextual engagement, and the volume of work previously given over to them testifies to their interpretative prominence.

As noted in the introduction, in terms of applying them to Jesus's ministry, John uses quotation *qua*-device less than its Synoptic counterparts. Whatever total one arrives at for the number of John's scriptural quotations, and the counting varies significantly among commentators,[8] it is by some degree less than that set forth by Matthew, Mark, or Luke. However, that only serves to underscore their potential interpretative significance in John—*less is more*, so to speak, and the relative paucity (and it is only relative, of course) prompts the reader to be attentive to John's distinctive mode of usage. As is well noted in Johannine scholarship, from 12.38 onward, the formula for introducing a quotation becomes one denoting the citation's specific *fulfillment* (a passive form of πληρόω),[9] and the change in introductory formula signals a "point of departure"[10] for the rest of the Fourth Gospel. This is significant, marking an interpretative heightening or sharpened focus in both chapters 12 and 19 (each with a double citation "bookending" the respective fulfillment discourse—12.38–40, 19.36–37), and connects to an intensification of the Johannine plot. Chapter 12 demarks the closure of Jesus's public ministry, whereas chapter 19 both announces Jesus's death and also makes an explicit statement in respect of the teleiosis of Scripture (19.28–30).[11] Evans's summary is thus apposite and worthy itself of direct quotation:

> The function of the Old Testament in the Fourth Gospel, as seen in the formal quotations, is not *ad hoc* but is systematic and progressive, showing that Jesus's public ministry (1.29–12.36a) conformed to scriptural expectations and requirements, while his Passion (12.36b–19.37) fulfilled scriptural prophecies. This progression is clearly indicated by the Scripture quotation formulas.[12]

It is further notable that the resurrection narrative contains no direct quotation, at least not one specifically cited,[13] and 19.37 therefore becomes both the closing as well as the climactic quotation within the Johannine Gospel.

The testimony of John 12.38 is consonant with this perspective. That is, before the Passion Narrative begins, before even the Upper Room discourse commences, non-response to Jesus, or non-belief in him, is vindicated by scriptural warrant. Although we are focusing on John 18–19, the (fulfillment) discourse to which John's Passion Narrative draws a climax has already been set in motion at an earlier stage in the Gospel. And in contrast to 1.19–12.36a, such warrant is no longer merely evidential or testimonial, but is specifically a matter of *fulfillment*, a more explicit, heightened category.[14] The introductory formula is therefore core to the communicative effect and derivative function of the given quotation. It does more than merely "introduce" the citation, but rather signals the essential interpretive lens through which the citation is to be read. This aspect also has ramifications for "non-quotations" too—or at least texts like 18.9 or 18.32, where a *logos* is specified as being fulfilled (bearing a similar introductory formula to 12.38) but where it is one whose "source" is the words of Jesus rather than the text of Scripture. We will revisit these "non-quotations" in chapter 5, as they have ramifications for the status of the Fourth Gospel, and for its own scriptural credentials.

This emphasis on "fulfillment" is therefore characteristic of how John employs the Jewish Scriptures in terms of speaking of Jesus's Passion. Even before the Passion Narrative, the four scriptural quotations all utilize the πληρόω formulation, and do so specifically in finding scriptural fulfillment for Jesus's death.[15] And this fulfillment lens offers a very different assessment on the scriptural basis for Jesus's death compared to that of the Synoptic authors. Take Matthew, for example. Twice, Matthew's Jesus contextualizes his death in terms of scriptural fulfillment (Matt 26.54, 56), but in neither instance is there an explicit quotation yielded to support that contention, strikingly so bearing in mind the frequency of such quotation formulae in the Matthean birth narrative (Matt 1.22–23, 2.5–6, 2.15, 2.17–28, 2.23). And unlike the Fourth Gospel, Matthew offers no fulfillment text to explain or signify Jesus's death.[16] Some aspect of the crucifixion scene, the breaking open of the tombs maybe (Matt. 27.51–53), or perhaps Pilate washing his hands (Matt 27.24), might have generated such fulfillment testimony, but it remains—at least in explicit quotational terms—somewhat lacking, and the Matthean silence serves to underscore the comparative intensity of the Johannine account. Why then—and with what ultimate effect—does the Fourth Gospel (alone) stress the fulfillment dimension to Jesus's *death*?

CRITERIA FOR ASSESSING A QUOTATION

Commentators reviewing the assessment of John's scriptural usage have tended to focus either on the *form* of the quotation or on its *function* in the Fourth Gospel, though studies have expanded their respective interpretive lenses in recent times. Sheridan, for example, assesses scholarly approaches to the evangelist's use of quotations within four categories: Methods, Sources, Formulae, and Function.[17] This is a useful heuristic split, but equally, it perhaps implies that the lenses are mutually exclusive. Our approach seeks to be more holistic. Although not slavishly applied, our consideration of the respective quotations will seek to be attentive to the following elements or features:

A. *Definition*—that is, *identifying that it is indeed a quotation being made*. This can be relatively straightforward in view of the signaled introductory formula, but it is not necessarily so. As noted earlier, there are different counts of the number of quotations across the Fourth Gospel, and such ambiguity extends to its Passion retelling. As we shall see, it is contested as to whether 19.28 qualifies in this regard, and if that is indeed the case, further questions arise as to what scriptural text is being quoted. Menken, for example, defines quotation as "a clause (or series of clauses) from Israel's Scriptures that is (or are) rendered verbatim (or anyhow recognizably) in the NT and that is (or are) marked as such by an introducing or concluding formula."[18] That is, the quotation's existence is demonstrated by both the introductory formula *and* the presence of an equivalent form within the Jewish Scriptures. For this reason, Menken does not include 17.12 or 19.28 within his analysis of the Fourth Gospel's quotations, as, in his view, they have quotation formulae but no quotation "text." Likewise, and perhaps reflective of a more redaction-critical motivation, discussion of a quotation may get merely overlooked because it does not appear to be explanatorily significant or to have sufficient text-critical interest. Menken omits discussion of John 19.24 on this basis.[19]

Definitions are helpful for scoping the exercise in hand, but equally can have limiting value if used too restrictively, or without attention to the wider implications of where things do not quite "fit." If only because of the variation—or even inconsistency—found within the Fourth Gospel on such "quotation" matters, we will instead work with a general, working conception of a quotation as a signalled reference to something textually external. It may not be an absolute, verbatim citation (and judgement on that is withheld), but rather the reader is demonstrably invited to make a connection with what follows. There will likely still be some ambiguity or inconsistency in this regard—John 18.9 signals fulfillment of a word Jesus had spoken rather than an external textual, referent point, and that verse will be considered in chapter 5 when we explore John's characterization of Jesus's words as Scripture. But for our present purposes of identifying a quotation's existence, our approach will be to assume a citation is being made—with the burden of proof falling to demonstrate that it isn't (and if so, what explanatory significance thereby arises).

B. *Source*—that is, *identifying the implied Vorlage for the cited text.* Although the scholarly consensus generally concurs that the LXX provides the primary source for the Fourth Gospel's quotations,[20] as we shall see, the precise provenance of John's citations still generates some queries. The *Vorlage* of 19.37, for example, warrants consideration both for its essential difference to the LXX and for its potential Masoretic influence; there is also the possibility that John is quoting merely from memory[21] and/or dependent upon oral tradition in some form. And there is an increasing attention to whether John is using composite quotations, with the precise *Vorlage* derived from a plurality of scriptural sources.[22] This all said, however, our study is less focused on source for source's sake; the sheer multiformity of the scriptural tradition warrants against this. The quotation's *Vorlage* is just one "variable" (choice of word deliberate) in the process of assessing its function within John's Passion, rather than—as has often been the case—the primary area of investigation.

C. *Method*—that is, *what interpretive methods or techniques does John utilize?* This may be through comparison with other contemporary exegetical approaches such as Qumran pesher,[23] or Rewritten Bible techniques. But it will also attend to matters of context, and how far the "original context" (however defined or articulated) shapes the evangelist's usage of the respective scriptural text. This is more than a *Vorlage* question, and attends to the degree to which the OT context is preserved or else reworked.[24] But equally we recognize that context is a slippery, and ultimately pluriform, term, and perhaps one by which not to get too bogged down. Hence we will want to understand it in broad terms, akin to Keefer's assessment of Hays's consideration of the NT's writers scriptural usage: "context refers to historical context, events in a narrative sequence, God's acts, and overarching themes, seeming to leave the meaning of OT context allusive and unspecified, or at least multifarious."[25]

D. *Lens*—that is, *what hermeneutical lens is operative?* This is linked to matters of method, and is perhaps the determinative or principal element of our consideration. We will want to be attentive to what Moo terms the "hermeneutical axiom" operative in the citation.[26] That is, what initiates, legitimizes or authorizes the application of the scriptural text to the Passion situation, and specifically to Jesus and his actions? What is John's warrant for doing so, and how do we discern or unpack that? To what extent, for example, is the Fourth Gospel's scriptural lens shaped by the evangelist's own christological assumptions, perhaps imposed onto Scripture in eisegetical rather than exegetical form? Particularly with the fulfillment burden the evangelist places upon Scripture—and its relationship to Jesus's actions, ministry and death—questions arise as to how the specific text is operative in that regard (why *that* text and not another) and/or whether/how a text functions *qua*-Scripture in that way. And bearing in mind its fulfillment characterization, how does the quotation relate to questions of scriptural promise and to the evangelist identifying a *sensus plenior* within the marshalled quotations? Such discussion will also come out further in our later chapters as we consider the wider lens or implications of John's scriptural usage. What does it do *with* and *to* Scripture? And how does it relate to Jesus's own words, which eventually acquire an authority of Scripture itself?

E. *Outcome*. Finally, we will want to consider the why/how of the particular quotation; what is the anticipated purpose or outcome of the situation? This might relate to the gospel writer's own intention—their theological or christological reflection, for example. But it might also pertain to wider implications, to the ongoing conception of Scripture, for instance, or to the sociocultural implications of scriptural usage. Such matters will become more pressing as we extend the discussion across the whole of the Fourth Gospel's use of Scripture, but they still warrant some consideration as we consider the individual quotations.

In sum, therefore, we will use quotations as organizational siting grounds for a broad consideration of John's appeal to Israel's Scriptures. This means that discussion of each instance is not limited merely to the citation itself, but will necessarily include wider consideration of the quotation's contribution to the overall Passion Narrative. Such an approach seems perfectly legitimate bearing in mind the fulfillment baggage the quotations carry in the Fourth Gospel. They function as interpretive keys to unlock the Johannine intertextual door—scriptural or otherwise—and hence form a framework for the subsequent consideration of the narratival and thematic allusions.

To engagement with the four quotations (19.24, 19.28, 19.36–37) we now turn. After their respective consideration, we will then draw out some salient overall features of how John uses quotation intertexts within its Passion narration.

QUOTATIONAL USAGE IN JOHN 19.24

Introduced by the now familiar ἵνα ἡ γραφὴ πληρωθῇ introductory formula (cf. 12.38; 13.18; 15.25; 17.12), the first explicit quotation within John's Passion does not occur until 19.24, so somewhat late on in the Passion retelling (and we will want therefore to comment further on the absence of quotation in the events of 18.1–19.22). Jesus has come to Golgotha for his

Table 2.1. Textual Comparison for John 19.24 Quotation

John 19.24	διεμερίσαντο τὰ ἱμάτιά μου ἑαυτοῖς, καὶ ἐπὶ τὸν ἱματισμόν μου ἔβαλον κλῆρον	They divided my clothes among themselves, and for my clothing they cast lots.
Ps 22.18 (21.19 LXX)	διεμερίσαντο τὰ ἱμάτιά μου ἑαυτοῖς, καὶ ἐπὶ τὸν ἱματισμόν μου ἔβαλον κλῆρον	They divided my clothes among themselves, and for my clothing they cast lots.

imminent crucifixion (19.17), but the evangelist offers little scenic description except for discussion of the titulus content (19.19–22) and the positioning of Jesus amidst two other figures (19.18). Therefore in plot terms at least, the subsequent reference to the fate of Jesus's clothing (19.23–24) seems somewhat odd, pedantic even, and a rather mundane, incidental event hardly warranting comment bearing in mind the overall brevity of the crucifixion account. But the evangelist nonetheless includes the incident, along with the accompanying fulfillment formula, quoting Ps 22.18 in that regard.

There is little question that the quotation is drawn verbatim from Ps 21.19 LXX,[27] and the citation therefore tends to occasion minimal *Vorlage* discussion from Johannine commentators.[28] Bearing in mind, as we shall see, John's liking for composite quotations[29] and their capacity thereby to invoke extended meaning or reference, the deployment of *just* Ps 22.18, with no other immediately obvious operative intertext, is notable and may be said to limit its intertextual capacity. But the apparent simplicity of 19.24 is deceptive. Rather than *Vorlage* matters, it is the interpretative questions that arise from its citation that generate further interest.

Some initial contextual comments regarding 19.24 are helpful. First, it is possible, likely even, that the Ps 22.18 citation is functioning as a *representative* scriptural text rather than as a specific Psalmic one, and/or that its status *qua*-Scripture is the determining factor in its usage. The clarifying ἡ λέγουσα is absent from several early manuscripts (א, B) and may therefore be a later addition, perhaps under the influence of the λέγει of 19.37.[30] If originally absent, rhetorical emphasis is placed on Scripture *per se*, rather than on the specific text (and the related event) being fulfilled.[31] Such an assessment seems perfectly plausible bearing in mind the gradual heightening in the volume of scriptural fulfillment for which the evangelist advocates, and which comes to some form of completion just a few verses later (19.28–30). Moreover, although it cites the psalm verbatim, the evangelist does not make the precise lexical association that would demonstrably authenticate the psalmic fulfillment (i.e., John 19.23 does not anticipate the ἱματισμός of 19.24/Ps 22.18). However, even if it is initially the *overall* Scriptural category for which John is seeking fulfillment, extending its logic to stipulate the specific significance of Ps 22.18 (and Psalm 22 more widely) is not contradictory. The appeal can be simultaneously both to the essence of Scripture *and* to a specific text; the respective lenses are not mutually exclusive.

Second, John 19.23–24 manifests a further incidence of characteristic Johannine irony (cp. 11.49–50), in that the fulfillment of Scripture is enacted by Roman soldiers. In the subsequent citation (19.28), Jesus's personal agency is specifically noted (and necessarily so for the scale of the "completion" event there enacted). But in this present example, it is the *opposition* who, however inadvertently, meticulously bring about scriptural fulfillment.[32] Other characters—beyond Jesus—thus have a participatory role to play in the fulfillment of Scripture, consciously or otherwise. This is the case elsewhere in the Fourth Gospel of course—Judas' agency in the fulfillment of Ps 41.9 in John 13.18, for example. But even so, in 19.23–24, Jesus is still effectively controlling or enabling that fulfillment—he is causing it to happen, and the soldiers' actions remain "scripted" within the wider fulfillment discourse.[33] The suggestion, though, that the soldiers' action enable them to receive the effects of Jesus's death seems to overplay the possibilities of 19.23–24[34]; the text itself gives no basis for such conjecture.

Third, the Synoptic Passion Narratives are familiar with the clothes-dividing tradition (Matt 27.35, Mark 15.24, Luke 23.34),[35] and their respective mentions likely also deliberately echo Ps 22.18, particularly bearing in mind their other Passion appeals to the Psalm (Mk 15.34/Ps 22.1, for example). John, however, intensifies the allusive reference and utilizes the specific quotational mode. Now, one is cautious about specifying the reasons for the more evident Johannine firmness, but it seems likely that John has *actively* chosen to strengthen what is more allusive in its synoptic counterparts,[36] a strengthening that is endorsed by the wider fulfillment hermeneutic established from 12.38 onward and driven by the perceived need to demonstrate unambiguous christological fulfillment. Such development, one suggests, would be not unwelcome to the Synoptics, and is certainly in the "spirit" of the Markan testimony. Likewise, it also correlates with the wider, early Christian association of Psalm 22 with Jesus's death, rendering it arguably the primary scriptural intertext in this regard.[37] The Psalm's usage in Heb 2.12, for example, likely also draws from such association. John's use of Psalm 22 therefore likely derives from tradition John has already received and, in terms of early Christian reception, it would be a perfectly appropriate "representative" text to deploy. Even if ἡ λέγουσα *is* a later addition, it nonetheless serves to give a specific text/events around which fulfillment may be found. As proposed above, the general *qua*-Scripture principle *and* the specific citation of Ps 22.18 are entirely complementary, and such both/and-ness would seem germane to the fulfillment(s) John seeks to articulate.

Fourth, and well-recognized within Johannine scholarship, the evangelist's appeal to Ps 22.18 seems to overlook the LXX's implied parallelism, thereby differentiating two distinct actions rather than conceiving them as parallel depictions of the same episode (cf. the similar, alleged misreading of parallelism in Matt 21.4–7). At a surface level at least, John's exegesis appears somewhat awkward or forced, and apparently ignorant of the implications of such parallelism.[38] But such accusations may be misplaced. Barrett, for example, ventures that a proper understanding of the intricacies of Hebrew parallelism is a later, post-Johannine phenomenon, and hence John should not be accused of having overlooked it here.[39] Alternatively, Carson proposes that

John does not actually *mis*read the parallelism, but rather reads the two stichs as representing the same "action," one made (together) in respect of both τὰ ἱμάτιά and τὸν ἱματισμόν.⁴⁰ Lots are cast for these garments and effect their distribution, and thus Ps 22.18 does not address the fate of the χιτών (19.23). Such a view is plausible bearing in mind the lexical dissimilarity between χιτών and Ps 22.18 (whereas both of Ps 22.18's τὰ ἱμάτιά and τὸν ἱματισμόν may be said to match the τὰ ἱμάτια of 19.23), but that then begs the question as to why the χιτών is included at all if it does not constitute part of the Psalm's address and (direct) fulfillment. Alternatively, John's interpretation may reflect contemporary exegetical practice, namely, to find divine insight in the whole text and explore its full interpretative potential. The parallelism is not so much overlooked, but rather actively set aside in order to exploit the full interpretative capacity the Psalm offered.

Fifth, the first-person voice of Ps 22.18 (and, by extension, John 19.24) serves to tie the action to Jesus himself. John retains the double reference to "μου" when one might have expected—if only for narrative consistency—an amendment to the third-person pronoun form. Such change of person is possible elsewhere for John,⁴¹ and it appears legitimate Second Temple exegetical practice to allow such lexical variation.⁴² But that is not John's action here, and instead, with the retention of μου, Jesus's voice continues to be heard, even at point of crucifixion, and even when the actions are those of a third party. The use of the first-person language aligns Jesus with the role of narrator, enabling his perspective on the scriptural fulfillment being achieved, and his own participation—however vicarious—within that process. The soldiers' role is rendered more secondary as a result.

Sixth, and to push the matter further, if it is indeed the case that the specific textual citation does "matter," Jesus becomes effectively the one speaking the Psalm. Even when not voicing the text in *narratival* terms, Jesus still "inhabits" the text, owns the Scripture in that way, and offers a further instance of how John ties together Jesus's actions and Scripture's witness, a theme we will explore further as our analysis ensues. In terms of such ownership, there is perhaps a parallel with Pilate's terse defense of the titulus' claim ("What I have written, I have written") in the preceding verse (19.22). Where Pilate's declaration only serves (ironically) to show his misunderstanding of Jesus's kingship, Jesus is able to declare the Psalm, and in contrast demonstrate his full understanding of it. He is the one who properly interprets the Psalm and pronounces its ultimate meaning. This would seem appropriate bearing in mind the subsequent fulfillment reference (19.28–30) which underscores Jesus's (sole) capability to bring about the perfection of Scripture.⁴³ It may also attest a particular emphasis or significance for oral delivery, assuming a predominantly non-literate culture and audience. That is, the "hearing" of the text—or a text whose mode of discourse is "oral"—may carry further weight than one that remains merely textual or "textified."

Let us turn, then, to the purpose of the quotation—what does it do? Generally speaking, scholars have tended to give less attention as to *why* this particular event is cited in respect of scriptural fulfillment, other than to suggest that it was a convenient tradition or source to which the evangelist is able to attach scriptural fulfillment. In and of itself, the specified event/practice would not have been particularly unusual,[44] and consequently begs the question as to why it warrants comment in such a brief narrative. And although the episode may well have been a familiar one to wider early Christian sources, and hence convenient in that regard, the sheer *oddity* of finding such explicit fulfillment in this episode is surely curious, particularly bearing in mind the weight John's strategy for seeking scriptural fulfillment seems to bear. The previous instances of declared fulfillment—(some) Jewish rejection of Jesus's ministry (12.37–40), Judas's "lifting his heel" against Jesus (13.18)[45] and the resultant, potentially sectarian division with Jewish communities (15.25)—can all claim to be integral elements of the Johannine narrative. Each is intrinsic to Johannine plot development and its relationship to Scripture, necessary content that gathers authority and significance because of its scriptural attestation. The subsequent citations (19.28, 19.36–37) likewise pertain to Jesus and the instance of his death, and, as we shall see, derive particular significance in that regard. But the events specified in 19.24 can scarcely make that claim, at least not at first sight. Even though the citation pertains to *Jesus's* clothing, their role in the plot—before one even gets to questions of fulfillment—remains somewhat limited. Or to put it another way, such fulfillment—on the surface at least—does not obviously relate to Jesus's death or to demonstrating its reality; the quotation can seem incidental, spurious even, and happens outside of the prevailing narrative flow.[46]

Moreover, the lexical dissimilarity between 19.23 and 19.24 raises further questions as to how Ps 22.18 can even be said to be "fulfilled." That is, Jesus's seamless χιτών (19.23) seemingly becomes the ἱματισμός of Ps 22.18, and John makes no attempt to amend the lexical disparity. At one level, then, one might suggest that it is the *event* that bears the burden of the fulfillment rather than the actual text; the (simple) need for scriptural warrant may be what drives the portrayal of the event. Psalm 22.18 provides a convenient—if somewhat odd—supportive text, but it has no other interpretative value; the seamless tunic is likewise included solely in the service of fulfillment and has no further significance beyond that fact.[47] If so, this would seem to have implications as to the scope and nature of *how* John conceives of nitty-gritty scriptural fulfillment, namely that it may be manifest beyond the limitations of lexical similarity (and/or the requirements for it) and is operative across a much wider lens/scope.

In sum, although the citation is surely driven by the desire for scriptural fulfillment (cf. the second οὖν (19.24) to reinforce the actions of the soldiers in respect of Ps 22.18), it remains ambiguous as to exactly how/why this event and/or psalm are employed to bear what appears to be a significant fulfillment burden. John 19.24 testifies to at least three ways in which this might be operative:

That "Scripture" as a whole is fulfilled, irrespective of the precise or specific text (*fulfillment qua-Scripture*)

That a particular scripture is fulfilled, and perhaps, by extension, its wider context (i.e., the whole of Psalm 22, rather than merely 22.18) (*fulfillment qua-text*)

That the described event or action matters in terms of fulfillment—and hence the cited text may be no more than a convenient bearer for such fulfillment. (*fulfillment qua-event*)

What motivates this specific instance of fulfillment beyond the burden of it being Scripture itself that is being fulfilled? Bearing in mind the brevity of John's Passion narration, what occasions its inclusion, and how does that inform notions of scriptural fulfillment? In the third instance above, what is it about the event that makes the connection?

1. *The division of clothing matters:* It is hard to see what—in and of itself—the division of clothing actually achieves in respect of John's retelling. The text implies that the separation of clothing and casting of lots have taken place (19.23), and 19.24c adds a confirmatory note to that effect, but that remains the extent of any commentary on the episode. Whereas the division of property belonging to an executed criminal was a perfectly feasible occurrence, there is no evidence that John's Jesus has much to split or distribute. Likewise, although it is perfectly plausible that Jesus was crucified naked, and much theological insight may be drawn from that possibility, such matters do not seem to be determinative in/for John's retelling. The removal of clothing perhaps echoes Jesus removing his outer robe in preparation for foot-washing (13.4),[48] but the latter stresses Jesus's own action in so doing, whereas 19.23 attributes the action to the soldiers; it is notable for *not* portraying Jesus's own enaction of the event. It may be that the division of clothing among the four soldiers mirrors the four women at the cross,[49] who each receive (in effect) a portion of the Beloved Disciple (19.25–27),[50] and in that sense, the implicit presence or memory of Jesus is confirmed. But again, that does not really necessitate scriptural fulfillment or the "demonstration" through the soldiers' actions, and technically it is

only Jesus's mother who passes over to the Beloved Disciple's care (19.26–27).
2. *The seamless garment matters:* Where the division of clothing seems unnecessary to the Johannine plot, the fate of the χιτών may have more significance, or at least it has evoked more curiosity from commentators. Where the Synoptics utilize the division of clothing tradition, albeit in allusive rather than fulfillment terms (Matt 27.35, Mark 15.24, Luke 23.34), John alone extends the reference to include the seamless garment tradition. Its absence from the Synoptic portrayal may well signal it being a Johannine creation,[51] but even if that is the case, such creation only serves to confirm that the seamless χιτών material forms an integral role within the Johannine portrayal.[52] The extra, otherwise unnecessary, detail given as to its construction (ἐκ τῶν ἄνωθεν ὑφαντὸς δι' ὅλου) may also testify to its prominence in the Johannine retelling; in terms of fulfillment purposes, at least, it would have been sufficient merely to have said it was ἄραφος.

So what might have occasioned the χιτών's inclusion, particularly in respect of the Fourth Gospel's fulfillment perspective? Fenton avers that the unity (or non-tearing) of the χιτών alludes to the synoptic account of the Temple curtain being torn,[53] particularly in the light of the Temple symbolism invoked by Jesus's death (cf. 2.18–22), but John gives no steer in that direction. The χιτών may carry priestly overtones,[54] but John has very little, if any, other sacerdotal patterning of Jesus.[55] It may have a more ironic aspect, consistent with John's other such usage, that at the same time that the soldiers are crucifying Jesus, they are (ironically) unwilling to tear his garment.[56] But it is more likely that the *unity* of the tunic matters, and this—rather than the particular item or its function—is what drives or necessitates the appeal to scriptural fulfillment.[57]

The precise referent for the implied unity is not absolutely clear, however, as there are several potential links (and they are not mutually exclusive). Jesus seeks after the unity of his disciples and subsequent generations (17.21–24), and the Fourth Gospel has also addressed the aspiration that Jesus will not lose any of his followers (17.12, 18.9—both instances are fulfillment statements).[58] David Strauss memorably spoke of the Gospel of John in terms of a "seamless garment," and that conjures the notion, albeit somewhat derivative, that the χιτών (maybe as the outer garment) testifies to the unity of the testimony of Jesus recorded and found within the Fourth Gospel.[59] If the division of the clothing into four and the preservation of the tunic are to map the "familial" scene of 19.25–27, then, likewise, one might identify a rhetorical parallel between the unbrokenness of the tunic and the anticipated unity of the new (Johannine) community as the Beloved Disciple welcomes

Jesus's mother into his home (19.27).⁶⁰ In related form, Jesus's body remains unbroken (19.33), as does the bread of the feeding (6.11) or the net of John 21 (21.11) and that may be said to mimic ecclesiological unity, so likewise the oneness of the tunic. Either way, the image of the χιτών's unbrokenness is of sufficient "significance" to warrant inclusion in John's retelling and thereby invite scriptural fulfillment in some form.

The presenting difficulty, of course, for the unity argument—as even its advocates concede⁶¹—is that the garment is taken away by the soldiers. If it is to be a metaphor or symbol of the Johannine Community's status, its use is somewhat counterintuitive or counterproductive.⁶² And after all, there is no *compelling* reason to conclude that the unity motif of the Fourth Gospel needs to be present within the Passion account.⁶³ Moreover, if the tunic's unity really is the presenting reason for the Psalm 22 citation, then it is interesting that both elements of Ps 22.18 are included and ascribed fulfillment credentials; the effect of the fulfillment would still have been achieved with just Ps 22.18b.

Furthermore, it is not as though the detail of the χιτών's composition is requisite for the psalmic fulfillment, and "[h]armony with the quotation from Psalm 22 could have been achieved without the insistence on the seamless quality of Jesus's garments."⁶⁴ Indeed, if as Carson proposes, John 19.24/Ps 22.18 does not address the fate of the χιτών, then the latter's inclusion may be on intratextual rather than intertextual grounds. For example, attending to its ἄνωθεν characterization, Fenik opines: "The untorn tunic woven from the top emerges as a symbol of Jesus's divine, heavenly existence that cannot be destroyed. The intact tunic bespeaks the truth that, despite the crucifixion, the life of the Son of God cannot be taken from him, because it has been 'woven' from above."⁶⁵ As such, it resonates with Jesus's prior declaration that power over him can only be given from above (ἄνωθεν—19.11); the χιτών becomes further visual evidence of the divine protection Jesus possesses.

Overall, it is hard to see how either of the soldiers' specified actions go about demonstrating scriptural fulfillment in any significant depth or fashion, or why they would be thought to be necessarily used as such. Moo ventures that the inclusion of the casting lots discourse (and hence the extended citation of Ps 22.18) derived merely from John's awareness of such seamless robe tradition, and thus need not have any further symbolic function.⁶⁶ Likewise, Köstenberger suggests John includes it because it is an event to which the evangelist is eyewitness,⁶⁷ hence reinforcing their authorial and testimonial credentials (cf. also 19.35), particularly in view of the subsequent community-founding events of 19.25–27. But this only re-presents the primary question, namely as to *why* both actions are included and seen as bearers of scriptural fulfillment. Even if, particularly for the χιτών material, the incident represents genuine and/or "historical" tradition for John, and has plausible association with Ps 22.18, that need only establish some testimonial or confirmatory relationship rather than requiring the driving πληρωθῇ classification. And the converse is also true. Because of the likely historical legitimacy of the practice of division of clothing, its inclusion in 19.23 is unlikely to be a creation merely to force accommodation to the Psalm.[68]

We might, therefore, turn the question the other way, and consider instead what the appeal to Psalm 22.18a achieves beyond being merely a suitable evidential foil for scriptural fulfillment. It may, for example, reflect the way in which "the evangelist stresses the divine providence present even in Jesus's most vulnerable moment,"[69] and that view is certainly plausible. But one might equally respond that John's Passion Narrative doesn't seem to focus on or even consider Jesus's vulnerability. Instead, the reverse seems to be the case—Jesus is in control as he carries his own cross (19.17), and is ironically "lifted up" unto glorification. As such, we might instead suggest that the citation of Ps 22.18 serves to emphasize the victory or achievement of the cruciform moment, underlining the irony that the moment of implied vulnerability so presented by Ps 22.18 is actually to be *not* vulnerable, but rather be vindicated in victory.[70] To do so, one suggests, is to take full, metaleptic account of Psalm 22, and of its wider content; indeed, the inclusion of both clothing stiches is part of a Johannine encouragement to embrace the full gamut of the Psalm, rather than doing so atomistically.

As has been well noted in respect of Mark's scriptural usage, its citation of Ps 22.1 (Mk 15.34) may also incorporate the full breadth of the Psalm's scope.[71] The righteous sufferer of 22.1 is the vindicated figure, the one both heard by God (Ps 22.24) and who declares God's praises (Ps 22.22). How might such maximal application extend to John's Passion Narrative? Obermann, for example, pursues the maximalist option, opining that Jesus fulfills the (whole) Psalm in terms of experiencing rejection by God.[72] Likewise Fenik ventures that, under the influence of the Psalm 22 citation, the episode demonstrates Jesus's "utter humiliation and deprivation of dignity," once more applying the full gamut of the Psalm's testimony.[73] However, such an assessment surely runs counter to the overall tenor of John's Passion retelling. As suggested above, Ps 22.1—at least in isolation—does not "work" for John, and its absence from John's account is entirely appropriate. The absence is found in Luke too, of course, but it becomes more noticeable in John bearing in mind the "ramping up" the Ps 22.18 *fulfillment* implies. One might say that, although Luke chooses to exclude the *eloi, eloi* lament, John simply *cannot* cite Ps 22.1—it goes against the very tenor of his portrayal of Jesus and God, and the portrayal of the cruciform, lifting up moment as Jesus's glorification.[74] Jesus is not—cannot be, even—rejected by God, particularly at his hour (16.32; cf. 8.29).[75] Similarly absent from John is the taunting of Jesus found in the Synoptics, content that seems to draw on Ps

22.8, and which might also seem to promote a (non-Johannine) portrayal of Jesus as one rejected by God and/or requiring external/divine salvation. At the very least, the John 19-Ps 22.1/22.8 tensions caution against any simple assumption of intertextual metaleptic transfer.

But that does not necessarily rule out a broader intertextual exchange with Psalm 22, beyond merely 22.18. *Pace* Obermann, we might suggest that John reads Jesus as fulfilling the figure of (the totality of) Psalm 22, but specifically its ultimate *reversal* of the notion of divine rejection and instead the definitive announcement of divine vindication. What might appear in the Psalm to be rejection is ultimately not so (22.22–31), and the integral vindication of the Psalm's protagonist—as one with whom God is very present—is brought to the fore. God is also vindicated by the process; the divine deliverance of the vindicated figure will be declared forever (22.30–31). This also ties back also to the contention above of the way in which Psalm 22 became, in an early stage of Christian thinking, inextricably intertwined with remembrance of Jesus's death. It is as if the NT writers could not talk about Jesus's death without talking about Psalm 22, and equally, could not talk about Psalm 22 without talking about Jesus's death.[76]

What, then, does Psalm 22 bring or add to the Johannine Passion? If we are to bring the full weight of the Psalm to the interpretative table, what is its intertextual added value? A contributory factor is the degree to which Psalm 22 is operative across the whole of John's Passion Narrative, rather than merely John 19.24/Ps 22.18. John 19.2–3 may have in mind, or at least reflect, the ridicule or mockery found in Ps 22.7–8. And it is possible that the wounds of Jesus (20.25) are also an echo of Ps 22.16. Köstenberger ventures that John's account of Jesus's death offers a midrash on Ps 22.15–18, the combination of thirst (19.28; Ps 22.15), pierced hands and feet (20.27; Ps 22.16) and preservation of bones (19.33; Ps 22.17).[77] The Fourth Gospel may also have made earlier allusions to Psalm 22, and if so, that would commend its wider usage in the Passion. Siliezar observes, for example: "It is not unusual that John alludes to an Old Testament text from which he has quoted elsewhere." He suggests three points within John 6 that might "be inspired by" Ps 22.26 (21.27 LXX); the language of fulfillment/satisfaction (John 6.12), the searching after Jesus (John 6.24) and the imagery of food that leads to eternal life (John 6.27).[78] One might also mention Ps 22.22 as a possible intertextual echo in John 17.6, particularly in view of that text's usage in Heb 2.12, and its connection there with Jesus tradition voiced by Jesus himself. And of course, the ultimate vindication of the lamenting figure—cf. 22.29–31—is intrinsic, integral even, to the ironic fulfillment hermeneutic that John seemingly seeks to unpack.

Also relevant, one suggests, is the broader context or milieu of Psalm 22. Richard Hays draws attention to John's use of Davidic psalms as potential testimony to/for Jesus's royal status, and the citation of Ps 22.18 in John 19.24 would seem to be a prime manifestation of this, particularly if, as observed above, the fulfillment *qua*-text aspect of the Psalm is in view. It might also allow other parts of Psalm 22 to bring further resonance to the Passion portrayal, beyond just the specific reference to v18. Daly-Denton seems to point in that direction, averring that "John's citation of Ps 21.19 exemplifies the principle that what is said is always heard against the background of the vast 'unsaid.'"[79] Although John does not explicitly specify it as such,[80] the speaker of the Septuagintal Psalm is David, and its attribution to Jesus here likely forms part of an extension to Jesus of that feature of the Psalm. As such, the Psalm's Davidic aspect carries the tenor of the one proclaimed—however unconsciously—as the King of the Jews (19.19–21) and also extends to its righteous sufferer aspect. John's Jesus comes to the cross dressed as a king (19.2–3)—or at least there is no mention of him being disrobed of this attire (it is not specified by the clothing episode). In particular, Daly-Denton has sought—with this and the numerous other Psalmic references across John—to view the citation of Psalm 22 as inculcating a Davidic tenor to the Fourth Gospel, thereby bringing David to the Johannine interpretative table.[81] Her ultimate position may go beyond what is possible, but she rightly draws attention to the resonance a text like Psalm 22 might have for John, and why it might be a suitable candidate by which the concept of scriptural fulfillment is outworked, and particularly its "royal" dimension. Addressing the specific choice of Ps 22.18, she comments: "His selectivity with regard to Psalm 22 is a hint that the one verse that he does decide to use will accord with his view that Jesus's death was actually a royal enthronement and the most complete manifestation of his glory."[82]

At the very least, with Daly-Denton, we might concur that it is kingship—Davidic or otherwise—that provides contextual focus to the Psalm,[83] and the idea of a righteous sufferer is derivative from this royal characterization. Meye Thompson arrives at not dissimilar conclusions. She speaks of those Davidic psalms used within the Passion Narrative as being "psalms of the rejected king,"[84] and hence commensurate with the kind of portrayal to which Daly-Denton appeals. To put in another way, Psalm 22 is a (necessary) part of what makes Jesus's Passion a *royal* death. The crowning of Jesus (19.2–3) is ironic, of course, and turns the notion of royalty on its head. But without the accompanying scriptural warrant, the irony inevitably breaks down. For Jesus to die a royal death, for the titulus' "King of the Jews" proclamation to have its full effect, for the cross to be the "throne"—and for that to receive ratification and/or not get reduced to unresolved irony or merely caricature—the Psalm 22 intertext is a necessary ingredient. Jesus's claim to kingship (18.36) remains merely a parody without the endorsement of scriptural fulfillment.

If Psalm 22 is casting a royal or Davidic lens onto the crucifixion scene, then such a lens may also offer further insight onto the unbrokenness of Jesus's χιτών. Daley-Denton, in particular, engages with several scriptural royal robe-tearing incidents as a window onto the Golgotha scene. For example, informed by Samuel that YHWH has rejected his kingship (1 Sam 15.26), Saul grasps Samuel's robe and rips it (1 Sam 15.27), the tearing demonstrative of the demise of Saul's Kingship (15.28). Similarly, the prophet Ahijah visibly illustrates the division of Jeroboam's kingship by tearing it into twelve pieces (1 Kings 11.29–31), indicative of the division that was to come. Such imagery, coupled with the Davidic tenor of Psalm 22 and juxtaposed with the seamless χιτών, may have explanatory value. Jesus's royal status is linked to the status of the robe; by contrast to his predecessors' attire, its non-breaking is evidence of his kingdom not being broken. The seamlessness—or non-division—of the χιτών underlines that, even in the cruciform moment—and climactically so perhaps—"Jesus's royal status remained intact and undiminished."[85] Of course, it is hard to identify specific methodological grounds to justify such echoes, but being at least attentive to their potential existence alongside the untorn robe does yield explanatory significance, whether "intended" or not by John. In a gospel so deepened with scriptural resonance, it is hard to ignore such echoes or insights and they enrich the portrayal John provides.

To press the matter further, without the "whole" Psalm in view, it is hard to see how—or why—John is finding fulfillment in the clothes-sharing episode beyond a mere "this-is-that" type of approach. Such a conclusion is possible, of course, and it would be akin to a quasi-pesher approach that finds fulfillment in particular episodes. However, the burden that the evangelist seems to want to place on fulfillment—and its overarching significance—leads us to conceive a more multi-layered lens and an embrace of the *whole* sense of the Psalm, "daringly read"[86] as Jesus's speech and forging the Fourth Gospel's christological-royal hermeneutic.

THE TITULUS INSCRIPTION (JOHN 19.19–22)

The ironic reversal implied by the Ps 22.18 citation is enhanced by its immediate context, and particularly the preceding discourse regarding the titulus inscription (19.19–22). Indeed, the latter provides a further reason or factor for the appeal to scriptural fulfillment in 19.24, specifically in respect of the γράφω/γραφή comparison so yielded. John effectively juxtaposes two competing claims to "γραφή" authority and plays them off against each other. Pilate's titulus γραφή, contested by the chief priests (19.21), seeks to claim authority for itself. Its three languages pronounce universal influence for the statement, and Pilate's defense of the titulus avowal appears to invest it with imperial authority. That is, Pilate declares that he himself has written (γράφω) the statement, claiming personal responsibility for its content (19.22; cf. also 19.19). The double use of γέγραφα (19.22) reinforces such procuratorial responsibility, both for the content of the τίτλος and for its apparent "γραφή" status. As Brodie succinctly opines: "Pilate had replied that the inscription, in fact, was like scripture."[87] At the same time, though, the evangelist falls short of calling the inscription γραφή—it remains a τίτλος, even though it is inscribed (γράφω) by Pilate, and therefore it is implicitly rendered inferior compared to the γραφή unwittingly fulfilled by the soldiers' actions (19.23–24).

This contributes further irony in terms of γραφή matters. It is the "junior" soldiers rather than the procurator who (properly) fulfil Scripture. The lifting up of the titulus γραφή (unconsciously/ironically) articulates the kingship of the one who is (ironically) "lifted up" on a Roman cross. Pilate is adamant about what he has written, but (ironically) demonstrates his *lack* of understanding of what he has written (γράφω). Unconsciously, "the chief agent of Roman imperial power in the Roman province of Judaea announces Jesus's sovereignty to all the world; he advances the Johannine Christology and subverts the imperial meaning of the cross."[88] Hence we might suggest that John conceives of the titulus inscription as *de facto* γραφή,[89] articulating both the testimonial function of Scripture demonstrated in the first half of the Fourth Gospel, but also representing in some fashion the scriptural fulfillment concept outworked in the Gospel's second half, and which reaches its telos in the subsequent verses (19.24, 19.28, 19.36–37).[90] To all intents and purposes therefore, even if mediated in ironic form, the titulus inscription, and the context/event it addresses, represents a further instance of Scripture fulfilled, of γραφή πεπληρωμένη. The cruciform titular—the cruciform γραφή—is fulfilled in the very mortal action the crucifixion enacts. It may even reflect or pronounce—in further ironic mode—the "fulfillment" of Ps 22.28, namely the proclamation of Jesus's kingdom manifest over the nations; if so, it gives further reason, as discussed above, for the wider sense of Psalm 22 being generated by John 19.24.

Pushing this further, if the titulus can be considered as effectively γραφή, or at least characterized as such in terms of authority and kingship, it could also be said to offer (and uniquely so, within the Fourth Gospel) explicit "scriptural" testimony for Jesus's kingship, or scriptural warrant for classifying the events of 19.16–30 as regicide. Hays rightly observes: "nowhere in John's fully developed drama of the trial and crucifixion does he make any gesture to explicate his christological redefinition of kingship in light of scriptural warrants. The redefinition is performed strictly by the authority of Jesus's own words and actions."[91] As we shall see, Jesus's "words and actions" absolutely have implications for Scripture and scriptural warrant, and Hays is right to draw attention to the lack of (prior) scriptural appeal in respect of Jesus's kingship. However, one might suggest, *pace* Hays, that John's characterization of the titulus inscription—as *de facto* γραφή—effectively does this, and offers written warrant, albeit derivatively and/or in characteristic ironic fashion, for Jesus's royal status. And to push that observation further, we might tentatively suggest that, for John, that which is written (γράφω) and which attests to Jesus's status or authority effectively assumes scriptural status (γραφή) for that reason (while still remaining merely a τίτλος).

Linked to this, also, is the response to the titulus. Many of the Jewish onlookers read its inscription (19.20), with some contesting the veracity of its claim. In so doing, they demonstrate their own misunderstanding of Jesus, intratextually reminiscent of John 12.37–41 perhaps, and thus one way that passage's scriptural fulfillment is achieved. Moreover, the chief priests' desire to change the text of the τίτλος, the wording of the effective γραφή, testifies to the relationship between scriptural fulfillment and Jesus. That is, Jesus's opponents arrive at their position not just because they "disbelieve" the γραφή, but also because they contest its very content.[92] Misunderstanding Jesus and misrepresenting Scripture are two sides of the same coin.

One further observation might be made in respect of the titulus and its potential ironic, textual claims. Mary Coloe draws attention to the phrasing of the appellation Ἰησοῦς ὁ Ναζωραῖος (19.19), the same nominal form used in terms of the one sought for arrest (18.5, 7). Rather than being "Jesus of Nazareth," as most translations render the phrase, Coloe conjectures that it is properly "Jesus the Nazarean," a deliberate nomenclature that derives not from Jesus's home but one that instead carries messianic overtones. It is premised, she ventures, on the Hebrew root *netzer* (cf. Isa 11.11), whose equivalent form *tzamah* (Zech 3.8, 6.12) also carries such messianic credentials. Drawing on Qumranic (4QpGen 5.3–4; 4QpIs[aa] 11) and targumic material, she conjectures "the hypothesis that by the first century CE the term 'Nazarene' had developed associations with a Davidic Messiah who would build the eschatological temple."[93] Such a connection probably requires a well-resourced reader to make it, but if there is indeed, some scripturally-resourced, messianic resonance to the Nazarene title, then it adds further weight to the fulfillment episode John is outworking, particularly bearing in mind the Davidic portrayal encapsulated within Psalm 22.

19.24—CONCLUSION

In the citation of Ps 22.18, we find scope for all three dimensions of scriptural fulfillment to be operative, and in mutually informing fashion. And in each instance, they are fulfilled in somewhat reversed or ironic manner. fulfillment *qua-Scripture* is enacted—but the divine purpose is (ironically) outworked through the agency of the opponent. Fulfillment *qua-Text* is portrayed, and through a specific text whose full scope reverses where it began, eliciting divine vindication of the one seemingly abandoned by God. Fulfillment *qua-Event* is outworked, but paradoxically so, in that the achievement of the divine purpose (including, one might suggest, the ongoing unity of the Johannine Community) is manifest through what appears to be loss and separation.[94]

As such, even though it remains a singular rather than composite quotation, and even though, as we will suggest, John's Passion seems to express a preference for the latter rather than the former, the citation of Ps 22.18 remains an explanatorily powerful intertext, one that enables an extended commentary on the crucifixion scene. Rather than being a wooden, simplistic pesher-style statement, the citation of Ps 22.18, proves to be a powerful one which carries a portfolio of elements and themes that are intrinsic to the Fourth Gospel's portrayal of Jesus's death—its royal status, its (ironic) enthronement and vindication of the suffering figure, and its (ironic) enactment by those outside of Israel.

QUOTATIONAL USAGE IN JOHN 19.28

The second fulfillment citation within John's Passion Narrative (19.28) occurs shortly after its predecessor (19.24) and such proximity contributes to the intensification and immediacy of the fulfillment motif.[95] The intervening section (19.25–27) is thus bookended by fulfillment discourses (19.24/19.28), and some kind of *inclusio* or chiasm is so generated, highlighting the transferral moment therein, and framing 19.25–27 as the birthing moment of the Johannine Community.[96] The significance of 19.25–27, and the following asyndetous μετὰ τοῦτο, is underscored by Jesus (then) knowing that all was now finished (19.28). The events of 19.25–27 therefore demark the completion of Jesus's missional task.[97]

Distinct for 19.28, though, is that the verbal form used in respect of scriptural fulfillment has changed from πληρόω (19.24) to τελειόω (19.28). Such a shift may be occasioned, in part at least, by the use of the cognate verb τελέω (19.28, 30),[98] perhaps for homophonic similarity, and/or with the double use of τελέω framing the τελειόω reference and ascribing it further emphasis accordingly.[99] The double use of τελέω resonates with John's demarcation of Jesus's death as the τέλος or climax of Jesus's work and love (13.1), and may itself offer a scriptural reminiscence of the completion of God's creational work (συνετέλεσεν—Gen 2.2). The switch to τελειόω—the only time John uses it of Scripture (19.36 returns to the familiar πληρόω)—serves to underscore the distinctive aspect of this instance of scriptural fulfillment, seemingly going one stage beyond that manifested through the previous πληρόω formulae.¹⁰⁰ At the τέλος of Jesus's work (13.1), at the moment when the narrator and Jesus synergistically announce the finish of his ministry/life (τελέω—19.28, 30),¹⁰¹ Scripture is distinctively—uniquely even—brought to fulfillment (τελειόω). This individual usage of τελειόω, deployed at the climactic moment of Jesus's cruciform death, gives further nuance and definition to the nature of the scriptural fulfillment found therein, and ties it explicitly to Jesus's actions.¹⁰²

Comparison with the Markan Passion portrayal may be helpful at this point, particularly in terms of mapping the chronological parallels with the Johannine rendering. In the Markan account, Jesus's voicing of Ps 22.1 (21.2 LXX—Mk 15.34) is "misheard" by onlookers as a call for Elijah's intervention (Mk 15.35–36), a response that is absent from the John's portrayal. Mark narrates the response to this, the offering of sour wine (ὄξος) up to Jesus (consistent with John at least in that detail—cf. John 19.29), as the event immediately preceding Jesus's death (Mark 15.37), as is likewise the case in John (John 19.30).¹⁰³ But by contrast, in the Johannine account—unsurprisingly—it is *Jesus* who initiates the drink offering. He declares his thirst (19.28), and the wine is offered in response to that declaration (19.29). As such, he is the one who is controlling the fulfillment of Scripture (even if the soldiers, assuming they are the ones who offer up the wine,¹⁰⁴ are once again participants in that fulfillment).

Two interpretative issues immediately arise in respect of 19.28's quotational usage—i) the format of the introductory formula, and ii) the content of the "quotation," and even its very "existence." As Vistar summarily quips: "The issue here is, what fulfills what?"¹⁰⁵

19.28—INTRODUCTORY FORMULA

Central to the interpretation of John 19.28 is how one renders the syntax of its pivotal phrase ἵνα τελειωθῇ ἡ γραφή.¹⁰⁶ Specifically, where and how does it perceive scriptural fulfillment being outworked? Two presenting syntactical options may be proposed:

A. As all was now finished in order to fulfil (the) Scripture, Jesus said . . .¹⁰⁷
B. Jesus knew that all was now finished, and he said (in order to fulfil the scripture) . . .¹⁰⁸

The respective renderings specify different—and contrasting—locations for scriptural fulfillment. The former associates it with the conclusion of Jesus's work, effectively aligning the completion of Jesus's death, the actioning of which Jesus himself controls, with the completion of Scripture. With this rendering, ἵνα τελειωθῇ ἡ γραφή functions essentially as an "adverbial modifier"[109] rather than as an introductory formula preceding a direct quotation (as, characteristically for John, it was in 19.24). Option B is more akin to the introductory formula mode, and locates the fulfillment with the subsequent (scriptural) statement. Jesus's declaration of thirst, whether as a concept or as a literal voicing of διψῶ, is what comprises the pronounced fulfillment.

As is invariably the case for such exegetical questions, a cogent case can be made for either reading. In favor of the former option is John's tendency (and likewise that of the NT) to have ἵνα introduce a final clause predicated on the antecedent verb (cf. the subsequent citation in 19.36, for example).[110] Likewise, there is the rhetorical and auditory association suggested by the juxtaposition of τελέω and τελειόω, such that they are mutually informing and associated concepts. Furthermore, the subsequent διψῶ appears to be a somewhat limited or brief citation, and—at first glance—not an obviously loaded text and thereby an unlikely candidate for carrying the burden of quotational fulfillment. Such brevity—and what might appear to be the absence of a signaled scriptural reference—therefore causes some commentators to ascribe only limited intertextual significance to Jesus's διψῶ declaration, and instead parse Jesus's thirst through John's previous discourse of the theme (particularly 7.37–39).[111] On such reading, Jesus's thirst is best explained in *intratextual,* rather than intertextual, terms. Though as we shall see, although such intratextual reference is surely at work here, it is likely in tandem with, rather than at the expense of, intertextual/scriptural engagement.

In favor of option B, λέγει is the sentence's main verb, and one would normally expect the ἵνα clause to be dependent on that rather than on the subsidiary verbal form εἰδὼς. Furthermore, John habitually places the citation/quotation after the (preceding) fulfillment formula, if only for rhetorical emphasis and expectation. John 19.31 offers a further example of a ἵνα statement preceding the main verb, and the ordering of 19.28 may also be occasioned by other factors, potentially deliberately so on John's part. Rather than emphasizing their similarity, it may serve to underscore the semantic difference between τελειόω and πληρόω, and thereby further alert the reader to the distinctiveness of this particular instance of scriptural fulfillment. John 17.12 uses the ἵνα ἡ γραφὴ πληρωθῇ formula, but does so without any succeeding text, and may therefore indicate fulfillment of Scripture *per se,* rather than anticipating a specific text. By contrast, the inclusion of διψῶ (19.28) allows for the possibility of that being the alluded/fulfilled citation, even if a somewhat brief one. And if further scriptural fulfillment is still to be found in subsequent verses/events (19.36–37), this implies that Scripture might not be *wholly* completed/fulfilled in 19.28, or at least not in the same terms as 19.24.

One might tentatively suggest that the ambiguity of 19.28's syntax is a feature that does not need to be resolved, but instead—as with other incidences of Johaninne indeterminacy—celebrated and further probed. That is, it would seem likely, probable even, that *both* renderings are anticipated by John, and both included accordingly.[112] If Jesus's death/exaltation is the climax of the Passion account, and indeed of the overall gospel narration, 19.28–30 is the moment at which that *telos* is achieved, and it warrants some form of literary flourish or distinction. We might therefore say that ἵνα τελειωθῇ ἡ γραφή functions as a "Janus" clause, one that can look both ways,[113] and profitably so; both syntactical renderings are to be embraced.[114] At this climactic moment, at the imminent point of Jesus's death, Scripture as whole is completed (τελειόω), *and at same time*, an individual scriptural text is invoked as demarking that process.[115] The achievement of both elements is mutually reinforcing, and through the agency of scriptural fulfillment, establishes the fundamental connection between Jesus's work and the corresponding *teleiosis* of Scripture. Jesus is both the one who knows and announces the completion of his work (19.28, 30), but is also the one who simultaneously enacts the fulfillment of Scripture. Kubiś draws attention to this contemporaneity, averring: "In 19.28b, the *logical* subject of the verb τελειόω is Jesus who, with full awareness (εἰδὼς), brings the Scripture to *perfect completeness*."[116] The duality of John 19.28 thus encapsulates the first two parts of our core hypothesis: Scripture is fundamental to John's explication of Jesus's death and its status is impacted through participation in such exposition.

How then is such Janus-type fulfillment enacted? We shall return later to the overall completion of Scripture and its accompanying implications,[117] and, for the moment, address the particular scriptural citation and what its fulfillment entails. The citation is brief to say the least, and indeed, could not be briefer: that is, διψῶ. It is prefaced, though, by λέγει; that is, Jesus is shown to be "speaking" the text, and/or the fulfillment is enacted through the specified action. The historical present heightens its narrative force. The front-loading[118] of the ἵνα clause draws attention to Jesus's verbal participation in this regard. That is, Jesus's "speaking" is an integral element of the scriptural fulfillment process, and serves to associate Jesus's speech/words with the authority of Scripture (and vice-versa), a further aspect we shall return to in chapter 5 (it being the third element of our core thesis). The brevity of Jesus's statement also gives some exegetical latitude, or at least moves on from requiring lexical equivalence, and points instead to a more thematic or narrative association.[119] Whereas the preceding fulfillment quotation (19.24) still necessitated fulfillment "action" on the part of the Roman soldiers, such action was driven—in John's narration at least—by the need for both parts of Ps 22.18 to be evidenced and manifest. John 19.28, by comparison, is far more general, and there is less lexical "demand" from the scriptural source, whatever its precise *Vorlage*. But although the demand for completion may be "lighter" than in other fulfillment instances, the Janus implications of 19.28's fulfillment render it the most significant example across the whole of John's Passion Narrative.

JOHN 19.28—A QUOTATION?

In view of its pithiness and the accompanying ambiguity of reference, does 19.28 genuinely qualify as a "quotation"? It depends, in many ways, as to how one defines a quotation or identifies the presence of one, and such methodological specificity has led many commentators to exclude it from the list of Johannine quotations.[120] There can seem good grounds for so doing—the brevity of the phrase, the different introductory formula, and the rhetorical Johannine neatness of seven specified quotations in the second half of the Gospel (12.38, 12.39–40, 13.18, 15.25, 19.24, 19.36, 19.37). More significantly the precise lexical form—διψῶ—doesn't appear within LXX testimony, somewhat telling in terms of quotational methodological precision. At the same time, the presence of some form of introductory formula, and the possibility of an accompanying cited scriptural text—however brief or however "re-presented"—points to at least some form of signalled citation, however one wishes to categorize it methodologically, and some commentators do therefore formally recognize it is a quotation.[121] And within our definition of a quotation laid out above, 19.28 does at least qualify for consideration as the introductory formula signals some form of anticipated citation.

Three accompanying observations might be made. First, the very declaration of Jesus as "thirsty" has tensions with John's prior narration, let alone it being the locus for climactic scriptural fulfillment. Although 19.28 recalls earlier references to Jesus's physical thirst (4.6–7), the episode at Jacob's well leads into wider discourse in respect of never being thirsty again (4.13–14). Jesus is subsequently the very source of living water (7.37–38), the epitome of the one who gives to those who are thirsty (7.38), but, in 19.28, he becomes "thirsty" himself in order for Scripture to be fulfilled (cf. also 18.11). This might represent—particularly following on from 19.24—a further instance of irony, or ironic reversal. That is, once more, scriptural fulfillment is enacted at a point of paradox or reversal; just as we saw an ironic fulfillment of Ps 22.18 (and the righteous suffer motif therein), so here we have the potential for a similar counter-ntuitive, counternarration even, instance of fulfillment.[122] Jesus becomes thirsty in order that others will never thirst again

(4.14, 6.35), and the water that subsequently flows out of Jesus's side (19.34) likely picks up the prophetic statement of 7.37–38.[123]

Second, Jesus assumes full authority for the citation, in terms of both its annunciation and its personification. As with 13.18 and 15.25, Jesus is the one who voices the scriptural "text." In these previous instances, the citation is only implicitly associated with Jesus himself; he is the object of the verbal idea within the quoted text. But in 19.28, the association is far more explicit—Jesus voices the text (as in 19.24), and owns it (along with its meaning/fulfillment) for himself. The unusual rendering of 19.28 noted above also "distances" the delivery from the previous introductory formula instances, and suggests something narratively different is happening. At this critical, climactic moment in the plot, Jesus effectively takes over the text for himself.

Third, we must clarify, technically at least, as to what kind of scriptural appeal or citation 19.28 is making, and whether it is indeed a citation at all. For those who pursue syntactic option A) above, there is, by implication, no explicit citation specified, and the focus is solely on Scripture's overall fulfillment,[124] or on a particular text that isn't actually specified.[125] But option B—as we are proceeding with it—does require classification in terms of its mode of appeal. For some, and with good reason, it is an unclear or unspecified scriptural reference, an appeal to Scripture rather than a formal quotation (the specific form διψῶ is absent from LXX MSS). Beutler terms it an "imprecise and ambiguous" citation,[126] whereas Brown is more cautious, preferring the more neutral term "scriptural element." Others term it an echo,[127] an allusion,[128] or scriptural proof,[129] or prefer the more uncommitted "citation."[130]

We will classify it as a "citation," not wanting to get bogged down in terms of precise definition. This seeks both to recognize that some form of scripture-sourced or scripture-directed appeal is being signalled, but it is being made in strange form—just the one word—and the distinctive mode is worthy of comment. The presence of an unmistakable, explicit quotation, when one seems so invited at such a critical narratival moment, is notable by its very absence. Instead, we have a hint at one, a hint at scriptural reference, but one which carries significant interpretative and intertextual baggage for the type of fulfillment John ascribes to Jesus. With some justification, therefore, Brawley describes 19.28 as an "absent complement"[131]—there is the promise or expectation of a fulfillment quotation, but one does not materialize (or at least not in expected form). Instead, the reader is given an echo or hint and invited to make the intertextual evaluation for themselves. At such a critical high point in the Passion narration, the reader is expected to make the connection, and is assumed to be well competent so to do. Hence to nuance Brawley's assessment, we would say that Scripture is not so much "absent" from the 19.28 presentation, but rather that it is presented, rendered— "quoted" even—in a variant form, and appropriately so, perhaps, in view of the different introductory verb (i.e., τελειόω, as opposed to πληρόω). Both the mode of introduction and the quotation/citation itself are distinctive within the Passion account and draw attention to the uniqueness of the intertextual move John 19.28 makes.

To what scripture, then, is the appeal being made? Some continuing reference to Psalm 22 is certainly possible bearing in mind its thematic usage in 19.24, and one might well expect ongoing resonance of its righteous sufferer motif into 19.28. If that is the case, Ps 22.15 would be the likely intertextual reference point; the Psalmist speaks of their strength being dried up and their tongue sticking to their jaw, both in an essentially mortem context (Ps 22.15). We noted above that John 19.24 might be working with Ps 22.15–18 as a whole unit of discourse, and the parched/thirst aspect of 22.15, addressed in John 19.28, would be a contributory factor in that regard. There is a possible echo, too, of Ps 22.31 in John 19.30,[132] though if so, it is more implicit and probably already assumes a Psalm 22/Passion Narrative association. Ridderbos further observes that Jesus's διψῶ cry equates to the suffering that the figure of Psalm 22 would have endured. Even if Ps 22.1 itself isn't cited, and even if Jesus's fate falls short of "extreme forsakenness," Jesus's appeal is a "lament wrung from him out of the depth of his suffering in which his solidarity with those who had lamented their suffering in Scripture consists above all in the fact that he and they took their suffering to God and laid it out before him."[133] Hence Ribberbos proposes that the scriptural citation is "not a proof of how strictly Jesus fulfilled Scripture,"[134] but one wonders whether such a proposal mistakenly underplays the efficacy and forcefulness of the scriptural appeal, particularly in light of the distinctive τελειόω introduction. That is, although there is indeed significant capacity for intertextual metalepsis and transferral of the Psalmic situation, *fulfillment* ultimately remains what drives the detail of the Johannine narration, both Jesus's thirst (19.28) and the soldiers' response to it (19.29).

The case for the emphasis on scriptural fulfillment becomes stronger when other textual candidates come to the table. Possible intertexts include Ps 63.1 or Ps 42.2, though these texts pertain more to spiritual rather than physical thirst,[135] whereas Jesus's need appears to be a physical one which the soldiers' actions address (19.29). Moreover, as with John 19.24/Ps 22.18, the Fourth Gospel is clear that God is not absent from Jesus, and to speak of thirst *for* God seems contrary to that fundamental premise. However, as noted above, the sheer oddity of Jesus—in control of his own destiny—apparently needing his thirst to be sated is, in and of itself, somewhat paradoxical; it appears, for some part at least, to be driven by the need for scriptural fulfillment, and hence there is no reason to restrict such thirst to the physical and exclude any spiritual dimension. After all, John has already juxtaposed physical and figurative thirst in its earlier discourse (4.13–14), and the reader has already been exposed to different—or contrasting—senses of δίψος. Moreover, the "power" of the intertextual reference is its capacity to incorporate the plurality of options and hold out several possibilities to the Johannine audience. That is, a *spiritual* thirst for God, the kind exuded within Ps 63.1 or Ps 42.2 would seem to accord well with other Fourth Gospel intratextual links;[136] earlier on in the Passion Narrative, Jesus speaks of drinking the cup his Father had given him (18.11), a willing advocacy of his forthcoming fate and thirst for God.

The spiritual dimension to Jesus's thirst may also equally be "sourced" from Ps 69.3, as the Psalmist therein is said to be waiting for God.[137] However, such waiting is accompanied by *physical* thirst (ἐβραγχίασεν ὁ λάρυγξ μου), and hence the craving experienced by the Psalmist is both spiritual *and* physical, perhaps in mutually informing fashion. This seems commensurate with the Johannine portrayal; it is hard to avoid the implication that the δίψος (19.28) is genuine and physical, and requiring some form of sating. As Ford notes, Jesus's "thirst is both for drink and for God. . . . So he is simultaneously at one with created life and with God."[138] Hence the majority of those commentators viewing 19.28 as a genuine citation locate Ps 69.3 as its probable provenance.[139] The likelihood of the Psalm being operative at this point is enhanced by its previous quotation in the Fourth Gospel (2.17—Ps 69.9 (Ps 68.10 LXX); 15.25—Ps 69.4 (Ps 69.5 LXX)) and the fact that the Psalmist is given ὄξος to drink (Ps 69.21; cf. John 19.29), just as Jesus is.[140] Where Psalms 42 and 63 would have proved better *Vorlage* candidates—for evincing the spiritual thirst, at least—they lack the ὄξος reference, an integral element within the Johannine portrayal. And although not explicit within the Passion narration, Ps 69.9b's assertion that the Psalmist bears the insults levied at God also seems commensurate with the broader Passion Narrative context (cf. 19.3, 19.15).

Even if there is consistency between Ps 69.3 and John 19.28–30 in terms of Jesus's thirst being both physical and spiritual, it remains the case that—in narrative terms at least—it is the *satiation* of Jesus's physical thirst that progresses the Johannine plot. Scriptural fulfillment is found in the accompanying action/narrative, not solely in Jesus's thirsty status. It is the giving *and* the receipt of the wine in response to the thirst that ultimately produces the fulfillment, not just the mere thirst alone. Even though Jesus knows all things are finished (19.28), he cannot announce "τετέλεσται" until the wine has been offered to and received by him (19.29–30). The "scriptural scene" which Jesus "orchestrates"[141] thus comprises 19.28–29—and not just 19.28; the thirst *and* the ὄξος are two sides of the same proverbial scriptural fulfillment coin. Hence the wider gamut of any intertextual association is necessarily brought to bear within the fulfillment motif—Ps 69.21 as well as Ps 69.3—and necessarily so. The reader must be sufficiently competent to make the double connection, of course. But with the appeal to both Ps 69.3 and Ps 69.21, John 19.28 represents the "recapitulation of a narrative moment,"[142] and/or initiates an intertextual shift to the whole backdrop of Psalm 69. If the reference to hyssop, and the previous appeal to the Psalm are indicative, it would seem that the wider aspect of Psalm 69—as with Psalm 22—is operative here. The evangelist is aware of the Psalm's wider context and its broader contours are operative both within John's Passion Narrative and across the Fourth Gospel as a whole.[143] The 19.28 citation may be a very brief one, but it carries with it a much wider intertextual template.

As such, and anticipating our subsequent discussion as to the overall teleiosis of Scripture, the broader reference beyond merely Ps 69.3 is indicative—the first fruits perhaps—of the much wider claim 19.28–30 makes in terms of scriptural fulfillment. The intertextual link John 19.28 initiates—particularly with such a brief citation—is not just to Psalm 69 and its depiction of a righteous sufferer, but to the full gamut of Scripture's testimony and fulfillment. As Köstenberger reminds the reader, the appeal to Jesus's thirst "fulfills the entire prophetic pattern of Scripture rather than merely matching an isolated trait of the psalmist's portrayal of the righteous sufferer."[144] Jesus being thirsty is hardly a significant aspect for the fulfillment of Scripture—as with the Ps 22.18 citation, invoking the Psalm's wider intertextual context is surely necessary. One might even suggest that trying to find a unique source for John's scriptural appeal is misguided, and inappropriately reductionistic. That is, as we shall continue to see, John's Passion Narrative draws on an amalgam of scriptural material, and its forcefulness is enhanced by simultaneous appeal to a plurality of scriptural passages. Although some "resonances" may be louder than others, the quieter ones remain integrally present and contribute to the overall intertextually rich picture John proffers. This is even more evident in the case of 19.28, its essential brevity paradoxically opening up a window onto a variety of sources.[145]

The question remains, however, as to the significance of Jesus's thirst, and to its spiritual-and-physical character. How is spiritual thirst satiated by physical drinking? Some commentators have found this tension problematic, overly problematic even. In an interesting assessment of the "thirst" question, for example, Leonard Witkamp observes that, if Ps 69.3 is operative within 19.28 (and in John's Passion more generally), this only serves to underscore Jesus's weakness, and runs counter to the Johannine portrayal of Jesus "in control." To avoid accusation, then, of unresolved paradox on John's part, Witkamp argues that the evangelist must be generating a distinctively *Johannine* reading of Psalm 69, particularly if/as the fulfillment dimension is to be achieved. For Witkamp, John's reading of Psalm 69 is shaped by—predicated on, even—Psalms 42 and 62, and Ps 69.3 becomes a *spiritual* thirst assuaged—however ironically—by the offering of wine.[146] He surmises: "Ps

69:21 indeed is the target text but that John did not read this psalm in a literal way (as modern interpreters do), finding in it a picture of the suffering of Jesus; rather, he read the psalm in a 'Johannine' way as a witness to the death of Jesus, giving it a spiritual interpretation in the course of his modification of his passion source."[147]

Witkamp is right to draw attention to the "Johannine" reading of the psalm, and to extend what he terms a "transliteral" reading that finds in Psalm 69 a quintessentially Johannine (i.e., spiritual) "thirst" to drink the cup the Father has given Jesus (cf. 18.11). But at the same time, one wonders whether his concerns as to the limiting implications Psalm 69 ascribes to the Johannine account are really warranted, and/or whether the Johannine reading is quite so divorced from or foreign to the "literal" one. John may offer a different or novel reading of the Psalm compared to its contemporaries, but it is not contrary to the Psalm's overall tenor or ethos. As we have noted, the Psalmist's thirst—even if physically manifest—is still occasioned by or linked to hoping or waiting on God (69.3b); the distinction in Psalm 69 (and especially 69.3) between physical and spiritual is more blurred than Witkamp allows, and the Psalm potentially offers John the scriptural template for precisely the spiritual-and-physical thirst satiation—and fulfillment—that the crucifixion scene embraces.

Furthermore, Witkamp is keen to downplay, remove even, any sense of a righteous sufferer from John's Passion, and particularly from its use of Psalm 69. A sufferer—however righteous—cannot achieve success, he ventures, and, of course, John's "Jesus is not merely a righteous martyr but deity in the flesh."[148] However, contra Witkamp, whereas Jesus's suffering in John's Passion is less than that of the Synoptics, it is suffering nonetheless,[149] *human* suffering even,[150] and there is no formal requirement to neglect the distress outworked within the Psalmic testimony. Moreover, as with Psalm 22, Psalm 69's tenor is the move from lament to praise, from suffering to worship and vindication (cf. Ps 69.30–36).[151] If John desires for the full contours of Psalm 69 to be at work, any suffering tension is ultimately resolved. It is true that the tenor of the Psalm does not absolutely "fit" the Johannine context, as John's Jesus is very much "in control" of events,[152] whereas the Psalmist laments their inability in the situation. But the irony of the suffering exemplified by the Psalmist, and so incorporated by John, is not that it limits the efficacy of Jesus's actions, but rather that—in intertextual terms—it is the very thing that *enables* their efficacy, and that of Jesus's God-given vocation. Suffering, akin to that found in Ps 69.3, and specifically manifest by the cruciform Jesus, becomes the medium for glorification and divine accomplishment. The suffering of the righteous one is *real* suffering,[153] and must be so for Jesus's actions to be atoningly efficacious. Hence Psalm 69 is a most appropriate text around which John might shape its Passion retelling; it *resolves* as much as problematizes the situation—or at least celebrates the paradox. And bearing mind John's conception of Jesus in both divine and human terms, it would seem somewhat suitable for Jesus's thirst—particularly when "defined" through intertextual links—to demonstrate both physical and spiritual aspects, and that both dimensions are intertextually evoked.

As with the quotation of Psalm 22 in John 19.24, the attribution of Psalm 69 to David is also significant. We might suggest that the suffering backdrop is integral to the Johannine Jesus's association with David, and with the royal/ Davidic patterning John draws out.[154] Hays, for example, moots the suggestion that "Jesus paradoxically fulfills the role of Davidic kingship precisely through his conformity to the extreme suffering portrayed in these Davidic lament psalms."[155] So also Carson: "granted the undergirding Davidic typology, the connexion is not merely analogical: the righteous sufferer of Ps. 69 prefigures, and thus predicts, the one in whom righteous suffering would reach its apogee."[156] Once more, it is the *paradoxical* or ironic, royal fulfillment to which John alludes, and the reader—admittedly, a competent one— should therefore not fear engagement with such matters.

We propose, therefore, that Jesus's thirst of 19.28 is indeed ironic, but not problematically so; indeed, it is a necessary, integral part of John's Passion portrayal. Tabb concurs, proposing that 19.28 meets the essential criteria for identifying irony within a narrative. First, he avers, Jesus's thirst is "double-layered"—that is, it is physical manifest, but ultimately looks higher, and searches after the divine. Second, there is tension between its self-evident physical dimension and that to which it points—the spiritual aspect. And third, the soldiers' offer of ὄξος is made in ignorance of that ultimate referent of Jesus's thirst.[157] However, to extend Tabb's analysis further, the reader's (full) recognition of such irony is premised upon the intertextual matrix to which 19.28 alludes, particularly the template of Psalm 69. One might arrive at a positive assessment though by intratextual means, but the intertextual lens is surely the determining factor, that which gives confidence for the success for the project. Scripture doesn't just testify to this—though that may be sufficient corroboration—but rather it is itself fulfilled, completed, perfected even through Jesus's thirst. Scripture—specifically Psalm 69—both confirms and the compounds the irony.

As we have seen, 19.28's reference to Jesus's thirst has intratextual implications too. Its (intertextual) appeal to Ps 69.3, 21 also has intratextual ramifications, taking the reader back to the Temple incident and the citation of Ps 69.9 therein (John 2.17). Jobes opines that the citation of Psalm 69 thus "bookends" the ministry of Jesus,[158] and that certainly provides a further Johannine *inclusio*. But particularly in respect of its fulfillment characterization in 19.28, one suggests the relationship is more than that; the *re-citation* of the Psalm in John's Pasion Narrative is what "completes" it, and/or brings it to fulfillment. Considering the citation of the Psalm in 2.17, Scott draws attention to the Johannine shift of focus: "By setting 'consume' (κατεσθίω) in the future, John gives the quote a proleptic focus alien to the narrative trajectory of the psalm, as also to the immediate narrative context in John 2."[159] The evangelist amends the aorist κατέφαγέν (Ps 68.10 LXX) to the future καταφάγεταί (John 2.17), and so sets up the expectation of the lemma's subsequent resolution within the Johannine narrative.[160] We suggest that John 19.28–29 achieves that resolution. Where 2.17, and the cleansing of the Temple, anticipate opposition and conflict, ultimately fatal, tied to the body of Jesus (2.21), 19.28–29 actualize such anticipation, and thereby "complete" it. The "drinking" of the wine symbolizes or represents the zeal that now encompasses Jesus, which he exudes and which now leads to his death (cf. 10.18—Jesus lays down his life of his own accord).[161] Putting it another way, the Temple incident, and the promise of both the destruction of the Temple and the construction of a new one (2.19), his body (2.21), emerges as the mission template for the Johannine Jesus. When Jesus knew that the mission was completed (τελέω—19.28), and prior to the τετέλεσται announcement of that fact (cf. τελέω—19.30), Psalm 69 is once more cited to articulate its accomplishment.

Three further points may be made in this regard. First, the completion of Jesus's work accompanies the "completion" of Ps.69.9, and, by implication the whole of Psalm 69. We suggest therefore that the fulfillment of Psalm 69 functions representatively in this regard, and *pars pro toto* for the full gamut of Scripture. Second, what was previously *written* (2.17) is now *spoken* by Jesus (19.28); Jesus assumes ownership of the written text, and voices it himself (the perfect tense of γεγραμμένον (2.17) has become the present tense of λέγει (19.28)). The words of Jesus and the text of Scripture become effectively intertwined, and the disciples' subsequent, post-Easter remembrance of the Temple episode likewise juxtaposes both aspects as equivalent. Or more specifically, the disciples remember the γεγραμμένον form, but they associate it with (the words of) Jesus (2.22). Such association is highly significant of course, and the juxtaposition of Scripture (and fulfillment) alongside Jesus's words are testimony to the equivalence of both aspects. Jesus words are/become 'scriptural' and Scripture is on a par with Jesus's testimony. We shall investigate this further, the final element of our thesis, in chapter 5.

Third, although we are making the case for Psalm 69 to be the primary text at work in John 19.28–30, it is not the only one; other accompanying scriptural intertexts are potentially operative within it. As we have seen, Ps 63.1 and Ps 42.2 might well be part of the intertextual matrix, working with Ps 69.9, and Ps 22.15 could equally be influential or operative in the unit; there is something of a "mosaic of thirst passages" operative in this regard.[162] But there are also other possibilities, ones whose existence would tie John's Passion Narrative more tightly to that of its Synoptic siblings, and engender more consistency between the respective accounts. Michael Licona, for example, reading Jesus's thirst as spiritual rather than physical, equates this with the *absence* of God, equivalent to Mk 15.34 and the citation of Ps 22.1. John 19.28 becomes, in Licona's view, a "dynamic equivalent translation" of the Markan testimony whereby "John has redacted Jesus's words but has retained their meaning."[163] John 19.28 fulfills Ps 22.1 rather than Ps 69.3, and John 19.28 and Mk 15.34 are rendered as effectively synonymous declarations. He further proposes that Jesus's τετέλεσται cry (19.30) mirrors the Lucan Jesus's declarative commitment of Luke 23.46, itself likely an allusion to Ps 31.5.[164] The association is, in our view, a less likely one, but were it legitimate, it would add further intertextual resonance to the fulfillment landscape of 19.28–30. Either way, it draws attention to the potential plurality of intertextual links John's Passion Narrative presents and informs the composite citations we will see in 19.36 and 19.37. It both illustrates the multiplicity of scriptural images upon which John may draw, and cautions against reducing John's sources—even for signalled quotations—to merely one specific *Vorlage*.[165] This becomes even more pertinent as we turn to John 19.36–37 and the composite quotation sources from which they seem to draw.

QUOTATIONAL USAGE IN JOHN 19.36

The next direct scriptural quotation comes forth in 19.36, and, after the shift in fulfillment terminology in 19.28, the customary ἵνα ἡ γραφὴ πληρωθῇ introductory formula is restored. The citation is also—as with the opening fulfillment quotations (12.38–40)—a paired one, with the πληρωθῇ attribution extending to include the citation found in 19.37. Along with 19.37, 19.36's quotation is used to unpack the fulfillment implications of 19.31–34 (cf. the directive ἐγένετο γὰρ ταῦτα —19.36). The parenthesis of 19.35 breaks the immediate flow of the discourse, a feature that warrants further comment,[166] but 19.36 would still seem to address the fulfillment implications of Jesus's legs remaining unbroken (19.31–33), with 19.37 then speaking to the consequences of piercing Jesus's side in verification of death (19.34). As with the preceding pair of linked quotations (12.38–40), they are "intended to affirm two separate, albeit related, points, with the second citation in each case providing an explanation of the origins or consequences of the 'fact' articulated by the first."[167] The double formulaic set of quotations is unique in John's Passion retelling, and this commends its significance or focal aspect, suitably attesting to its rhetorical climax. John 19.36–37 also forms a fitting *inclusio* to the fulfillment doublet of 12.38–40, and there is good reason to see (pun intended) the 19.36–37 unit (and particularly 19.37) as revisiting and replaying the seeing/(dis)believing motif established in 12.37–40. Just as a double quotation demarks Jesus's withdrawal from public ministry, a further double quotation signals the end of Jesus's life.[168]

The Synoptic Passion Narratives do not make the same connection in respect of Jesus's bones, neither the principle itself nor the attestation through scriptural reference (fulfillment or otherwise). The content may derive from (apologetic) pre-Johannine tradition, namely the rabbinic view that resurrection took the form in which one died, with the Fourth Gospel wishing to remove a potential obstacle or objection to Jesus's resurrected form. However, that is hard to prove either way. And on surface reading at least, the argumentation of 19.36 appears to be more straightforward. In response to Jesus's legs not being broken, the evangelist marshals scriptural testimony vindicating or affirming that principle; no further explanation or clarification is offered, nor would its inclusion appear necessary. Hence there could be something akin to a pesher-style equivalency claimed by John; the scriptural text—whatever its origin—simply relates to Jesus's bones remaining unbroken (19.33) and evidencing that fact. But if that were simply the case, then an introductory formula akin to ἡ γραφὴ εἶπεν (cf. 7.42) would have easily suited Johannine purposes. That is, it would suffice merely to know scripture affirmed or testified to the actions of 19.33. But instead, once more, John situates the incident in terms of scriptural *fulfillment*, a weightier, more profound claim which, as with the previous incidences, has warranted (and generated) far more interpretative significance. As with 19.24 and 19.28, a deeper, more robust intertextual engagement is also invited; 19.36 manifests a decisive Johannine twist, with the apparent contextualization of Jesus's death specifically in terms of the Passover lamb.

Coupled with the burden of fulfillment is a debate as to the origin—or origins—of the cited text. The provenance of ὀστοῦν οὐ συντριβήσεται αὐτοῦ (19.36) is fundamental to its capacity for intertextual address. Several candidates may be suggested, none of which are a direct match with the Johannine text form (see Table 2.2).

Bearing in mind its previous Passover references, and the wider patterning of John's Passion Narrative according to Paschal traditions,[169] the Exod 12.10,[170] 12.46 and Num 9.12 options would seem appropriate sources,[171] even if not used verbatim.[172] All three texts make essentially the same point. Although Num 9.12 uses the third rather than second person plural, the instruction remains consistent, namely to preserve the integrity of the Passover Lamb, all of whose bones are to remain unbroken. The ambiguous αὐτοῦ[173] also enables the switch between lamb and Jesus, so "works" in that regard, even if the gender to which αὐτοῦ alludes ends up functionally changed.[174] But making such a connection assumes that the intertextual association is premised more on narrative patterning than on lexical similarity,[175] and it is the thematic

Table 2.2. Textual Comparison for John 19.36 Quotation

John 19.36	ὀστοῦν οὐ συντριβήσεται αὐτοῦ	None of his bones shall be broken
Exod 12.10	καὶ ὀστοῦν οὐ συντρίψετε ἀπ' αὐτοῦ	You shall not break a bone from it
Exod 12.46	καὶ ὀστοῦν οὐ συντρίψετε ἀπ' αὐτοῦ	You shall not break a bone from it
Num 9.12	καὶ ὀστοῦν οὐ συντρίψουσιν ἀπ' αὐτοῦ	They shall not break a bone from it
Ps 34.20 (33.21 LXX)	κύριος φυλάσσει πάντα τὰ ὀστᾶ αὐτῶν, ἓν ἐξ αὐτῶν οὐ συντριβήσεται	The Lord will guard all their bones; not one from them will be broken

parallels that ultimately forge the connection. The frequent Passover backdrop already assembled by John leads the reader to make the Paschal Lamb association (cf. 1.29); one set of intertextual exchange thus shapes the further instance, and we will explore the prior Passover backdrop in more detail in the next chapter.[176]

Although John 19.36 shares most of the words of the three Pentateuchal texts, there remains a significant lexical distinction, in outcome as well as form. Where Exod 12.10, 46 and Num 9.12 all use the active voice, and attend therefore to the agency of the breaking action, John 19.36 underscores the reverse. By using the passive voice, it is the effect *on* the figure that is significant, and the distinction seems integral to the Johannine purpose. The soldiers do not attempt to break Jesus's legs because, with Jesus already dead, it is unnecessary so to do. Their inaction is not mandated, or motivated, by external warrant, scriptural, imperial, or otherwise, but is rather sheer pragmatic reality. The sparing of the *crurifragium* is occasioned by Jesus himself, as the one who has controlled the timing and mode of his death, and John goes to some lengths to avoid any soldierly agency in its happening. Hence there is something of a reverse parallel with the soldiers' actions of 19.24, in which John also found scriptural fulfillment. In the former example, the soldiers' actions unwittingly full Scripture through their "predicted" deeds; in the latter one, it is their *inaction* that is doing so.

Vorlage-wise, it is possible, of course, that narrative circumstances have merely occasioned the change of person and voice.[177] Reim, for example, posits that John is working from a Hebrew form of Num 9.12 and that οὐ συντριβήσεται manifests a legitimate Greek rendering of it.[178] Montenaro also seeks to restrict the Psalm's reference to the Pentateuchal voice, and avers that the form found in John 19.36 is a "memory variant" of Exodus 12.10/ Num 9.12. The textual form is occasioned by oral usage of Scripture, rather than it being a deliberate attempt to combine the Pentateuchal texts with other scriptural testimony. He opines: "it is simpler to imagine that John's memory has varied the voice of συντρίψετε or συντρίψουσιν and dropped the preposition than that he intentionally combined the passages, presumably by preserving the grammatical structure of the Exodus/Numbers passage but preferring the passive voice of the Psalm."[179] Such a scenario is possible, of course, but the precision of συντριβήσεται—and particularly the variant passive voice—doesn't make it a compelling choice. This then gives grounds to look beyond the Pentateuchal examples, not to exclude them, but rather to widen the scope of John's intertextual engagement. After all, the Pentateuch has not been a source for the evangelist's scriptural citation thus far, and if there were an Exodus/Numbers *Vorlage* in 19.36, it would be the Gospel's only such explicit instance.[180]

A more pressing case can be made for a reference to Ps 34.20 (Ps 33.21 LXX), and, for a number of scholars, this is the preferred solution to the question of 19.36's *Vorlage*. Even if John overlays it with a Passover tenor, they suggest that the Psalm remains the primary or focal quotation source.[181] The key premise for such attribution is the Psalmist's use of the specific συντριβήσεται form, in association with τὰ ὀστᾶ (recognising, of course, its plural rendering compared to the singular ὀστέον of John 19.36 and the Pentateuchal texts). Williams, for example, ventures that συντριβήσεται may function as a "*divine* passive,"[182] and, as noted earlier, this seems consistent with the Johannine portrayal and Jesus's and/or God's ultimate "responsibility" for the non-breaking of the bones. The full extent of Ps 34.20—and its appeal to divine protection of the suffering figure's bones—is also commensurate with the immediate Johannine narrative context.[183] Garland conjectures that the definite usage of "the righteous" (Ps 33.20 LXX—albeit in plural rather than singular form), and without a following "sufferer(s)" may also extend a messianic dimension to the Psalm, and hence John uses it for such messianic (rather than righteous sufferer) associations. But this seems to impose too much interpretative burden on the text. Indeed, the plural referent of Ps 34.19–20—righteous *ones*—differs from the singular αὐτοῦ of 19.36, and Ps 34.20 lacks, at least in explicit form, the Johaninne ὀστοῦν οὐ phrasing (19.36) found in all three Pentateuchal/Passover texts. Hence, *of itself*, or without some form of redaction or editing, just as with the Pentateuchal examples, Ps 34.20 still isn't the perfect fit for the alleged *Vorlage* of 19.36.

Hence it seems plausible, necessary even, to see the citation in John 19.36 as somehow derivative from both streams or sources, rather than reducing it to just one primary *Vorlage*, and a number of commentators now recognize such a blending, or multiple sourcing.[184] Menken is probably representative in his assessment: "The best explanation for the peculiar textual form of the quotation in John 19.36 seems to be that here elements from Ps 34(33).21 have been combined with the elements from the Pentateuch texts."[185] However, we might go further and, with Williams, define the quotation as a genuine *composite* citation, a deliberate Johannine strategy whereby citations are fused together from multiple sources in service of the diverse—maybe even divergent—interpretative needs. It is more than the respective Psalm and Torah texts being "analogous passages" in terms of their frame of reference,[186] though that, of course, necessarily remains the case. More specifically, as Williams rightly observes, John's overall presentation of Jesus is "composite," and hence its deployment of scriptural sources, used in the service of the characterization of Jesus,[187] may be similarly amalgamated or merged.[188] She proposes that eight of Fourth Gospel's fifteen direct quotations may be classified as composite, further indicative of it being a characteristic Johannine tendency, and one that testifies to a wider, more diverse intertextual landscape, resisting simplistic or reductionistic *Vorlage* discussion.[189]

What then does this composite quotation do or achieve? In primary terms, it intertextually combines the respective motifs of the righteous suffer of Psalm 34 and the unblemished Pentateuch Passover Lamb, enabling *both* scriptural motifs to function in tandem, in mutually informing fashion, and so evoke a wider interpretative horizon in respect of Jesus's death. It may even—*gezara shawah* style—draw Psalm 22 back into the portrayal too, with the Psalmist's capacity to count all their bones (Ps 22.17).[190] With the 19.36 citation, John is both consistent with (and maybe intensifies)[191] the Synoptic tradition in terms of a righteous sufferer (and thereby with its own usage of Ps 22.18 in 19.24 and Ps 69 in 19.28), but at the same time expands its remit and scope with the thematic Passover material that is so integral to the Fourth Gospel's Passion retelling. Such combination may have prior parallel in the text of *Jubilees*, specifically *Jub.* 49.13: "and not break any bone thereof; for of the children of Israel no bone shall be crushed." Menken proposes that this text explicitly sets out the handling of the Paschal Lamb, but also exhibits the influence of Ps 34.21 through the appeal's emphatic "not a single one" nature. As such, *Jub.* 49.13 proves "a causal connection was made between not breaking the bones of the paschal lamb and the deliverance of Israel, expressed in terms of the bones of the Israelites not being broken, and that the Pentateuchal provision about not breaking the bones was combined with Ps. 34(33).21."[192]

Of course, in *Jubilees*, Israel is identified explicitly with the righteous sufferer, and only implicitly (if at all) with the Passover Lamb itself, whereas the Johannine Jesus inhabits—and fulfills—both roles, a principle Menken rightly concedes. But equally, this example at least attests to the *possibility* of the composite quotation, and the capacity of an astute or informed reader to recognize its plurality accordingly.[193] Such dual imaging gives further reason to conceive the *Vorlage* as drawing on several sources and resists simplifying or reducing it to merely one source. Indeed, the "compositeness" of the quotation is both deliberate and necessary for John's christological purposes, as no individual source sufficiently enables that alone. Rather than being merely one such image, the figure of 19.36 becomes the "righteous one of the Psalms who is protected and vindicated by God and, *at the same time*, he is the true Passover Lamb whose bones will not be broken."[194]

In sum, the quotation in John 19.36 is brief and concise, but its brevity contrasts directly with the interpretative outcome it generates (an assessment we found similarly for both 19.24 and 19.28). It carries significant intertextual baggage, and appropriately so for the conclusion of the Passion Narrative, bringing to a *telos* the Passover Lamb theme that the evangelist develops from 1.29 onward and also restating the righteous sufferer imagery implicit in the 19.24 and 19.28 quotations. As such, and as was suggested for both 19.24 and 19.28, the quotation in 19.36 carries intratextual as well as intertextual import.

But its significance may go even further than such lamb-ic narration. That is, akin to the casting of lots for clothing in 19.24, in 19.36, the Fourth Gospel finds scriptural fulfillment in the mundane, in the ordinary, in that which would not ordinarily warrant comment; fulfillment is found in what has *not* taken place. As Brawley observes: "The notice that none of Jesus's bones were broken actually conjures up a non-event that ordinarily would draw no attention. Scripture gives meaning to something that did not happen."[195] The capacity and scope for scriptural fulfillment, and the extent to which it drives John's Passion narration, demands that what *doesn't* take place, as well as what does, thus contributes to the evangelist's overall intertextual portrait. The burden for demonstrating scriptural fulfillment within the Johannine Passion, the task of demonstrating that John's Jesus died κατὰ τὰς γραφὰς, is a heavy one indeed.

QUOTATIONAL USAGE IN JOHN 19.37

With the subsequent scriptural quotation of John 19.37 (cf. Zech 12.10), the double citation introduced by 19.36 is completed. Technically, in this second element of the scriptural pairing, John specifies merely the *saying* of the citation[196] rather than its fulfillment, and thus the Zechariah element could be viewed as subsidiary or lesser in that regard.[197] More likely, however, particularly in view of its climactic position, and as the second element of the parallel quotation of Isa 6.10 in John 12.40 likewise lacks the explicit fulfillment preface, 19.37's γραφή also anticipates "fulfillment," carrying the πληρωθῇ designation by extension and with equal weight.[198] The respective source texts of 19.36–37 are not so explicitly associated elsewhere in contemporary literature, and it is relatively unusual for the Fourth Gospel to align two citations together onto one event as part of its narrative commentary.[199] Hence it seems likely that John deliberately juxtaposes them for cumulative fulfillment effect. This notion is further evidenced by the *inclusio* 19.36–37 forms with the previous Johannine double OT citation (12.38–40; cf. Isa. 53.1, 6.10), thereby bookending the discourse in respect of Jesus's death through scriptural fulfillment demarcation.[200] Scripture is used both to frame the declaration of its own fulfillment and to inform the very events that determine such fulfillment.

It is similarly possible (and complementary with the *inclusio* proposed above) that Zechariah 9–14 bookends the wider portrayal of Jesus's Passion. John 12.15 quotes Zech 9.9 in respect of the triumphal entry (12.15) and Zech 12.10 is similarly cited here (19.37), at the end of the Passion scene, thereby establishing a "Zechariah *inclusio*,"[201] a contrasting one that moves from celebration (Zech. 9.9) to piercing and death (Zech. 12.10).[202] Bynum surmises: "When taken together, the two citations demonstrate John's dialogue with Zechariah as he encloses the passion narrative in the hope, joy and irony of Zech 9–12."[203] This is in synchronicity with similar use of Zechariah 9–14 material in the Synoptic evangelistic Passion Narratives,[204] and further suggests that that textual unit proved to be a suitable source for the NT writers when seeking to make sense of Jesus's death κατὰ τὰς γραφὰς.

The quotation of 19.37 is the only clear instance in John's Passion Narrative where γραφή denotes a specific passage from Scripture (ἑτέρα γραφὴ), rather than merely signalling a generic appeal to Scripture *per se*.[205] It is also the one introductory formula in the Passion account that utilizes a present active indicative verbal form,[206] and such "present-ness" may add further energy and ongoing action to its climactic effect. As we shall discuss further in chapter 4, Scripture continues to speak *after* its specified teleiosis (19.30), and 19.37's λέγει usage confirms this temporal, continuous aspect. Hence even in paired form with 19.36, and even if/as it lacks the explicit πληρωθῇ designation, there is extra rhetorical significance ascribed to 19.37's content, manifesting the veritable climax of John's program of scriptural fulfillment.

MATTERS OF *VORLAGE*

Quite what *comprises* such rhetorical significance remains more elusive, however. If there is any neatness or tidiness to the bookending function of the 19.37 citation, such neatness is lost when one considers the nitty-gritty detail of its usage. Scholars are almost universally agreed that the cited text is Zech 12.10, and there is no other obvious alternative. But the specific *Vorlage* of the Zechariah text remains contested, as the version found within

John 19.37 lacks any absolute match in terms of extant, contemporary form. Debates as to its precise provenance are well-rehearsed and longstanding,[207] and they can easily end up as merely arguments from silence, but they still warrant some consideration if we are to assess the overall function of the citation and its reception.

As is evident from the texts specified below, Zech 12.10 LXX lacks any matching word to the rendering of John 19.37. It has some similarity to later Greek recensions, but these likely post-date the 19.37 text form. Neither does it—or even can it—follow the MT verbatim, as the MT specifies the object of the observation in first-person terms (אלי) rather than 19.37's third (εἰς ὃν). Most significantly, Zech 12.10 LXX reads "mocked" rather than "pierced." Although the former may have some limited resonance with earlier parts of John's Passion (e.g., 19.3), such ridiculing has ceased by the time of the crucifixion itself. John instead ascribes significance to the rhetorical effect of ἐκκεντέω, which is evident in the MT tradition (דקר), and hence it is plausible that John has deliberately quoted the Hebrew form *against* or in tension with the LXX rendering.[208] Various solutions have thus been proffered for John's (choice of) *Vorlage*:

- The evangelist employs their own (Greek) translation of the Hebrew,[209] ascribing it a particular christological flavor in so doing.[210] This accounts for the similarity to the Hebraic tradition, but gets around—or sidesteps—the difficulties with the particular MT text form.
- Similarly, the *Vorlage* is the evangelist's own creation, but one based on an existing Greek source.[211]
- It is an existing (Christian?) Greek translation of the Hebrew,[212] functioning in effect as a pre-existing testimonium.[213]
- It is a form found within an existing recension of the Greek text.[214]
- It is a form testified to in another Greek MS.[215]
- It is a composite *Vorlage*, that is, drawing on another scriptural text(s), in addition to Zech 12.10.[216]

What can we say in respect of the *Vorlage* question? All of the above options are possible up to a point, but none are absolutely compelling. The

Table 2.3. Textual Comparison for John 19.37 Quotation

John 19.37	ὄψονται εἰς ὃν ἐξεκέντησαν	They will look on the one whom they have pierced
Zech 12.10 LXX	καὶ ἐπιβλέψονται πρός με ἀνθ᾽ ὧν κατωρχήσαντο	They will look to me because they have danced triumphantly
Zech 12.10 MT	והביטו אלי את אשר דקרו	They look on me whom they have pierced

choice of verb (ἐκκεντέω) may suggest a pre-existing testimonium, particularly in the light of Rev 1.7, but one would surely expect the same verbal form in 19.34 to indisputably demonstrate the text's fulfillment. In short, there is no neat or easy solution to the quotational form of Zech 12.10 found in John 19.37.

Rather than merely Zech 12.10 being the sole operative source, therefore, it is possible that other scriptural intertexts may also be functioning in 19.37, particularly bearing mind similar source amalgamation in the preceding verse (19.36). Williams, for example, ventures that Isaiah 52–53, a text with some similarities to Zech 12.9–13, also contributes to 19.37's *Vorlage*, generating "a deliberate evocation of the Isaianic connection between seeing and lifting up," concepts similarly aligned earlier in the Johannine narrative (3.14, 8.28, 12.32). Specifically, Williams proposes that John 19.37's ὄψονται—somewhat different to LXX's or Theodotion's ἐπιβλέψονται—derives from Isa 52.10 LXX (also ὄψονται) and the public visualization of YHWH's salvific actions before all the nations. It also draws on the repeated exhortations to look on the one who is lifted up (Isa 52.13), both the Servant's exalted and glorious status (52.13), as well as their horrific appearance (52.14). John's previous references to being lifted up are associated with seeing as indicative of, or leading to, belief (3.14, 8.28, 12.32). Although "seeing does not *guarantee* believing,"[217] the evangelist surely hopes that it will do so (cf. 20.31),[218] and hence Williams' proposal of a similar combination seems perfectly plausible, thereby occasioning a further composite quotation in the Johannine Passion Narrative, this time a combination of Zech 12.10 and Isa 52.10.

With such "compositeness" likely operative in 19.36 too, the pairing and mutual fulfillment of the two quotations of 19.36–37 show further sibling similarity in respect of their composite generation. It also serves to underscore the way in which Isaiah 53—and to a lesser degree Isaiah 52—might function as a template for the Passion scene, a concept to which we will return in the next chapter. Ridderbos, for example, muses that the context of John 19.37, and its imagery of piercing evokes a "figure strongly reminiscent of the man of sorrows in Isaiah 53."[219] Polinksi takes the mooted Isaianic backdrop even further, contending that John intertextually associates the righteous ones of Ps 34:19–21 with the Righteous One of Isa 53.11, and hence the Isaiah 53 context is already in place in John 19.36 and subsequently extends over into 19.37 too.[220] And if Isaiah 53 is contributing to 19.36–37, as it does to the programmatic statement of 1.39, then respective Servant Song intertexts function to bookend John's overall discourse of Jesus's death.

However one ultimately resolves the *Vorlage* question, the version that the evangelist deploys is both consistent (obviously) with John's narratival purposes and broadly coherent with the Hebrew text form (though the MT's look on *me* rather than on *him* remains intriguing). Indeed, assuming some form of apologetic usage, one suggests it cannot be otherwise, else its argument in respect of Jesus's death and scriptural fulfillment would simply have been rejected. If there is any sense of John seeking to convince non-believers through its appeal to Scripture, particularly at the gospel's rhetorical climax, then the "text(s)" to which it appeals must surely have been familiar and recognizable both to its audience and to the Fourth Gospel's interlocutors. Or to put it another way, if the evangelist felt free to amend its scriptural sources, without limit, then it might have done a much better job of so doing, by matching the verbs of 19.34 and 19.37, for example. As such, one might easily overlook the *Vorlage* question as either unresolvable or merely secondary to it being driven by John's presentation of Jesus. Our position is that the text in view is Zech 12.10 in Masoretic form, but with some evangelistic creativity informed both by the particular first-person orientation of Zech 12.10 and by combination with Isa 52.10's ὄψονται.

SCOPING THE ZECH 12.10 QUOTATION—
WHO AND WHAT?

Although a significant task in and of itself, focusing merely on the citation's *Vorlage* can distract from querying *why* Zech 12.10 is used, and why so at the zenith of the Fourth Gospel's narrative. What is it about this text in particular that the evangelist finds so compelling that it warrants such climatic Passion fulfillment? And why is it that, post-the teleiosis of 19.28, Scripture can still be said/need to speak? For example, it is not the case that the verbal usage of 19.34 (νύσσω) necessitates the citational form of 19.37 (ἐκκεντέω); indeed, the different forms suggest that something more significant than mere lexical affinity is at play.[221] And if it were purely a matter of finding a convenient pretext for foretelling messianic piercing, other, better options were available.[222] Bearing in mind the influence of Isaiah 53 across the second half of the Fourth Gospel, and its potential contribution to 19.37's *Vorlage*, a case for Isa 53.5 might be made. But John does not go there—at least not explicitly so. Instead, what is it about Zech 12.10 that leads the evangelist to place it at the pinnacle of John's Passion Narrative?

In order to answer this question, two related matters warrant initial consideration. First, who pierces Jesus? Significantly perhaps, it is ambiguous as to who John anticipates being the subject(s) of 19.37's two actions (ὄψονται and ἐξεκέντησαν), and this raises several interpretive possibilities. Although the default option may be to attribute the same subject to both verbal actions, that is not necessarily the case; the shift in tense, and the potential differentiation implied by the sub-clause, allow for two different subjects to be operative. The agent of ἐξεκέντησαν (19.37) is probably assumed to be the Romans, but

John technically ascribes the prior piercing to one soldier (19.34), and that may account for the verbal change in 19.37, drawing attention to the corporate implications of an action undertaken by one individual. The agent may equally be—or include—οἱ Ἰουδαῖοι, as they are the ones who initiate the process of confirming death and removal of the bodies (19.31).[223] But perhaps the most straightforward option is to take seriously the absence of an explicit subject for ἐξεκέντησαν; that is, it is presumably the soldier's "historical" action that initiates the matter (so 19.34), but the citation's imprecision in terms of subject enables its wider application and rhetorical extension. The reader vicariously participates in the piercing too, occasioning the verbal change between 19.34 and 19.37, the latter representing their metaphorical complicity in the action. An individual Roman soldier may have pierced Jesus (νύσσω—19.34), but the Fourth Gospel stresses that wider humanity is the agent of ἐκκεντέω (19.37).

Second, who *sees*—who is the agent of ὄψονται? This is even more ambiguous, and equally even more significant. If different subjects are permitted, then options are open, and the differing time scales evidenced by the different tenses (future and aorist) leads in that direction. The subject of ὄψονται includes the initial eyewitness of 19.35 (probably the Beloved Disciple), but, as with ἐκκεντέω, it likely extends to incorporate a wider audience, those whom John invites to consider as to their response to Jesus, and ideally to do so from the perspective of belief in him (cf. 20.30–31). Hence the subject of the seeing is most likely the audience or reader of the Fourth Gospel, those who have seen and come to believe based on what they have "visualized."[224] Although not required syntactically, for 19.37, the implied subjects of "seeing" and "piercing" are effectively the same.

Linked to the "who?" is the "what?" In such a tight, ambiguous phrase, the two aspects are inextricably linked and mutually informing. Whoever the implied "seer" is, their focus is on the pierced Jesus. As is the case for the entire Passion Narrative, Jesus is the focal point of the episode, and the one upon whom fulfillment has come. In terms of "what" is seen, it is—at least—the act of piercing Jesus's side; the *pierced* Jesus is the focal image, and importantly, one suggests, not the cruciform Jesus. The anticipated visualization of 19.37 is not of the crucifixion act, but instead, of the subsequent piercing. The distinction is a significant one—crucifixion and (non-)crurifragium are different "events" for John and have different interpretative significance. John's template for Jesus's death is crucifixion, and that is requisite for the predictions pertaining to his lifting up and the mode of death to be fulfilled (12.32–33). But the evangelist is equally clear that Jesus himself chooses when to die (19.30), and in that sense the Romans do not "kill" him or put him to death. The piercing thus achieves or demonstrates something different, confirming Jesus's death rather than causing it, and drawing attention instead to the fluid outflow the piercing occasions.

This distinction is therefore determinative for what is conceived within 19.37's anticipated visualization, that is, what is used to evidence what, and when/how the testimony of the figure of 19.35 accompanies it. Broadly speaking, three "events" are invoked in 19.33–34: the non-breaking of Jesus's legs, the piercing of his side, and the resulting evulsion of blood and water. And there are two scriptural citations, the first of which (19.36) is the warrant or fulfillment of the first of the events (19.33). The question then becomes whether the "seeing" of 19.37 includes just the action of the piercing or whether it also incorporates the fluid outflow. Some seek to distinguish the latter two events and their accompanying witness. The Zech 12.10 quotation would offer scriptural warrant/fulfillment for the act of piercing (event two), and the figure of 19.35 offers (truthful) confirmation of the outflow of the blood and water (event three). If so, this would have interesting implications for the role of Scripture in John's Passion Narrative, namely that the spectacle of ultimate significance—blood and water—is evidenced *outside of* Scripture, and instead only by human testimony, by the figure at the cross (likely the Beloved Disciple) and serving to vindicate their authority accordingly.

Where previously Scripture has been used for testimonial purpose, its "silence" on the blood/water would be somewhat out of Johannine character. Although, it is true, John never explicitly unpacks the significance of the fluid flow, and although 19.37 does not exhaust the intertextual commentary upon it, it still seems more reasonable to associate the "seeing" action of 19.37 with both the piercing *and* the flow of fluids. Indeed, the double reference to ὁράω (19.35, 37) seems to equate the two evidential/confirmatory sources, and if so, Zechariah's fulfillment includes, at least in part, to whatever the blood and water attest. The intratextual evocation the 19.34 image generates also requires intertextual—that is, scriptural—warrant, and appropriately so at the very moment of scriptural fulfillment. The outcome or result of the piercing matters as much as the physical action, the future ὄψονται (19.37) anticipating a wider "seeing" that leads to belief. It is of the same interpretative significance as ὁ ἑωρακὼς of 19.35; the latter figure—Beloved Disciple or otherwise—is a "catalyst of belief" occasioned by their equivalent act of "seeing."[225] The Beloved Disciple's human testimony is further, complementary confirmation, and brings Scripture and the perspective of the Johannine Community into close juxtaposition. The Beloved Disciple is also found to be participating in the fulfillment of Scripture; his testimony is true because it is aligned with, and anticipated by, Scripture. We might even venture that the Beloved Disciple's testimony is thereby "fulfilled" by its integration with the climactic fulfillment of Israel's Scripture.[226]

INTERPRETATION OF THE QUOTATION

John's use of "pierced" (19.37) seems particularly pointed (no pun intended), and one might assume that the specific verbal/text form is driven by the need to find fulfillment in the piercing action of 19.34. It could be that the Zech 12.10 fulfills merely a testimonial function, confirming the significance of the piercing. On such a reading, it is Scripture *per se* that is fulfilled rather than a specific appeal to Zechariah itself.[227] Or the citation may have a more ironic tone in that the soldiers—by piercing Jesus—inadvertently fulfil Scripture, and thereby participate in a divinely-approved action. But that, too, would be a rather limited use of the Zechariah text, and overlooks the visual focus of 19.37; ὄψονται is the main verb, and, particularly in the future tense, thereby anticipates a wider optical significance than merely "proving" that the piercing has taken place. Likewise, the different piercing verb of 19.37 (ἐκκεντέω) suggests that the evangelist uses Zech 12.10 as more than just a convenient text of Scripture, and the distinctive ἑτέρα γραφὴ introductory formula also draws attention to the specificity of the Zechariah text. The piercing action is just the mode of confirming death;[228] the Fourth Gospel is more interested in what is forthcoming from Jesus's side—the blood and water—and the Beloved Disciple's visual confirmation of that fact. Moreover, the emphatic future of ὄψονται distances, divorces almost, the physical timing/activity of the piercing from the act of "seeing" it effects. Menken, for example, hints at the possibility of resurrection influence here—the anticipated seeing of Jesus in John 20 (20.18, 20, 25, 29).[229]

Hence it seems probable that Zech 12.10 has a wider interpretative function in respect of John 19.37. This has been the case, of course, for the previous quotations in John's Passion, and the wider intertextual and intratextual links are germane to the interpretation of the quotation; they resist such "minimalistic" analysis. The verbal shift between 19.34 and 19.37 suggests that the Zech 12.10 source is utilized for more than lexical convenience, and this invites wider consideration of the Zechariah backdrop, particularly as the Zechariah *inclusio* points toward a specific Johannine interest in that scriptural text.

The immediate context to Zech 12.10 offers a cautionary note, however, particularly with its more negative milieu. The broad setting is one of mourning (cf. Zech 12.10–14), and Rev 1.7 picks up the lament motif in its citation of Zech 12.10. The act of piercing is for mourning over a firstborn child (12.10), and such mourning extends across Jerusalem and across tribes and families. It is hardly a cause for celebration, and contrasts with the celebration of the triumphal entry that occasioned the previous Zechariah appeal (John 12.15; Zech 9.9). Although John does not explicitly evoke the quotation's lamenting context, there is mourning in terms of Nicodemus' and Joseph's response (19.38–42), along with that of Mary Magdalene (20.11–13), but that is well after the citation.[230] In 19.37, *looking*, rather than mourning, takes center stage.

But it is at this point of mourning that hope breaks in, and, within the Hebrew text at least, specifically the opening of a fountain that will cleanse the residents of Jerusalem from sin and impurity (Zech 13.1). It is hard not to hear an echo of the water from Jesus's side (19.34) at this point, a matter to which we will return in chapter 5. Other aspects of Zechariah 12–13 may also be intertextually invoked. The piercing of Jesus resonates with the striking of the Shepherd (Zech 13.7; cf. Mk 14.27), particularly bearing in mind Jesus's prior shepherd self-identification (John 10:11–14), or Zech 13.7 may even have been picked up earlier on in the Fourth Gospel (16.2). Zechariah 12.10 emphasizes how the mourning compares to that for a firstborn/only son, echoes perhaps of the *Akedah* (Genesis 22) if that is somehow on John's radar. Likewise, the cleansing fountain of Zech 13.1 may have resonance from earlier on in the Gospel (4.10, 7.38).[231] This would reinforce the notion that the piercing, rather than being a *negative* motif, instead becomes a positive one, the source of living water, and that which comes forth from Jesus's side (cf. 7.37–39). As such, Jesus's piercing reveals that his death is both sacrifice (19.36)—and one associated with blood—but also one that ultimately yields life (John 10.10).[232] Hence Sheridan's observation that "the wider evocative context of Zech 12.10 has little to do with John 19.37" is not persuasive, or rather it remains predicated on the particular reading of 19.37 she proposes.[233] Kubiś's contrasting statement—"it is incontrovertible that John alluded to the entire context of Zech 12.10"[234]—may express an equivalent overconfidence in this regard, but it is hard to ignore the potential associations between Zechariah 12–13 and John's Passion retelling, and the evangelist's specific choice of fulfillment passage seems both deliberate and interpretatively fruitful.

If the implied *Vorlage* is, then, MT-related, and if the Zechariah context is to be taken seriously, how is John addressing the MT's "personal" dimension? Köstenberger draws attention to the way in which the "on me" (אלי) of the Hebrew is lost in the Johannine rendering, or at least the ambiguity of the phrase is sidestepped.[235] The oddity of the Masoretic version is that YHWH—rather than a third party—is the one who is pierced, but the Fourth Gospel's third-person rendering (ὄν) loses that aspect. Indeed, one might well have expected John to exploit this feature—playing on the piercing of the "Word become flesh"—but if so, it is lost or thought too subtle to reproduce in the exact MT form. Sheridan suggests a different vocalization of אלי such that it just becomes equivalent to אל,[236] but that doesn't seem necessary if the evangelist is undertaking the more christological reading we propose below.

For the narrative presentation and Christology of the Fourth Gospel suggest that the full "divine" gamut of Zech 12.10 may still be in play, the shift to the third person notwithstanding. It is quite possible that John has utilized the Zechariah text precisely because it specifically addresses YHWH as the object of the piercing action. Other instances of the piercing of a representative figure might well have been available, and indeed, the verbal mismatch between νύσσω (19.34) and ἐκκεντέω (19.37) serves to underscore the variation. That is, the appeal to Zech 12.10 is not conditioned by the demands of verbal equivalence or terminological specificity. On that basis, Isaiah 53 and, more recently/explicitly, Psalm 22, have been on the Fourth Gospel's radar and such texts could well have provided the fulfillment source for 19.37.[237] The specific appeal to Zech 12.10, and at such a climactic, teleological point in the gospel account, suggests that it offers John a very particular "take" on the piercing narrative, and one whose significance goes well beyond merely recounting the physical action. Rather than the piercing of YHWH being something to be avoided, Zech 12.10 MT offers scriptural testimony, scripture *fulfilled* in the piercing of Jesus, namely that God—that is, YHWH—is indeed the One who is pierced. Zechariah 12.10 becomes the evangelist's effective trump card, yielding ultimate scriptural warrant for the impact of Jesus's death, namely Jesus's divine identity. Rogers concludes on such grounds: "The warrant for John's appropriation of a text like Zech 12.10 . . . rests in his Spirit-given theological presupposition that Jesus is God, that he is the revelation of God's glory."[238] One might therefore suggest that John resolves the prominent internal tension within the Zechariah account, namely the idea that YHWH can be pierced. Jesus's piercing both demonstrates that tension and fulfills the Scripture which attests it.[239] As Rogers again succinctly states: "John seems to answer the *sui generis* problem, God is pierced, with the *sui generis* answer, Jesus is God."[240] The pinnacle of Scripture's fulfillment is its christological claim to the divine identity of Jesus.

Some commentators read the impact of the Zech 12.10 more cautiously, it must be said. The shift of personal pronoun, for example, leads some to view 19.37 in essentially representative terms—that is, departing from an explicit YHWH focus and instead describing a figure whose action somehow acts in place of God. Brown notes, for example, that if 19.37 was intended to prove or demonstrate Jesus's divinity, then the first-person aspect of Zech 12.10 MT could/should have been preserved, thereby tying 19.37 more explicitly to the Zechariah *Vorlage*.[241] But such preservation would sit less easily with 19.36, whose third-person aspect is necessary, and perhaps also lessens the force of looking on the one actually physically pierced by the soldier's action. And as Kubiś astutely observes: "According to Zech 12:10, regardless of the textual tradition in which this oracle is conveyed. . . . , the one on whom they look is *always* identified as *God*."[242]

This reading of Zech 12.10 is consistent with the Fourth Gospel's wider purposes and offers a fitting climax to the evangelist's presentation of Jesus and the exhortation to believe (20.31). Because Zech 12.10 presents God as the pierced one, and as Jesus is the one pierced, then Jesus must be God. Through its citation of Zech 12.10, 19.37 underscores John's focus on the *identity of the one seen*, rather than on the physical act of piercing, recapitulating the visual invitation of 1.39 and 1.46. It requires significant awareness of the Zechariah oracle, of course, of the (divine piercing) tradition associated with it, and it builds significant theological reflection on that basis. But that is somewhat appropriate, one suggests—the *gravitas* of the theological claim is contingent on the profundity and depth of the citation. John 19.37/ Zech 12.10 evidence a high point in the explication of Jesus's divine identity, commensurate with Jesus's death being the locus for the manifestation of the divine glory. Such manifestation is endorsed and mediated by the Jewish Scriptures, and the act of Jesus's piercing realizes the fulfillment of those Scriptures, specifically Zech 12.10. As Hurtado notes: "John does not replace the God of the Old Testament with Jesus. Instead, there is this amazing linkage and extension to Jesus of Old Testament ways of referring to God."[243] The reader is also taken back to 1.18, and the Prologue's contention that no-one has ever seen God. John 19.37 reverses or nuances that claim—to see the pierced Jesus is to see the (pierced) God—and a further bookend or *inclusio* to the account with 19.37 is so formed. For the Johannine evangelist, looking onto the pierced/divine one ultimately becomes the source of eternal life (cf. 20.31).

CONCLUSION—QUOTATIONAL USE IN JOHN'S PASSION NARRATIVE

What then might we say in overall terms as to the use of scriptural quotations in John's Passion Narrative? At the very least, quotation as the *mode* of citation has interpretative significance. Aside from any fulfillment implications, it draws the reader's attention to the specific matter in hand and (what may seem like) "[p]etty detail repeatedly takes on notable importance."[244] But we might also tentatively identify some habits or consistent features of the evangelist's quotational practice. These are only provisional at this stage, premised just on the quotational evidence, and they will need to be re-visited in our subsequent chapters as we come to more widespread conclusions as to John's use of Scripture. But for the moment, we might draw out the following principles that are manifest through the Passion Narrative's inclusion of signaled quotations:

1. Composite Nature

There is a multi-layered, multi-dimensional aspect to John's quotational usage. It is not monochrome. In several of the instances we have discussed, tracing the *Vorlage* of the quotation suggested that its source is composite (19.36, 19.37), and necessarily so. The imagery and context drawn on by the quotations derive from several sources, and it is the combination of those reference points that informs the usage of the cited lemma. There appears to be an amalgam or plurality as to the way quotations are rendered, and this encourages consideration of whether such compositeness—or multivalency—exists for other types of John's intertextual usage. We will have this in mind when considering John's use of allusions in our next chapter.

This has wider implications too, one suggests, for the process of seeking after a quotation's *Vorlage*, the task which has previously so dominated Johannine OT/NT discourse. Our discussion suggests that there is still merit in seeking after such matters and that there is explanatory insight so derived.[245] But equally, it cannot be done with certainty or overconfidence. Within the Passion Account, John 19.24 apart, there is significant plurality for each quotation's *Vorlage*. Changes can be made to the cited form—and legitimately so—without the scriptural text's authority or integrity being undermined. Textual alterations appear permissible to make sense of Scripture, particularly in its capacity for fulfillment. And such changes, and the resulting elements of the composite quotation, are motivated by the Fourth Gospel's presenting narratival and christological perspectives. The *function* of the quoted text is as important as its form.[246] Williams's summary is thus an appropriate one: "Among the distinguishing features of John's composite citations is that they have been deliberately shaped to align closely with the distinctively Johannine presentation of Jesus."[247] Unsurprisingly bearing in mind 20.31, the specific quotational lexeme and the Fourth Gospel's christological purposes are inextricably intertwined.

2. Christological Lens

The meaning derived from the quotations it cites is ultimately driven by John's christological perspective. Simply put, John's "interpretation of Scripture is determined by his view of Jesus" and the perceived need to legitimate Jesus's cruciform death.[248] The cited texts serve John's portrayal of Jesus and the Passion scene, rather than vice-versa. John's choice of text(s), John's "composition" of them, serves to demonstrate the way in which Jesus's death demonstrates their fulfillment. In that sense, we might, with Hays, speak of John "reading backwards," with the crux of the christological Passion effectively forming the Fourth Gospel's interpretative starting point.[249] The evangelist has read retrospectively, discerning texts that support its analysis, even if the cited texts themselves do not appear overtly prophetic. John's christology, and likewise its theology (cf. 19.37), drives the narrative's use of scriptural quotations, and it is that perspective, rather than the specific citational text form, that is hermeneutically primary.[250] For example, of the first two quotations, Ford opines: "The division of his clothes by the soldiers is crucially understood through Psalm 22 and his thirst through Psalm 69."[251] Ford's use of "crucially" is probably meant to stress importance, but one wonders if—unconsciously or otherwise—he has also drawn out an important *double entendre* in respect of John's scriptural usage. That is, 19.24 and 19.28 draw out the crucial—or *cruciform*—aspect of the reading of the two Psalms, and that aspect is fundamental to their integration into John's Passion re-narration.

Pushing this further, the utilized quotations are intrinsic to the question of Jesus's identity, arguably the central motif or question of John's Passion retelling. King, Lamb, YHWH, the one who controls Scripture—all such images derive from the quotations John's Passion Narrative employs. Source, method and lens are all shaped—decisively one suggests—by the operative Johannine christological hermeneutic.

3. Quotation and Fulfillment

Integrally linked to this christological perspective is the fulfillment characterization the Fourth Gospel ascribes to the cited quotations. The fulfillment aspect is not unique to the Passion Narrative (cf. 12.38, 13.18, 15.25, 17.12), and the reader comes to chapters 18–19 already prepared for such scriptural authentication. But John's Passion retelling intensifies the volume, and its reader is left in no doubt that Jesus's death is explicitly κατὰ τὰς γραφὰς. The cross is no accident or misapprehension, but rather the very event to which the Scriptures decisively point,[252] and which leads to their fulfillment and ultimate perfection. Such fulfillment takes a plurality of forms. As with John 19.24/Ps 22.18, it may be fulfillment of the specific text, fulfillment of the whole entity that is Scripture, or fulfillment of the event to which the text is addressed.

However, *why* such fulfillment can be said to happening is less obvious, or at least John does not explicitly specify. There is no causal statement of the type presented in 12.39 or 12.41, and the reader is invited to take responsibility for unearthing that aspect themselves and drawing conclusions accordingly from the presenting narrative context. But a wider principle applies nonetheless. With the intensification of fulfillment present in the third triptych element, John effectively implies that the "true meaning of Scripture cannot be found within the text itself, but only *in its fulfillment in Jesus.*"[253] We will explore this aspect further in chapter 4.

Matthew Scott describes the Fourth Gospel's fulfillment hermeneutic well, contending that its "teleological approach to quotation licenses a reworking of the scriptural voice that it speaks in the mode of its fulfillment."[254] The events to which John aligns the quotations are seemingly mundane or routine, and of themselves should invite little comment and/or their content would normally be overlooked. But attribution of the fulfillment designation is critical; it invests the event (and in the case of the *crurifragium*, even the non-event—19.36) with substantial interpretive significance. Furthermore, the evangelist only quotes as much of the scriptural source(s) as is necessary to demonstrate that the requisite fulfillment has been achieved. This contrasts, for example, with the quotational technique of the Epistle to the Hebrews, where a lengthy citation is given even if/when only a small portion or phrase of it is germane to the epistolary argument.[255] The sheer brevity of the Passion quotations (especially 19.28, 19.36–37) is therefore noteworthy, particularly as the shorter the quotation the more intertextual, fulfillment weight it carries. As we shall see in chapter 4 and the declaration of the overall teleiosis of Scripture, the claim for this is premised upon a single word quotation (διψῶ—19.28). Less is more, so to speak.

Is this fulfillment of individual, specific scriptures, or of Scripture as a whole? We might suggest that, in terms of the Passion's quotational usage at least, the answer is both/and rather than either/or. Scripture is both wood and trees as far as the Passion Narrative is concerned. On the one hand, we have seen the Fourth Gospel's pressing concern to emphasize the fulfillment of the wider curvature of Scripture—that is, the text *qua*-Scripture—without the attribution to the specific or implied source. All four quotations lack such attribution or any directive signalling as to their "author" or associated voice, and John instead focuses essentially on their fulfillment *as Scripture*.[256] There is no reference to Isaiah's participation, for example, as in John 12.37–41, nor any explicit reference to the Davidic context of Psalm 22 or Psalm 69 (even if, as we have suggested, such Davidic association is germane to John's usage of the respective Psalms). Hence, with Jobes: "When John's use of Scripture is considered as a whole, John seems to be more interested in presenting Jesus—his life, words, deeds/signs, passion, death and resurrection—as the fulfillment of Scripture in general rather than the fulfillment of individual passages of the Old Testament."[257]

But at the same time, and with quintessential Johannine paradox, we have shown that the origin(s) of the quoted text is far from incidental, and, indeed, is critical to the evangelist's interpretive purposes. John is interested in specific passages—independently or combined together—rather than in just the basic fulfillment of Scripture, and particular passages (Psalm 22, Psalm 34, Psalm 69, Zechariah 12–13) are specifically chosen because of their individual testimony and fulfillment capacity. Considering the origins of the two

Isaianic citations in John 12.38–40, Jonathan Lett avers: "Attention to the phenomenon of intertextuality suggests that exegesis ought not be so quick to pluck John's scriptural citations from their original contexts."[258] We concur with Lett, and suggest the principle extends to the Passion quotations too. Rather than pulling the reader away from the scriptural record, John's intertextual citation draws them toward the source material and its wider context/milieu. Lett further argues, persuasively one suggests, that as John's use of Israel's Scriptures is so *embedded* in the Gospel text, its lens so attuned to fulfillment, to see citations as atomistic, unrelated to context is to misconstrue John's perception of Israel's Scriptures and their fundamental, specific shaping of the Johannine kerygma.[259]

4. Ironic Interpretation/Reversal

Irony pervades the way in which John's Passion Narrative conceives of quotations being fulfilled. This, of course, accords with the essential irony of the Johannine Passion, and potentially of the Fourth Gospel as a whole, namely that "Jesus's task is completed (cf. 19.30) at the very same point that the opposition appears to have succeeded in executing its own lethal intentions."[260] Jesus's humiliation—the division of his clothing, the thirst only sated by sour wine, his dead body pierced by a Roman spear—all receive scriptural warrant, and necessarily in virtue of the Fourth Gospel's fulfillment lens. There is important "continuity" with the quotation's broader context, but such continuity is revealed in surprising or counter-intuitive fashion, with the "lifting up" on a Roman cross proving to be Jesus's royal enthronement rather than his disgrace. Daly-Denton's summary encapsulates the ironic tendency well: "it is the sight of Jesus in mock royal regalia, having just undergone a Roman scourging and about to lay down his life, that shows what the word 'king' means."[261] The accompanying detail reinforces this irony. The completion of Jesus's task—τετέλεσται (19.30)—is announced once he has consumed the ὄξος handed to him. Whereas his opening sign turned water in abundant volumes of good wine and so revealed Jesus's glory (2.11), so the fulfillment of that glory—on a Roman cross—is (ironically and/or in reverse fashion) manifest by drinking of sour wine.

The accompanying motif of scriptural fulfillment only reinforces the ironic way in the Fourth Gospel sees this outworked—"the completion of the Scripture reveals that this humiliating death accomplishes God's purposes."[262] And recognizing the scriptural basis for the respective quotations is critical for discerning their ironic interpretation, for the ironic play breaks down if the full scriptural warrant is not found. John's Passion quotations are therefore far from being atomistic citations or proof texts. When shorn of its scriptural backdrop, or bereft of its context, the quotation's interpretation will inevitably look bizarre or contradictory, and often without resolution. But if/ as the wider context is brought the fore, the inherent truthfulness to the quotation's usage is manifest for all its ironic character.

5. *Sporadic Nature*

It is well established in Johannine scholarship that the Fourth Gospel uses significantly fewer quotations compared to its Synoptic counterparts.[263] Although the close proximity of the four quotations intensifies their cumulative effect, and although this gives particular attention to the crucifixion scene and its scriptural warrant, it remains the case that much of John's Passion Narrative is empty of direct quotation. It is the third part of the Passion triptych that bears the quotation/fulfillment burden, drawing rhetorical focus to the fulfillment Jesus's physical death occasions. The absence of any scriptural citation—fulfillment-wise or otherwise—in the trial or burial scene, for example, is notable. But such absence may serve to underscore the necessity for locating scriptural fulfillment with the manner and evidencing of Jesus's *death* as the primary matter in hand. Once 19.37 has confirmed the scriptural warrant for the evidencing of the spearing of Jesus's side, it follows, up to a point at least, that the work of both Scripture and Jesus is in some sense done. As we shall see in chapter 4, this has implications for John's conception of Scripture, its *Schriftverständnisses*, and for the wider scriptural fulfillment enterprise which John's Passion undertakes.

6. *Intertextual <-> Intratextual*

Our analysis has suggested that one cannot effectively assess John's use of scriptural quotations in isolation. The quotations stand on their own feet, of course, and their intertextual effect is significant, as we have seen. However, the full impact or effect of the quotation is as much an intratextual as an intertextual exercise; the reader draws on other parts of the Fourth Gospel to assess the use of the quotation and to how it might shape John's wider evangelistic enterprise. The Paschal Lamb connotation to John 19.36; the paradox of Jesus's thirst (19.28) as the one who promises the Samaritan woman that she will never be thirsty again (4.13); or the significance of the outpoured blood and water that 19.37 invites onlookers to see and believe—all embrace prior Johannine features or images but without the quotation itself detailing them. Attending to the Fourth Gospel's use of Scripture is necessarily intratextual as much as intertextual.

7. Quotations Demonstrate Significance

Overall, whereas other citations apply fulfillment to Jesus's words (18.9, 18.32), and where in other parts of the Passion Narrative, as we shall see, the citational mode is allusion rather than quotation, the presence of back-to-back, explicit quotation is both prominent and seemingly necessary for John's evangelistic purposes. That is, at the very pinnacle of John's evangelistic discourse, and in order to address the core crux of the crucified messiah, the reader is left in no doubt as to the κατὰ τὰς γραφὰς nature of the event. Allusion can invariably be, as we shall see, a more potent or generative intertextual tool, but, by its very nature, is more contested or ambiguous in its interpretation. By contrast, explicit quotation is clearly signalled, and the reader is demonstrably aware as to the scriptural warrant/fulfillment of the crucifixion scene. When the evangelist seeks interpretive weight and significance, signalled, direct quotation is their default option.[264]

NOTES

1. Myers, *Characterizing Jesus*, 9–16; Sheridan, *Retelling*, 12–37; Daise, *Quotations in John*, 1–20.
2. Menken, *Quotations in the Fourth Gospel*.
3. Daise, *Quotations in John*, 3.
4. So Evans, "Quotation," 79–83; cf. also Stanley Porter, "The Linguistic Function of Biblical Citations in John's Gospel," in *Biblical Interpretation in Early Christian Gospels. Volume 4: The Gospel of John*, ed. Thomas R. Hatina, LNTS 613 (London: T&T Clark, 2020), 121–36.
5. Freed, *Quotations*, 129.
6. Four of Fourth Gospel's (likely) nineteen quotations are located in 19.23–37.
7. Menken, *Quotations in the Fourth Gospel*, 212.
8. For example, Menken, *Quotations in the Fourth Gospel*, 12 counts seventeen, with 17.12 and 19.28 excluded as they manifest an introductory formula but without a specific quotation; whereas Schuchard, "Form Versus Function," 23–45 limits the count to merely thirteen, omitting four found in Menken's list (i.e., 7.38, 7.42, 8.17 and 12.34) as they do not explicitly replicate the text of the LXX. They are a construction of the evangelist and/or reference scriptural concepts rather than specific texts. See the comparison of commentators' respective "counts" in Daise, *Quotations in John*, 212.
9. So, prior to the Passion Narrative: John 12.38, 12.39–40, 13.18, 15.25.
10. Evans, "Quotation," 81.
11. The assessment of Thompson, "Psalms," 267 is explicit in this regard: "Those texts cited in the second part of the Gospel focus specifically on Jesus's rejection or death."

12. Craig A. Evans, *Word and Glory: On the Exegetical and Theological Background of John's Prologue*, JSNTSupp 89 (Sheffield, UK: JSOT Press, 1993), 174.

13. John 20.9 alludes to an unnamed scripture—and likely refers intratextually back to 2.17—but no actual textual citation is made.

14. Menken, "Observations," 131 draws attention to Obermann's helpful distinction between "implicit" and "explicit" fulfillment of Scripture, namely: "Scripture is explicitly fulfilled in Jesus's passion, and implicitly in his preceding ministry." See Obermann, *Erfüllung*, 348–50.

15. Cf. Köstenberger, "Use of the Old Testament," 53: "the first four OT quotations in the second half of John's Gospel all focus on people's rejection and hatred of Jesus and declare that this unprovoked and baseless animosity was in keeping with God's sovereign plan."

16. The only fulfillment quotation in Matthew's Passion Narrative attests to the death of Judas (Matt 27.9).

17. Sheridan, *Retelling*, 12.

18. Menken, *Quotations in the Fourth Gospel*, 11.

19. For Menken, *Quotations in the Fourth Gospel*, the interpretative questions pertain to source and evangelistic redaction; distinctive is the consideration of how John's editorial perspective might have redacted established *Vorlagen*, and hence the hunt for unknown sources becomes less pressing. Where a citation merely repeats the *Vorlage*, there is less evidence as to the evangelist's perspective—or at least it becomes essentially an argument from silence.

20. So Freed, *Quotations*, 130. Also Menken, *Quotations in the Fourth Gospel*, 205: "It is evident that the LXX is the Bible of the fourth evangelist."

21. As suggested by Charles Goodwin, "How Did John Treat His Sources," *JBL* 73 (1954): 61–75.

22. See especially Catrin H. Williams, "Composite Citations in the Gospel of John," in *Composite Citations in Antiquity. Volume 2, New Testament Uses*, ed. Sean A. Adams and Seth Ehorn, LNTS 593 (London: Bloomsbury, 2018), 94–127.

23. By pesher, we understand the particular mode of biblical interpretation present in Qumran literature whereby a scriptural text is interpreted as specifically fulfilled within the experience of the Qumran community. The Fourth Gospel might make similar connections in terms of Scripture being fulfilled in its readers' own time, though it does not use the interpretation/pesher designation that distinguishes the Qumran practice. On the Pesharim, see Timothy H. Lim, *Pesharim* (London: Sheffield Academic Press, 2002).

24. On the question of "context" in OT/NT studies, see Arthur Keefer, "The Meaning and Place of Old Testament Context in OT/NT Methodology," in *Methodology in the Use of the Old Testament in the New: Context and Criteria*, ed. David Allen and Steve Smith, LNTS 597 (London: T&T Clark, 2019), 75–85.

25. Keefer, "Context," 77n13, drawing on Hays, *Echoes*, 156–57, 161.

26. Douglas J. Moo, *The Old Testament in the Gospel Passion Narratives* (Sheffield, UK: Almond Press, 1983), 8.

27. Psalm 22.18 MT has an imperfect form (יחלקו), but the LXX renders the aorist διεμερίσαντο, which John 19.24 follows.

28. For example, Menken, *Quotations in the Fourth Gospel* omits 19.24 (along with 10.34 (Ps 81.6) and 12.38 (Isa 53.1)) from his analysis of Fourth Gospel quotations for that reason. This perhaps illustrates the degree to which twentieth-century research on John's use of the Jewish Scriptures was driven by interest in *Vorlage* concerns—that is, more straightforward source instances tended not to warrant further enquiry.

29. See Williams, "Composite Citations," 94–127, and subsequent sections.

30. Roger L. Omanson, *A Textual Guide to the Greek New Testament: An Adaptation of Bruce M. Metzger's Textual Commentary for the Needs of Translators* (Stuttgart: Deutsche Bibelgesellschaft, 2006) classifies it as type C variant, that is, generally uncertain as to whether it is original or not.

31. So Beutler, "Use," 149. He continues: "The narrowing of 'scripture' to this individual verse seems to be secondary."

32. John Fenton, *The Passion According to John: With Introduction, Notes, and Meditations* (London: SPCK, 1961), 50: "The soldiers, like Caiaphas and Pilate and the Jews, are unconsciously playing their part in a play they do not understand."

33. Myers, *Characterizing Jesus*, 170. She continues: "Even their [i.e., the soldiers] menial tasks show the truth behind Jesus's claims."

34. Cf. John Paul Heil, *Blood and Water: The Death and Resurrection of Jesus in John 18–21*, CBQMS 27 (Washington, DC: Catholic Biblical Association of America, 1995).

35. Margaret Daly-Denton, "The Psalms in John's Gospel," in *The Psalms in the New Testament*, ed. Steve Moyise and M. J. J. Menken (London: T&T Clark, 2004), 133: "John is on common ground with the synoptics."

36. Rudolf Schnackenburg, *The Gospel According to St John*, vol. 3 (Tunbridge Wells: Burns & Oates, 1982), 272 proposes such a (later) development to the Synoptic record, premised upon particular sources available to John. Cf. also Stibbe, *John as Storyteller*, 176.

37. See Moo, *Old Testament*, 287–88; Allen, *According*, 177.

38. Brown, *Death*, 954n41 notes the suggestion that the Aramaic of a Psalm 22 targum might have formed part of the Fourth Gospel's mindset, as the targum distinguishes between clothes and cloak, but rejects it as an interpretive possibility as there is no evidence of its being extant in the first century.

39. C. K. Barrett, *The Gospel According to St John: An Introduction with Commentary and Notes on the Greek Text* (London: SPCK, 1978), 550–51. Other commentators, though, have queried this premise; cf. Lindars, *Apologetic*, 91: "John must not be held to be ignorant of the most consistent characteristic of Hebrew poetry. John knew that Ps 22.19 meant what the Synoptists made of it . . . but *purposely* chose to take it literally."

40. D. A. Carson, *The Gospel According to John: An Introduction and Commentary* (Leicester: Apollos, 1991). Likewise, Andreas J. Köstenberger, "John," in G. K. Beale and D. A. Carson (eds.), *Commentary on the New Testament Use of the Old Testament* (Grand Rapids, MI: Apollos, 2007), 501 suggests that the second line of the psalm is elaborating on the first, and John's usage so "involves an element of midrash."

41. See 19.37, for example.

42. So Susan Docherty, "New Testament Scriptural Interpretation in its Early Jewish Context," *NovT* 57 (2015): 15, following Samely: "this practice of allocating a new speaker or referent to a scriptural passage is widespread in rabbinic interpretation, and involves the specification of the speaker, or addressee, or time of utterance of words which appear ambiguous or undetermined in their original context, especially where they contain first-person direct speech." Whereas John's christological hermeneutic may be motivating the vocal re-assignment, its re-allocation onto Jesus's lips is standard exegetical practice.

43. Although the soldiers do offer up the wine on hyssop (19.29) and are therefore included in that way, the actual fulfillment (the double use of τελέω language (19.28, 30) is solely Jesus's responsibility. Likewise, the text being fulfilled—whatever its *Vorlage* might be—is a first-person verb (διψῶ) which Jesus himself once more cites (and gives further instance of Jesus voicing the Psalms—cf. Rom 15.3).

44. Barrett, *Gospel*, 550.

45. Probably the same scripture alluded to in 17.12.

46. So Porter, "Linguistic," 130: "this quotation is not part of the narrative proper but belongs to the commentary of the omniscient author who sees in the casting of lots and not dividing of Jesus's garment that Scripture is fulfilled." Likewise Green, *Death of Jesus*, 298: "The elaboration of this scene found in John 19.23–25a is clearly secondary in an attempt to show how the OT was precisely 'fulfilled.'"

47. So Lincoln, *Gospel*, 476: "the evangelist's concern to find an exact fulfillment of Scripture quite adequately accounts for the inclusion of this description of the tunic." Likewise Rudolph Bultmann, *The Gospel of John: A Commentary* (Oxford: Basil Blackwell, 1971), 671: "One could ask whether the episode has a particular meaning for him, but there is nothing to indicate as such."

48. Thomas L. Brodie, *The Gospel According to John: A Literary and Theological Commentary* (OUP, 1993), 546. Brodie also perceives in the action something of a descent from kingship to nakedness (546); that may be a more persuasive contrast bearing in mind the irony of the cruciform lifting up.

49. Schnackenburg, *Gospel*, 273.

50. Brown, *Death*, 955n44 describes attempts to make such a connection as "far-fetched," but the immediate proximity of two fourfold "gatherings" has at least some symbolic potential, however outworked.

51. Frey, *Theology*, 163: "We can even assume that John actually created or fictionally imagined the scene." Freed, *Quotations*, 124 also points toward some form of Johannine creation: John's "effort to interpret and supplement the Synoptic account led to the discovery and use of the Ps text."

52. Cf. Stibbe, *John as Storyteller*, 176—"the idea of the tunic is the centre of theological symbolism in this Episode."

53. Fenton, *Passion*, 51: the curtain is torn ἀπ' ἄνωθεν (Mk 15.38) and Jesus's garment is woven ἐκ τῶν ἄνωθεν (John 19.23).

54. Lindars, *Apologetic*, 91.

55. That is perhaps more a case for Revelation—cf. Rev 1.13–16, for example. See, though, Helen K. Bond, "Discarding the Seamless Robe the High Priesthood of Jesus in John's Gospel," in *Israel's God and Rebecca's Children: Christology*

and Community in Early Judaism and Christianity, ed. David B. Capes et al. (Waco, TX: Baylor University Press, 2007), 183–94, for a more positive assessment of John's priestly depiction. She contends that John's Jewish readers would have understood χιτών in priestly terms, and particularly in terms of one worn by the priest for the Day of Atonement (Lev 16.4). (She concedes, though, that this robe is never said to be seamless, a factor which seems significant for John's interpretive purposes here). Bond continues: "In the same way that Jesus transcends and supersedes the temple, so he transcends and renders redundant the earthly high priest; everything that Jewish Christians once looked to the high priest to achieve is now accomplished to the full in Christ" (192).

56. Marianne Meye Thompson, *John: A Commentary*, NTL (Louisville, KY: Westminster John Knox, 2015), 399.

57. See *inter alia* Culpepper, "Theology," 26–28.

58. Keener, *Gospel*, 1140 doubts the ecclesial/disciple allegorical solution on the grounds that Jesus does lose the tunic, and hence the unbroken/wholeness argument is undermined.

59. So John Ashton, "John and the Johannine Literature: The Woman at the Well," in *The Cambridge Companion to Biblical Interpretation*, ed. John Barton (Cambridge, UK: Cambridge University Press, 1998), 259. The χιτών's "receipt" by the soldiers may also have missional implications, the offer of life conceptually bound up within the garment.

60. Cf. Culpepper, "Theology," 35: "The fact that the tunic is not torn reflects God's intent that the community of believers should be one." Advocating the relationship between the unity of the tunic and that of the Church, see also Schuchard, *Scripture within Scripture*, 127–32.

61. Brown, *Death*, 955–58.

62. J. Ramsey Michaels, *The Gospel of John* (Grand Rapids, MI: Eerdmans, 2010), 953, is thus dismissive of any symbolism deriving from the χιτών. So also Moo, *Old Testament*, 256: "nothing would indicate that χιτών is symbolic of the church."

63. See Schnackenburg, *Gospel*, 274.

64. Senior, *Passion in John*, 106.

65. Juraj Feník, "Clothing Symbolism in the Elijah-Elisha Cycle and in the Gospel of John," *Studia Biblica Slovaca* 13 (2021): 66.

66. Moo, *Old Testament*, 255–57.

67. Köstenberger, "John," 502; so also Carson, *Gospel*, 614.

68. Freed, *Quotations*, 101.

69. Myers, *Characterizing Jesus*, 167.

70. Hence Daly-Denton's suggestion that the seamless/untorn robe points toward the divine vindication of Jesus may well be a valid assessment (Daly-Denton, "Psalms," 132).

71. See Holly J. Carey, *Jesus' Cry from the Cross: Towards a First-Century Understanding of the Intertextual Relationship between Psalm 22 and the Narrative of Mark's Gospel*, LNTS 398 (London: T&T Clark, 2009); also Holly J. Carey, "Psalm 22 in Mark's Gospel: Moving Forward," in *New Studies in Textual Interplay*, ed. Craig A. Evans, et al., LNTS 632; London: T&T Clark, 2021), 121–37. For a

different perspective, advocating a more limited application of Psalm 22, see Stephen P. Ahearne-Kroll, *The Psalms of Lament in Mark's Passion: Jesus' Davidic Suffering*, SNTSMS 142 (Cambridge, UK: Cambridge University Press, 2007).

72. Obermann, *Erfüllung*, 282–97.

73. Feník, "Clothing Symbolism," 64.

74. Ville Auvinen, "Jesus and the Devout Psalmist of Psalm 22," in *Jesus and the Scriptures: Problems, Passages, and Patterns*, ed. Tobias Hägerland, LNTS 552; London: T&T Clark, 2016), 134 avers that Ps 22.1 was available to the Fourth Gospel, either through its sources, or through Mark directly, and hence it is a definite decision (as with Luke) *not* to include it.

75. Daly-Denton, "Psalms," 132; Thompson, "Psalms," 270.

76. Thomas J. Parker, "Jesus and Scripture: A Comparative Study of Hebrews, James, 1 and 2 Peter and Their Use of the Old Testament and Jesus Traditions" (PhD Dissertation: Vrije Universiteit, 2022).

77. Köstenberger, "John," 502.

78. Carlos Raúl Sosa Siliezar, *The Savior of the World: A Theology of the Universal Gospel* (Waco, TX: Baylor University Press, 2019), 140.

79. Margaret Daly-Denton, *David in the Fourth Gospel: The Johannine Reception of the Psalms*, AGJU 47 (Leiden: Brill, 2000), 213–14.

80. Daly-Denton observes that Davidic authorship is effectively a "given."

81. Daly-Denton, *David*; see also Daly-Denton, "Psalms," 119–37.

82. Daly-Denton, "Psalms," 132. Cf. also John Ashton, *Understanding the Fourth Gospel* (Oxford: Oxford University Press, 2007), 464: "by replacing the anguished appeal recorded by Mark and Matthew with a shout of triumph, John transforms the cross into a throne."

83. Juel, *Messianic*, 103.

84. Thompson, "Psalms," 270.

85. Daly-Denton, *David*, 218.

86. Matthew Scott, *The Hermeneutics of Christological Psalmody in Paul: An Intertextual Enquiry*, SNTSMS 158 (Cambridge, UK: Cambridge University Press, 2014), 64. He continues: John's "teleological approach to quotation licenses a reworking of the scriptural voice so that it speaks in the mode of its fulfillment" (64).

87. Brodie, *Gospel*, 547. He further observes how the clarifying statement of 19.24 (Οἱ μὲν οὖν στρατιῶται ταῦτα ἐποίησαν) reinforces the notion of actual fulfillment, and hence matches the previous re-statement of Pilate's writing (ὃ γέγραφα, γέγραφα—19.22). In both instances, double/repeated attention is given to the respective action, thus likewise reinforcing the comparison of the two different types of γραφή—inscription and Scripture. Likewise, also Keener, *Gospel*, 1138: "The finality of Pilate's claim about 'what I have written' . . . may remind the reader of every other use of 'written' to this point in the Gospel—every other use refers to Scripture."

88. Arthur M. Wright, "The King on the Cross: Johannine Christology in the Roman Imperial Context," in *Johannine Christology*, Stanley E. Porter and Andrew W. Pitts, Johannine Studies 3 (Leiden: Brill, 2020), 136.

89. So also Wright, "King on the Cross," 136.

90. Hence *contra* Beutler, "Use," 148, who ventures that "where John speaks of 'writing' in the context of the titulus" seems "to be irrelevant for the question of Holy Scripture." The very juxtaposition of two contrasting types of γράφω/γραφή material richly contributes to how the Passion Narrative conceives of the role and function of Scripture.

91. Hays, *Echoes-Gospels*, 326.

92. There are echoes here, too, of the previous fulfillment quotation (15.25), and the contested interpretation of Scripture found there. See further the discussion on 15.25 in chapter 4.

93. Mary L. Coloe, *John*, Wisdom Commentary 44 (Collegeville, MN: Liturgical, 2021), 478. See also Mary L. Coloe, "The Nazarene King: Pilate's Title as the Key to John's Crucifixion," in *The Death of Jesus in the Fourth Gospel*, ed. Gilbert van Belle (Leuven: Leuven University Press, 2007), 839–48.

94. We might also say that taking this approach to John's use of Ps 22.18 also serves to remove the primary stumbling block to the χιτών = unity association. That is, the mode of "reverse" or "ironic" fulfillment renders the contrary to/of the assumed premise.

95. Köstenberger, "John," 502: "The reference in 19.28 to Scripture being fulfilled builds on 19.24 . . . and continues the evangelist's emphasis on Jesus's actively bringing about the respective events of his passion."

96. See the further discussion of this unit in chapter 3.

97. Cf. Senior, *Passion in John*, 114: "the Church will be born at the moment of Jesus's death."

98. Köstenberger, "John," 502.

99. Some have speculated that the use of τελειόω derives from other early Christian source material, but it is more likely a Johannine flourish, particularly in view of the τελ-related imagery at work here. Cf. Brown, *Death*: "*teleioun* is more appropriate than *pleroun* for this particular reference to Scripture because this is the final fulfillment, the *telos*, the end." Indeed, we might suggest that John is making a claim in respect of Scripture that goes beyond mere fulfillment—and is more akin to the notion of perfection; hence the different verb is both appropriate and necessary on such grounds. See the further discussion in chapter 4.

100. We do not regard πληρόω and τελειόω as synonymous or equivalents. Others do see them as synonymous (Bultmann, *John*, 674n1; Leonard Theodor Witkamp, "Jesus' Thirst in John 19:28–30: Literal or Figurative?," *JBL* 115 (1996): 493); Evans, "Quotation," 80 avers that it is "virtually identical in meaning to the ἵνα πληρωθῇ formula." However, as we shall discuss in chapter 4, John's usage distinguishes their respective meanings; the teleiosis declared in 19.30 is distinctive for the character and status of Scripture *per se*. Cf. Hengel, "Old Testament," 33: "Only here in the entire gospel does the Evangelist speak of a *teleioun* of the Scriptures, an increase over the previous formulaic *pleroun*, which expresses the 'ultimate fulfillment' of all christological prophecy in the Scriptures, which in turn reach their goal in the death of Jesus." Hengel's language, although rightly drawing attention to the verbal heightening, may even undervalue the implications of the τελειόω claim; see our discussion in chapter 4.

101. Lieu, "Narrative," 150: "narrator and Jesus speak and think the same language." Such commonality therefore also serves to commend the role and perspective of the Johannine narrator.

102. See particularly Obermann, *Erfüllung*, 350–64 for the emphasis on the distinctiveness of the 19.28 claim to scriptural fulfillment and its resulting, climactic implications. "Die Vollendung des Willens Gottes und die Vollendung der Schrift fallen zusammen in dem einen Geschehen am Kreuz, da dort beide in letztgültiger Konkretion Gestalt gewonnen haben" (364). We will explore this further in chapter 4.

103. And of course, there remain other key points of difference. John has the soldiers, rather than the onlookers, offer the wine, and has hyssop rather than a sponge as the specified means of distribution (19.29).

104. Only Luke's Passion Narrative explicitly makes the soldiers the ones offering up the wine (Luke 23.36), and one might normally be attentive to the ambiguity in John. But whereas it is theoretically possible that the women assume the role of drink-bearers, it is most logically the action of the same soldiers of 19.23–24. This is also consistent with the context of Ps 69.21, where the ὄξος is proffered by opponents rather than by supporters.

105. Deolito V. Vistar Jr, *The Cross-and-Resurrection: The Supreme Sign in John's Gospel*, WUNT 2/508 (Tübingen: Mohr Siebeck, 2020), 195.

106. The fact that this clause appears nowhere else in the NT is further testimony to its rhetorical, climactic significance.

107. Jobes, *John*, 277; Michaels, *Gospel of John*, 961; cf. also G. Bampfylde, "John XIX 28: A Case for a Different Translation," *NovT* 11 (1969): 247–60. "The 'scripture' has nothing to do with the thirst of Jesus except by way of a paradoxical contrast. Instead, 19:28 should be translated in some such way as this: 'After this, Jesus, knowing that everything had been completed in order to bring the scripture to fruition, said, "I thirst"'" (260). He contends that the "Scripture" of 19.28 is Zech 14.8, in tandem with Ezekiel 47.

108. Witkamp, "Thirst," 494; Keener, *Gospel*, 1146; Carson, *Gospel*, 619; Vistar Jr, *Cross-and-Resurrection*, 195; Barrett, *Gospel*, 553. Likewise, BDF 478.

109. Daise, *Quotations in John*, 6n19.

110. Brian Tabb, "Jesus's Thirst at the Cross: Irony and Intertextuality in John 19:28," *EQ* 85 (2013): 339.

111. Cf. Culpepper, "Theology," 32: "it seems doubtful that the significance of Jesus's thirst is to be found primarily in the nuances of the earlier text [i.e., Psalm 69] . . . Instead, we must once again look for the meaning of Jesus's thirst within the Gospel itself."

112. So also Edward W. Klink, *John*, Zondervan Exegetical Commentary on the New Testament 4 (Grand Rapids, MI: Zondervan Academic, 2016), 809.

113. The NASB's rendering comes close to this: "Jesus, knowing that all things had already been accomplished, in order that the Scripture might be fulfilled, said. . . . "

114. One thinks, by comparison, of the debates within Pauline scholarship as to the extent/nature of the phrase πίστις Χριστοῦ, and whether it should be rendered as a subjective or objective genitive (cf. Gal 2.16). Rather than seeing the options as mutually exclusive, it is entirely possible that Paul has in mind *both* senses of the phrase,

and wishes to exploit the plurality accordingly. One might make the same observation too of the infamous crux of John 7.38, and the referent of αὐτοῦ therein (and notably so in view of its scriptural designation). Rather than having to adjudicate between the believer or Jesus being its referent, and thus the source of the living water, potentially both senses may be possible and genuinely so. We shall return to this text in chapter 5.

115. Brown, *Death*, 1070–74 seems to follow this trajectory; cf. also Raymond E. Brown, *The Gospel According to John*, AB 29 (London: Chapman, 1971), 2.908. So also Obermann, *Erfüllung*, 356. Martine Windal, "«J'ai soif» L'accomplissement de l'Écriture en Jn 19, 28," *Revue des Sciences Religieuses* 89 (2015): 25–46 points to the equivocalness of the text—that both senses are possible—and avers that translations accordingly need to preserve both aspects.

116. Adam Kubiś, *The Book of Zechariah in the Gospel of John*, EBib 64 (Pendé: J. Gabalda, 2012), 215.

117. See chapter 4.

118. Tabb, "Thirst's helpful expression."

119. Robert L. Brawley, "An Absent Complement and Intertextuality in John 19:28–29," *JBL* 112 (1993): 427 observes: "the significance of John 19.28–29 lies obscure under a veil of brevity."

120. Menken, *Quotations in the Fourth Gospel*; Schuchard, *Scripture within Scripture*, xiii-xiv; Daise, *Quotations in John*, 17; Porter, "Linguistic," 132; Köstenberger, "Use of the Old Testament," 54 is perhaps typical in this regard, averring that "Jesus's words on the cross, 'I'm thirsty,' fulfil Ps 69:22" but without formally classifying the utterance as a "quotation."

121. *Inter alia* Evans, "Quotation," 80; Reim, *Studien*, 160; Clark-Soles, *Scripture*, 222.

122. Stephen D. Moore, *Poststructural-Ism and the New Testament: Derrida and Foucault at the Foot of the Cross* (1994), 56–57 points to the inherent tension as problematic: "The hierarchical opposition established at the well is inverted as the cross, the ostensibly superior, pleromatic term (living water, Spirit) being shown to depend for its effective existence on the inferior, insufficient term (literal well water), contrary to everything that the Gospel has led us to expect." But this is to overlook the characteristic irony of the Fourth Gospel, and particularly the way in which the scriptural appeal of 19.28 outworks the ultimate achievement of the one who claims (physical) thirst. Likewise, Koester's assessment of Moore's critique: "Moore fails to note that paradox is fundamental to the Gospel's message and that it functions along with irony"—so Craig R. Koester, *Symbolism in the Fourth Gospel: Meaning, Mystery, Community* (Minneapolis: Fortress Press, 2003), 203.

123. Though not all commentators view this paradox as problematic—quite the reverse. Cf. Thompson, *John*, 400: "it is precisely the Word *made flesh*, capable of thirst, that offers thirst-quenching water."

124. Jobes, *John*, 277–78.

125. Bampfylde, "John XIX 28," 252.

126. Beutler, "Use."

127. Brawley, "Absent."

128. Daly-Denton, "Psalms," 135; Tabb, "Thirst," 342 specifies it as a "formal allusion," Obermann, *Erfüllung*, 364 as a "herausgestellte Anspielung."

129. Köstenberger, "John," 503.

130. Sheridan, *Retelling*, 28.

131. Brawley, "Absent," 427–43.

132. Richard Duane Patterson, "Psalm 22: From Trial to Triumph," *JETS* 47 (2004): 228; Rebekah Eklund, *Jesus Wept: The Significance of Jesus' Laments in the New Testament*, LNTS 515 (London: Bloomsbury, 2015), 40.

133. Herman N. Ridderbos, *The Gospel According to John: A Theological Commentary* (Grand Rapids, MI: Eerdmans, 1997), 617.

134. Ridderbos, *John*, 616–17.

135. David F. Ford, *The Gospel of John: A Theological Commentary* (Grand Rapids, MI: Baker Academic, 2021), 382 also moots Ps 143.6 as a possible intertext.

136. See Senior, *Passion in John*, 117.

137. Psalm 69 is cut from similar righteous sufferer cloth to Psalm 22. And, as with Psalm 22, its usage by John likely draws from pre-existing Jesus/Passion tradition. But John, even more than with Psalm 22, puts its own particular stamp on the Psalm's fulfillment.

138. Ford, *The Gospel of John*, 382.

139. Koester, *Symbolism*, 218.

140. Michaels, *Gospel of John* contends that Ps 69.9 is not the antecedent text; indeed, he only considers Ps 69.22 in this regard, and notes that the only word in common is ὄξος: "It is unlikely, therefore, that this text is in play."

141. Myers, *Characterizing Jesus*, 167 neatly summarizes 19.28–29 in such terms.

142. Scott, *Hermeneutics*, 65n8.

143. Tabb, "Thirst," 343: "The multiple appeals to this psalm in the Fourth Gospel (2:17; 15:25; 19:28) strongly suggest that the evangelist appeals to the Old Testament with an awareness of the context."

144. Köstenberger, "John," 503.

145. Cf. Daly-Denton, "Psalms," 135: "It is precisely the lightness of the one-word evocation of Ps 69.22 that suggests to the reader a deeper thirst of Jesus."

146. He calls this a "transliteral" reading.

147. Witkamp, "Thirst," 503.

148. Keener, *Gospel*, 1148.

149. See Frey, *Glory*, 210–212. Frey points out that ancient readers would have been well aware of the suffering crucifixions entailed and thus "could also imagine what was not explicitly narrated" (210).

150. Hengel, "Old Testament," 33: "The thirst of the Crucified One is at the same time an expression of his creatureliness and has antidocetic character."

151. So again Richard B. Hays, *The Conversion of the Imagination: Paul as Interpreter of Israel's Scripture* (Grand Rapids, MI: Eerdmans, 2005), 111: "correlated hermeneutically with the story of Jesus's death and resurrection."

152. John emphasizes Jesus's knowledge of the presenting situation (19.28), for example.

153. Cf. Richard Bauckham, *Gospel of Glory: Major Themes in Johannine Theology* (Grand Rapids, MI: Baker Academic, 2015), 60: "John recounts no supernatural accompaniments: no darkness at noon, no earthquake, no tearing of the temple veil. What happens is just what always happened at crucifixions, in all their pain and humiliation." So also Moo, *Old Testament*, 362.

154. Tabb, "Thirst," 345: "It is preferable to see the reference to Psalm 69 in John 19:28 as *typological*, with Jesus as the Davidic righteous sufferer *par excellence*."

155. Hays, *Echoes-Gospels*, 326. So also Thompson, "Psalms," 279: "On John's reading, the Psalms present Jesus, not as a desperate King seeking protection from his enemies and rescue by a seemingly absent God, but as a righteous King vindicated by God against those who falsely accuse and pursue him."

156. D. A. Carson, "John and the Johannine Epistles," in *It Is Written: Scripture Citing Scripture: Essays in Honour of Barnabas Lindars, SSF*, ed. D. A. Carson and H. G. M. Williamson (Cambridge, UK: Cambridge University Press, 1988), 249. Even if one is cautious about extending a "prophetic" dimension to Psalm 69, the "analogical" King David-Jesus relationship still warrants attention.

157. Tabb, "Thirst," 350.

158. Jobes, *John*, 278.

159. Scott, *Hermeneutics*, 65.

160. Menken, *Quotations in the Fourth Gospel*, 37–45 attests the change to the evangelist, rather than it being part of received tradition. With the change of tense, "the quotation from Ps 69.10 should mean here that Jesus's zeal for God's house will cause his death on a cross" (40).

161. Cf. Benjamin J. Lappenga, "Whose Zeal Is It Anyway? The Citation of Psalm 69.9 in John 2.17 as a Double Entendre," in *Abiding Words: The Use of Scripture in the Gospel of John*, ed. Alicia D. Myers and Bruce G. Schuchard, SBLRBS 81 (Atlanta, SBL: 2015), 141–59, who proposes that the "zeal" of the citation of Ps 69.9 may have a "double entendre" and extend to Jesus's opponents, that is, unbelieving Jews. Lappenga's analysis is perhaps more plausible than persuasive, but it further attests the complexity and multi-layered nature of John's intertextual engagement.

162. Garland, "fulfillment," 242.

163. Michael R. Licona, *Why Are There Differences in the Gospels? What We Can Learn from Ancient Biography* (New York: Oxford University Press, 2017), 166; similarly Senior, *Passion in John*, 116–17.

164. Licona, *Differences*, 166.

165. One thinks here of Michelle Fletcher's work on pastiche techniques for assessing scriptural usage in Revelation. The Apocalypse draws on and merges a plurality of scriptural images and motifs, rather than merely a specific or individual one. See Michelle Fletcher, *Reading Revelation as Pastiche: Imitating the Past*, LNTS 571 (London: Bloomsbury, 2017).

166. See, further, the discussion on 19.34 in chapter 5.

167. Williams, "Composite Citations," 116.

168. Hence we find this inclusio more prominent than the one implied by the bookending Zechariah quotations (12.14–15/Zech 9.9 and 19.37/Zech 12.10—cf.

Schuchard, "Form Versus Function," 45), but the latter one still has significant communicative effect.

169. See further chapter 3. Ridderbos, *John*, 622 strongly dissents from the notion that 19.36 alludes to Passover Lamb, or related, imagery: "this pericope contains no allusion to the Passover, and Jesus's death is not related to Passover or the Passover Lamb anywhere else in this Gospel."

170. Freed, *Quotations*, 125 contends that Exod 12.10 is "the most likely direct source" of the citation. Similarly, Mark Edwards, *John* (Oxford: Blackwell, 2004), 186, though erroneously locating it to v37 rather than v36.

171. Carson, *Gospel*, 627 deems the Passover Lamb texts to be the primary ones for John 19.36.

172. Variant readings of John 19.39 are assimilations to Exod 12.10—so Menken, *Quotations in the Fourth Gospel*, 148. He also notes that similar assimilation may be found in LXX MSS, accommodating the form found in John 19.36.

173. Brown, *Death*, 1185 observes that such ambiguity also extends to the "its" of the Lamb and/or the "his" of the suffering psalmist.

174. Technically, the antecedent noun for Exod 12.46 is τὸ πασχα (12.43), so αὐτοῦ (12.46) is neuter gender, and John thus switches it to masculine if/when the citation is applied to Jesus. Brawley, "Absent," 429 ventures that this "violates the context of Exod 12.46," but such an assessment surely overlooks the interpretative flexibility Second Temple interpreters might employ.

175. As noted by Brown, "Metalepsis," 29–41. She rightly ventures of John's use of creation imagery: "this storied feature from Genesis into John's Gospel is easily overlooked if we only focus on pronounced verbal connections between the two texts and ignore the storied ones" (32). We explore the ramifications of this further in chapter 3.

176. Cf. Paul M. Hoskins, "Deliverance from Death by the True Passover Lamb: A Significant Aspect of the Fulfillment of the Passover in the Gospel of John," *JETS* 52 (2009): 287: "Passover is a visible and repeated element of the Gospel of John and rules for the Passover sacrifice come to the forefront in relation to Jesus in 19:36." He further avers: "In John 19, one finds John's most explicit Scripture citation connecting Jesus to the Passover lamb" (296).

177. As Moo, *Old Testament*, 315 rightly points out: "Changes in person . . . are frequent in the application of OT texts to NT situations."

178. Reim, *Studien*, 52.

179. Andrew Montanaro, "The Use of Memory in the Old Testament Quotations in John's Gospel," *NovT* 59 (2017): 152.

180. Garland, "Fulfillment," 246.

181. Menken, *Quotations in the Fourth Gospel*. Dodd, *Interpretation*, 424; Ridderbos, *John*, 622–23; Thompson, "Psalms," 278–79; Lars Olov Eriksson, *"Come, Children, Listen to Me!": Psalm 34 in the Hebrew Bible and in Early Christian Writings*, ConBOT 32 (Stockholm: Almqvist & Wiksell, 1991), 121–23.

182. Williams, "Composite Citations," 118.

183. Brown, *Death*, 1186: "the motif of this psalm (God answers the call of the afflicted and delivers the just: 34.7, 20) would fit the Johannine scene well."

184. Lindars, *The Gospel of John*, 590; Senior, *Passion in John*, 122; Andreas J. Köstenberger, "Exodus in John," in *Exodus in the New Testament* ed. Seth M. Ehorn, LNTS 663 (London: T&T Clark, 2022), 106; Nathanael R. Polinski, *That the Scriptures Might Be Fulfilled through Perfect Christian Worship* (Eugene, OR: Pickwick, 2019), 105: "The pentateuchal texts express the prohibition against breaking any bones in the Passover lamb. The psalm attests to God's providential care of the Righteous (One)."

185. Menken, *Quotations in the Fourth Gospel*, 152.

186. Menken, "Old Testament (2002)," 42. Menken does speak of a "combination" of the respective passages, but without explicitly saying it is a composite quotation.

187. Myers, *Characterizing Jesus*, passim.

188. Williams, "Composite Citations," 118.

189. The citation in 19.36 is therefore more than a paraphrase—contra Jobes, *John*, 281.

190. So McWhirter, "Messianic," 143: "John seems to have searched Ps. 22:16–17 for all its worth, finding a concise description of Jesus's crucifixion as well as valuable links to Exod. 12:46; Ps. 34:20; and Zech. 12:10."

191. So Joshua J. F. Coutts, "Revelation, Provision and Deliverance: The Reception of Exodus in Johannine Literature," in *The Reception of Exodus Motifs in Jewish and Christian Literature*, ed. Beate Kowalski and Susan Docherty, TBN 30 (Leiden: Brill, 2021), 280.

192. Menken, *Quotations in the Fourth Gospel*, 164, see also 161–64.

193. Menken, *Quotations in the Fourth Gospel*, 164. He continues: in *Jub.* 49.13, "we have a clear pre-Johannine instance of the same biblical passages as we found in John 19.36" (164).

194. Catrin H. Williams, "'Seeing,' Salvation and the Use of Scripture in the Gospel of John," in *Atonement: Jewish and Christian Origins*, ed. Max Botner, et al. (Grand Rapids: Eerdmans, 2020), 134, emphasis added.

195. Brawley, "Absent," 434.

196. Such speaking language is a familiar mode of Jewish interpretation—cf. Rom 4.3, 9.17, 10.11. Brown, *Gospel According to John*, 938 terms it "a fixed rabbinic formula for introducing another citation." The present tense of λέγει is also notable in that Scripture is speaking—and continues to "speak"—even after it has been τελειόω-ed (19.30).

197. Lindars, *Apologetic*, 268–69 ventures that 19.37 captures the essence of 19.36, at least in apologetic terms, in that Jesus was pierced, but no bones were broken. The respective quotations are doing far more than this on their own terms, and there is no need to see them as so closely aligned. However, with Lindars, one can well imagine that usage of Zech 12.10 might be motivated by apologetic reasons and/or form part of the wider apologetic explanation of why a cruciform death was required for the Messiah.

198. The adverbial πάλιν is also present in both instances (12.39, 19.37), further matching the respective second quotations and carrying forward the fulfillment capacity of the preceding one. Likewise, the plural ταῦτα (19.36) would also seem to

imply that *both* the non-breaking of bones (19.36) and the piercing (19.37) evidence scriptural fulfillment.

199. Sheridan, "Pierced," 192.

200. Myers, *Characterizing Jesus*, 69. Hays, *Echoes-Gospels*, 285 also speaks of 19.36–37 sounding a form of closure to the book of the passion (13.1–19.42)—"the closing cadence at the end of a movement in a symphony."

201. See Bynum, "Quotations," 47–48.

202. Though, as we shall suggest, John construes the piercing as ultimately positive or salvific and, in effect, an ironic cause for celebration.

203. Bynum, "Quotations," 73. He continues, stressing the way in which Zechariah 9–14 gives the framework for the Johannine Passion—"the era of renewal envisioned by Zechariah has come" (73).

204. Cf. Brown, *Gospel According to John*, 954: "chs. ix-xiv are an important OT source for citations about Jesus." Also Hays, *Echoes-Gospels*, 82.

205. Beutler, "Use," 149—the inclusion of ἑτέρα would seem to testify in this regard. As noted above, ἡ λέγουσα (19.24) is absent from early MSS.

206. Bynum, "Quotations," 65.

207. See especially Menken, *Quotations in the Fourth Gospel*; Schuchard, *Scripture within Scripture*, 141–49; Bynum, *Fourth Gospel*, passim. Also Sheridan, "Pierced," 194–98; Williams, "Composite Citations," 119–24.

208. Cf. Paul Miller, "'They Saw His Glory and Spoke of Him': The Gospel of John and the Old Testament," in *Hearing the Old Testament in the New Testament*, ed. Stanley E. Porter (Grand Rapids: Eerdmans, 2006), 128.

209. Freed, *Quotations*, 114.

210. Schnackenburg, *Gospel*, 293.

211. Schuchard, *Scripture within Scripture*, 141–49.

212. Michaels, *Gospel of John*, 976; Menken, "Minor Prophets," 87 concludes therefore that "John's quotation . . . represents an independent early Christian translation into Greek of the Hebrew text."

213. Dodd, *Interpretation*, 427–28, Lindars, *The Gospel of John*, 590; Köstenberger, "John," 504.

214. Brown, *Gospel According to John*, 938 suggests a proto-Theodotion form.

215. So Bynum, *Fourth Gospel*. He proposes an origin in the 8HevXIIgr scroll (or "R").

216. Williams, "Composite Citations," 119–24.

217. So Craig R. Koester, "Narrative-Critical Interpretation of John 20," in *Come and Read: Interpretive Approaches to the Gospel of John*, ed. Alicia D. Myers and Lindsey S. Jodrey (Lanham, MD: Fortress Academic, 2019), 141, emphasis added. Cf. also Lieu, "Narrative," 151: "the effect of such 'looking' is left for the reader to determine."

218. On the motif of "seeing" in the Fourth Gospel, cf. Miller, "They Saw His Glory," 134–46.

219. Ridderbos, *John*, 623.

220. Polinski, *Scriptures*.

221. We noted the same point in respect of 19.24.

222. Bret A. Rogers, *Jesus as the Pierced One: The Use of Zechariah 12.10 in John's Gospel and Revelation* (Eugene: Pickwick, 2020), 79.

223. Sheridan, "Pierced," 194–98.

224. Polinski, *Scriptures*, 137.

225. Williams, "Composite Citations," 122n85.

226. We return to the blood/water discourse, and its scriptural origins, in chapter 5, particularly in terms of how the imagery of 19.34 draws both on Israel's Scriptures and the γραφή the Fourth Gospel itself attests.

227. Brant, *John*, 255, for example, seems to head in this direction. She ventures that scriptural testimony is marshalled to show that the opponents, unconsciously or otherwise, are participants in the divine plan to which Scripture attests.

228. Contra Barrett, *Gospel*, 559, who proposes: "It is not the look but the piercing that fulfills prophecy that interests him." Instead, we venture, the burden is on the *visualization* of the scene—the piercing is merely the link action that enables what is seen.

229. Menken, *Quotations in the Fourth Gospel*, 182–83.

230. Bynum, "Quotations," 69.

231. So Klink, *John*.

232. Klink, *John*, 817s.

233. Sheridan, "Pierced," 208. Her analysis in this way is more intratextual than intertextual.

234. Kubiś, *Book of Zechariah*, 484.

235. Köstenberger, "John," 505.

236. Sheridan, "Pierced," 196.

237. See, for example, Rogers, *Pierced*, 88–89.

238. Rogers, *Pierced*, 104. Similarly Kubiś, *Book of Zechariah*, 217: "The message was straightforward; on the level of Zechariah: the pierced God is the Messiah and the pierced Messiah is God; on the level of the FG: the pierced Jesus is both the pierced Messiah and the pierced God."

239. Rogers stresses that the tension of Zech 12.10 is one present within the Jewish text itself, and that Johannine appropriation/usage of it does not merely derive from a Christianized reading. Cf. also Garland, "fulfillment," 249: "from John's perspective, the Scripture reveals that Jesus was destined to be pierced."

240. Rogers, *Pierced*, 78.

241. Brown, *Gospel According to John*, 955–56.

242. Kubiś, *Book of Zechariah*, 189.

243. Larry W. Hurtado, *Lord Jesus Christ: Devotion to Jesus in Earliest Christianity* (Grand Rapids, MI: Eerdmans, 2003), 379.

244. Brawley, "Absent," 434.

245. So also Daise, *Quotations in John*, 5–12 in his defense of continued examination of the Fourth Gospel's quotational use.

246. Cf. Miller, "They Saw His Glory," 129: "Function determines form in John's use of Scripture." On the form versus function question more generally, see Schuchard, "Form Versus Function," 23–45.

247. Williams, "Seeing," 132–33.

248. Menken, "Old Testament (2002)," 43. Cf. also Obermann, *Erfüllung*, 409–22.

249. Hays, *Reading Backwards*, 77: "a reading backwards that reinterprets Scripture in light of a new revelation imparted *by* Jesus and focused *on* the person of Jesus himself."

250. So Miller, "They Saw His Glory," 128–33.

251. Ford, *The Gospel of John*, 369.

252. Lieu, "Narrative," 151: "each moment of Jesus's crucifixion happened in order to fulfil Scripture."

253. Miller, "They Saw His Glory," 131, emphasis added.

254. Scott, *Hermeneutics*, 64.

255. Cf. the citation of Jer 31.31–34 in Heb 8.8–12. Hebrews only really addresses the phrase "new covenant," and ignores the rest of what is an otherwise lengthy quotation.

256. So Thompson, "Psalms," 269–70.

257. Jobes, *John*, 277–78. Also Lieu, "Narrative," 151: "Scripture, like Jesus's passion, functions as a unity and not as a patchwork of details to be matched."

258. Jonathan Lett, "The Divine Identity of Jesus as the Reason for Israel's Unbelief in John 12:36–43," *JBL* 135 (2016): 161.

259. Lett, "Divine Identity," 159–73.

260. Andrew T. Lincoln, "The Lazarus Story: A Literary Perspective," in *The Gospel of John and Christian Theology*, ed. Richard Bauckham and Carl Mosser (Grand Rapids, MI: Eerdmans 2008), 214.

261. Daly-Denton, *John*, 203.

262. Garland, "fulfillment," 243.

263. See *inter alia*, Hays, *Echoes-Gospels*, 284.

264. Luther, "Authentication," 160, for example, differentiates between quotations and allusions as follows: "The FG refers to Scripture *implicitly* through allusions and references in terms of content, language, form, or theology and *explicitly* through quotations" (emphasis original).

Chapter 3

Allusion Usage in John's Passion Narrative

In our previous chapter, we considered John's use of signaled scriptural quotations and their form and function within John's Passion Narrative. We suggested that they provide a structural framework for the Fourth Gospel's use of Israel's Scriptures, and demonstrate how particular texts function intertextually as focal points for articulating the substance and impact of Jesus's death. We drew particular significance to the fulfillment introductory formula John attributes to those texts, and hence to the interpretive burden each quotation bears. We also noted how the quotation could be a composite one derived from several texts, so enabling a wider interpretative terrain, and/or with John also utilizing the citation in an atypical or ironic form. The seven principles elucidated at the end of chapter two suggest that the brevity of John's four Passion quotations contrasts dramatically with their explanatory depth.

Signalled quotations are, however, just one (albeit highly significant) aspect by which John's Passion Narrative invokes scriptural interaction. Although they offer a primary lens onto the Fourth Gospel's scriptural usage, and while they draw out key motifs such as fulfillment, kingship, and divine identity, we also noted some limiting features in respect of how they function within John's Passion retelling. In particular, quotational usage—at least with an accompanying scriptural text—occurs only in the third part of the Passion triptych, and, if quotations were the only measure of intertextual scriptural engagement, then our core hypothesis would be necessarily reduced to just the crucifixion scene. If we are wanting to demonstrate that the *whole* of the Fourth Gospel Passion Narrative draws on Israel's Scriptures, we must necessarily attend to other modes of intertextual engagement.

PRINCIPLES FOR HANDLING JOHN'S USE OF ALLUSIONS

Compared to quotations at least, more common across the Fourth Gospel are multi-layered allusions and echoes of the Old Testament, resonances to its narratives, characters, imagery, and plot. Coutts, for example, rightly opines that "John's engagement with Scripture exhibits a preference for allusion and the evocation of scriptural themes and images over explicit citation of texts."[1] With its climactic chorus of direct citation, the crucifixion scene may be less demonstrative of this principle than earlier parts of the Fourth Gospel. As we have argued, the quotations surely carry a significant weight of interpretative significance for John's Passion, still functioning as the "route in" for unpacking the Johannine portrayal of Jesus's death. But allusive modes of reference nonetheless remain integral pieces of John's scriptural jigsaw, and particularly so for the first two scenes of the Passion triptych; quotations are the tip of a much bigger intertextual iceberg. In this third chapter, we consider such allusions and echoes, and how John accesses them and guides the reader accordingly.

Richard Hays, perhaps the leading exponent of attending to the New Testament authors' capacity for intertextual allusion, notes: "John's manner of alluding . . . relies upon evoking *images* and *figures* from Israel's Scripture."[2] That is, rather than by including specific texts as the trigger for an allusion, John tends instead to allusively evoke a theme or concept by drawing on their associated imagery and context. Hence partly for heuristic reasons, but more for the fact that it best manifests the evangelist's allusive practice, this chapter will consider the evocation of particular scriptural themes or motifs rather than seeking to isolate individual verbal allusions (which are simply more limited and less potent). In so doing, we shall see that the frequency of these intertexts matters, in that John's continued appeal to the concept increases the volume of the allusion. It is this accumulated, aggregated aspect of the allusions that give them their force, their corporate rather than their individual impact.[3]

Allusions are potent intertexts, and potent in two particular ways. First, where quotations generally tend toward the particular or specific situation, allusions, whether textual, narratival or thematic, have the potential to open up a wider trajectory or scope of enquiry, what Shin terms their capacity to function "as the metonymic evocation of a larger signification system."[4] Although the alluding phrase or word itself may be short, they educe a much broader discourse of reference. And this is particularly the case when John makes thematic allusions; as we shall see, apparently simple references to a garden (18.1) or to hyssop (19.29) have the capacity to evoke extensive narratives of Creation or Passover.

Second, an integral aspect of an allusion's function is that the reader is given work to do, to resolve or outwork the allusion for themselves. Williams draws attention to the way in which ancient authors set forth intertextual hints or allusions, but did so elusively (or allusively?!), merely hinting at potential connections and inviting the reader themselves to make the wider connections.[5] This raises questions as to the required competency of the reader, as we noted in chapter 1, and our analysis will be attentive to what might be expected of them in terms of their scriptural awareness. And it also means that a plurality of interpretive outcomes are possible, and those who desire certainty in this regard will likely be frustrated by John's intertextual tactics. Questions inevitably arise as to how one adjudicates on the merits and validity of any mooted allusion. At the same time, though, this surely enhances the richness of the intertextual process; because the reader has a role to play, because they are given the capacity to make connections and come to their own interpretative conclusions, a fuller scope of intertextual possibilities so arise.[6] And because readers likely pursue allusions in different ways, this informs the indeterminacy that is a frequent part of the Johannine plot—the reader is charged with resolving for themselves those ambiguities or tensions the Gospel invokes. Our approach therefore will tend more to the maximalist end of the spectrum in terms of an allusion's potential plausibility. This is not to adjudicate on its likelihood, but rather to moot its existence as possible, and leave it with the reader to arrive at their own assessment of its probability.

We will consider three thematic allusions in detail, advocating that they give significant intertextual shaping to the Fourth Gospel's Passion retelling. We look at John's evocation of Creation imagery, and the extent to which the evangelist portrays Jesus's death as the completion of the Creation process. We map the way in which the Fourth Gospel works with the motif of Passover, and particularly how John brings it to a thematic climax in the Passion account. And third, we consider the way in which the imagery of the Suffering Servant (Isaiah 53), inaugurated at the end of Jesus's public ministry, continues to be an operative theme across the Johannine Passion. Along, then, with some more minor lexical allusions, we draw some general conclusions as to how scriptural allusions function in John's Passion Narrative, and particularly how they complement its accompanying quotational usage.

CREATION IMAGERY IN JOHN'S PASSION NARRATIVE

Perhaps the strongest, most repeated, allusive motif across John's Passion Narrative is the referencing of creation imagery,[7] and particularly its Genesis dimension. Genesis 1–3 has, after all, been a frequent resource thus far for John's retelling,[8] even if by allusional rather than formal citation means. Whether the replaying of the creation moment "in the beginning" (John 1.1), whether the debate over Jesus and God working on the Sabbath (John 5.16–24), or whether the "creation" of sight for the man born blind (John 9.1–41), Genesis 1–3 has provided the evangelist with a template for intertextual remembrance and association. Its extension to, and culmination in, the Passion scene should therefore come as no surprise. As previously suggested, Jesus's cruciform τετέλεσται cry (19.30) likely echoes the climax of a new creation moment,[9] or even the final completion of the creation announced in Gen 2.1–2.[10] On the basis of such an echo, Wright opines: "John is inviting his readers to understand the events concerning Jesus, particularly his death, as the culmination of the vast story of creation and new creation."[11] Moreover, Genesis imagery continues after the Passion account, whether by Mary Magdalene's "mistaking" Jesus for the gardener (20.15), or through Jesus's breathing the Paraclete, re-capturing the divine breath of life into the first human figure (20.22; Gen 2.7). In the light of such prominent Genesis/Creation imagery, Daly-Denton passionately ventures that "Jesus's death ushers in the new aeon that was envisaged as an eternal Sabbath."[12] How, then, is this creation/sabbath portrayal outworked across the Passion account?

Creation Imagery: Garden

We suggest that the theme is established from the outset of John's Passion retelling, thereby foregrounding it as a fundamental element of John's intertextual tapestry. The Passion account opens with Jesus and his disciples leaving the upper room, crossing the Kidron valley, and entering a place specifically identified as a garden (κῆπος—18.1). John's explicit reference to Jesus and the disciples entering the garden—an otherwise incidental detail—underscores the deliberate nature of the activity; the garden is established as the "stage" for the next episode of John's narration. The garden motif so becomes the primary locus for explicating the events of Jesus's Passion, with several, subsequent reminders of the narrative location for John's retelling (18.26, 19.41; cf. also 20.15). Admittedly, there appear to be two discrete κῆπος locations specified, one across the Kidron valley (18.1) and another at Golgotha itself (19.41), and they are clearly distinguished.[13] But equally, both are designated as a κῆπος, and thus "garden" forms an *inclusio* to the Passion retelling, being both the entry and exit point of the Johannine account. Lieu rightly surmises therefore that "the whole passion narrative becomes identified as belonging to a 'garden.'"[14] Moore offers a slightly more cautious horticultural assessment—"the works of salvation (the Passion, Crucifixion and Resurrection) all take place in one, albeit metaphorical garden"[15]—conceding a more symbolic dimension to the garden motif. But such symbolism directs the reader even more toward the intertextual significance of the garden image, alongside its precise, physical location.

So although garden terminology is not infrequent scriptural language, it seems likely that John's Passion Narrative is making some form of allusion—or narrative connection—to Genesis 1–3.[16] John does not give any justification for why a garden location is chosen or required, and the Genesis associations it generates may therefore be its ultimate driver. A new, distinct discourse unit is starting—that is, the Johannine Passion Narrative—and the specific detailing of a κῆπος (18.1) would seem unwarranted unless Genesis echoes, and the implications afresh of Ἐν ἀρχῇ (1.1), are to be unpacked. It is true that Gen 2.8f uses παράδεισος rather than κῆπος (John 18.1), and that has led several commentators to query, on lexical grounds, the existence of any such Genesis allusion.[17] However, there are other instances where the two terms are used synonymously,[18] and the lexical variance in 18.1 may be merely because paradise language in the Johannine or NT milieu meant something quite different. Lexical precision cannot be the sole grounds for adjudicating on wider, narrative connections. And in glass half-full terms, one must equally account for why there appear to be so many Genesis 1–3 connections across John 18–20 if no allusion is intended.[19] The Synoptic accounts make no reference to garden imagery in terms of the tomb's location in either the Passion or Resurrection narrative,[20] and this would further seem to underscore its significance for John and/or at least invite the question as to *why* it is included if it were not for allusive purposes.

The case for a garden backdrop established by 18.1 is strengthened by further references to such imagery.[21] Jesus's placement in the middle of the two other crucified figures (19.18) recalls the placement of the Tree of Life in the midst of the garden (Gen 2.9), particularly bearing in mind the life-giving, liberative outcome to Jesus's death.[22] Mary Magdalene famously mistakes the resurrected Jesus for a gardener (20.15), an error that underscores the divine "creator" allusion in respect of Jesus's identity.[23] And the reader is also reminded of the garden backdrop prior to Jesus's death. In Peter's third denial, for example, the instance that generates the cock's crow (18.26), he responds to the accusation of Malchus's relative that the latter had seen Peter with Jesus in the *garden* (18.26). The precise specification of κῆπος seems unnecessary unless it is bearing Genesis imagery; but if the latter principle is conceded, then a much wider intertextual evocation is potentially operative.

What, then, does the garden intertext do? In view of the volume of garden references, we suggest that it symbolically evokes the scene of Genesis 1–3, and the accompanying narrative therein. Jesus's divine presence in the garden equates with that of Eden, with the disciples symbolically cast as representative humans. John's reminder that Jesus and the disciples had previously met in the garden a number of times (18.2) may also be significant, underscoring it as the primary place for divine-human encounter. Jesus's action of coming out (ἐξῆλθεν—18.4) may suggest a walled garden, and hence imply a "potential" παράδεισος,[24] but such a link seems unnecessarily forced. Nonetheless, the garden setting offers a symbolic backdrop that echoes the clash between God and the world, with Jesus portrayed in divine terms. It is, after all, the location of three ἐγώ εἰμι statements (note the emphatic repetition in 18.8 to reinforce understanding) which give substance to such divine characterization.[25] It may also invoke a playful reworking of the garden scene and the visual theme to which John frequently alludes (cf. 1.29). Where, in Genesis, God is only encountered in auditory form, Jesus—as God—is now visible, one to behold (19.37), and the "seeing" of this is integral to the inculcation of belief (19.35; cf. 1 John 1.1–3). And juxtaposing the wider Genesis and John narratives has evident parallels too: "This then was the scene of the great act of disloyalty, when Judas, a disciple chosen to find life in Jesus, handed over his Lord to his enemies. It was in a garden, according to the biblical narrative, that the first great act of disloyalty took place when Adam deliberately disobeyed the Lord who had brought him to life from the dust."[26] The "betrayal" of the John 18 garden evokes the "betrayal" of its Genesis 3 equivalent. And as such, it informs Jesus's declaration that those who belong to the truth are those who listen to his voice (18.37). In so doing, they contrast with Adam, who listened Eve's voice (Gen 3.7), rather than to that of God (Gen 2.16–17, 3.1). Similarly, the testing scene of Genesis 3—and Adam and Eve's "failure" within it—occasions the opening of their eyes (Gen 3.7), further imagery resonant with the frequent Johannine emphasis on "seeing."

Genesis 3 may well also form the template for the Petrine denial scene. Peter—like Eve and Adam before him, in another garden—is found to be denying God, and replaying their dishonesty. Such imagery has already been alluded to—however problematically—in 8.44, and Peter is conceivably personified as having diabolic or devilish origins. His threefold denial is lying (cf. 8.44), and demonstrative of the kind of dishonesty previously found within Eden. Moreover, the servant claims that he "saw" Peter in the garden with Jesus (18.26). Visual language is, of course, key terminology for the Fourth Gospel, as we have seen in the last chapter, and it would seem to be the case too here. It is ambiguous as to whether the slave was part of the arresting party, so it is not clear as to whether he is being duplicitous or not. But his response to Peter may further pattern him too as a quasi-serpent figure, tempting—or testing—Peter, inducing the denial from him accordingly. Pushing the allusion further, the Genesis serpent imagery might also extend to Judas too. Such interpretation may derive more from modern perspectives on demonology than from the Fourth Gospel itself, but in the light of the prevailing garden/Eden backdrop, Judas's characterization in devilish terms (13.2) at least allows for this allusive possibility.

At some point, we suggest, the combination—or volume—of garden references starts to "stack up," and, despite the doubts of some commentators,[27] commends the horticultural scriptural allusion accordingly. Even if the Fourth Evangelist does not *intend* the allusion, intertextual linkage and meaning-generation is possible, particularly for the attentive reader, and it may be that the other Adamic allusions (see below) also add weight to the mooted allusion and sustain it accordingly. The garden milieu contrasts with the non-verdant location to which Jesus subsequently departs and in which his opponents are encountered (i.e., the High Priest's courtyard (18.15) and the *stone* pavement—the *Gabbatha*—of Pilate's praetorium (18.13)), and this becomes, in effect, a place of non-divine encounter. It is entirely possible, of course, that the garden motif is merely a convenient, contemporary stock image—like the vine (15.1) or the shepherd (10.11)—without it necessarily requiring a precise scriptural source or origin. But equally the options are not mutually exclusive; just as the other (stock) images have scriptural connotation, it is possible that garden too has a stock value, but one from which an informed reader can fruitfully gain further intertextual scriptural insight.[28]

The primacy of the garden imagery may also circumvent the passing reference to the Kidron valley (18.1) and overlook its intertextual potential. As Christos Karakolis observes, like with the garden reference, the inclusion of the Kidron detail is odd or unnecessary, somewhat superfluous even. Its inclusion may therefore also be premised on intertextual grounds and provide a further scriptural allusion at the very outset of the Passion account. King David is said to make a similar journey, crossing the Kidron Wadi and ascending the Mount of Olives (2 Sam 15.23).[29] He does so while fleeing from Absalom, and, with the specific Kidron identification, it is possible that John is equating Jesus's impending passion with Absalom's revolt.[30] There are similarities perhaps between the two accounts, as Karakolis conjectures, and there may be the sense of an enrichening intertextual reference, but the reader has to do a fair amount of work to make the connections, premised essentially just on one word—Kidron. At the same time, the mooted allusion underpins some of the Jesus-David patterning we observed in respect of the citation of Ps 22.18 (John 19.24), and underscores (from the outset of the Passion) that Jesus enters the garden as "king."[31] The manifestation of (and challenge to) his kingship will be a core theme of the Johannine Passion (cf. 19.2–3, 19.14, 19.19–21).[32]

Tradition also ascribed David's tomb to a garden location. With Jesus's tomb likewise in a garden, and with his burial portrayed as one fit for a king in terms of the volume of spices it occasioned (19.39), it is possible that John is drawing a further Davidic connection in respect of Jesus's kingly death.

Raymond Brown, although generally skeptical as to the Genesis allusions in relation to garden imagery, still moots the possibility of a symbolic allusion in John 19.41 to Neh 3.16 LXX and the garden location of David's tomb (cf. Acts 2.29, which seems to attest it as a familiar situation).[33] It is hard to pronounce confidently as to whether the tomb allusion was intentional on John's part. But it does "fit" both with the wider Davidic kingship motif John has sought to unpack by intertextual means, and likewise with the subsequent Jewish exchange with Pilate regarding Jesus's kingship (18.28–19.15), the second part of the Passion triptych. We might say, then, that the Kidron reference of 18.1 sustains the "royal" connotations of the garden imagery, and sharpens its intertextual function in monarchical terms.

One further comment might be made, and that is the limited extent of the garden discourse beyond the arrest episode, there being no Gethsemane discourse between Jesus and his disciples such as is found in the Synoptics. John 17.12 and 18.11 parallel the Markan Gethsemane account, and suggest that John is cognizant of that tradition, but has instead actively chosen to omit it from the Passion account.[34] Such absence may serve to underscore—or at least does not detract from—the prevailing Genesis backdrop to chapters 18–19. But it is likely also contingent upon the overall Johannine Passion portrayal of a confident, assured Jesus (compared to the Markan apprehension and hesitation). Mark's Gethsemane discourse fits ill, for example, with the conception of the good shepherd who avowedly lays down his life for the sheep (John 10.11).[35] In narratival/sequential terms, John 17 putatively evokes aspects or elements of the Synoptic Gethsemane tradition,[36] but a closer thematic equivalent is 12.27–36, and notably so bearing in mind the appeal to Psalm 6.3–4 in John 12.27. That is, John has reworked "Passion" content and placed it within the account of Jesus's public ministry. But in doing so, the evangelist preserves its scriptural resonance, albeit sourced from a different Psalm and uttered with a different Jesus characterization. Mark's Gethsemane account has Jesus apprehensively appealing to the language of Psalms 42 and 43, praying that the approaching "hour" might pass (Mark 14.35). By contrast, John places Psalm 6 content on Jesus's lips as he questions whether he should "pray" the request to be saved from death (12.27). Jesus declines to do so (12.27), commensurate with the Johannine pattern that anticipates the cruciform death as victory and glory. There is no uncertainty or hesitation on Jesus's part as the hour of his glorification has come (12.23).

This comparison with Mark is somewhat stark—in both narrative and conceptual terms—and it has relevance for our assessment of the Fourth Gospel's scriptural usage. It may be that "John was 'struggling with an unwelcome bit of tradition' in this regard"[37] and hence the positioning of such tradition, and the scriptural warrant it invokes (or doesn't invoke) is conditioned by the Fourth Gospel's wider evangelistic concerns and its presentation of Jesus.

Assuming John is aware of such Gethsemane tradition, its "relocation" (and the accompanying re-positioning of the scriptural connections) to either chapter 12 or chapter 17 is thus salient to our assessment of the scriptural characterization of the Johannine Passion. The absence of the material from the John 18–19 is shaped by Johannine editorial purposes, and what is included is equally shaped by such concerns. John does not want to "compromise" the presenting garden image within the Passion retelling, its scriptural evocation being such a key ingredient for the account of Jesus's death therein. But the re-positioned material is nonetheless still dependent upon Scripture; John's Passion content retains its κατὰ τὰς γραφὰς warrant even when the evangelist relocates it outside the specific Passion Narrative parameters.

Creation Imagery: Adam

Alongside the garden motif, the creation backdrop to John's Passion narration is further underpinned by allusions to other features of Genesis 1–3. In particular, the exhortatory imperative of 19.5—"Behold the Man" (ἰδοὺ ὁ ἄνθρωπος)—may be said to have Adamic reference, functioning specifically as an allusion to Gen 3.22 and/or carrying the Adamic notion of the one that bears the image of God. The "*ecce homo*" proclamation has no parallel in the Synoptics, and hence manifests a particular Johannine Passion distinctive. Its rhetorical flourish also warrants some form of explanation or interpretation, as it is not obvious why the phrase is included in the trial proceedings, and contributes nothing formal to the course of Jesus's trial.[38] Moreover, it is not evident as to why Pilate would even want to draw attention to Jesus's *humanity*, at least not without also drawing attention to the humiliation of the figure. Hence an otherwise bland statement assumes potential significance, while remaining unclear as to what that significance might be. As Beutler summarily quips: "These words of Pilate are as well-known as they are difficult to understand."[39] Might an intertextual approach help explain their inclusion/ function?[40]

The declaration of 19.5 parallels that of 19.14, the latter stressing the mutually informing irony of the impending humiliation of the one proclaimed as king (19.14), but whose crown is one composed of thorns (19.5). Both instances draw attention to Jesus's identity, and both are brief, interjectional summons to "behold" (ἰδοὺ/ἴδε) Jesus. If 19.14 somehow sheds intratextual light on 19.5, if the two verses are somehow associated, then that has potential implications for 19.5's scriptural evocation. The earlier Johannine invitation to "behold"—the imperatival exhortation to regard the Lamb of God (1.29, 36)—also draws on scriptural imagery (as we shall suggest, the Passover Lamb), as does the similarly exhortatory ἰδοὺ of 12.15, quoting

Zech 9.9. Hence it seems perfectly plausible—invited, even—to assume a scriptural resonance or association to the parallel invocation of 19.5.

Bearing in mind the kingship context of 19.14 and beyond, it is possible that the 19.5 imperative also draws upon monarchical imagery. If so, it establishes the kind of royal figure that will be lifted up at Golgotha, and anticipates the regal characterization of the Psalm 22 Davidic figure (19.24). The ironic fulfillment of Psalm 22 we suggested John 19.24 generates is likewise manifest in the ironic proclamation of kingship in 19.14, along with the similarly ironic royal claims of Jesus's titulus (19.19) and Pilate's misunderstanding of them (19.21–22). As with 19.21–22, Pilate does not understand the deeper significance of both of his prior declarations, 19.5 and 19.14. Just like Caiaphas (11.49–52), and just like his own response to the titulus, the wider significance of Pilate's statement of 19.5 is ironically outworked. Shin even goes as far as to suggest that 19.5, and particularly 19.14, appropriate "the motif of Jesus's kingship in such a way that Pilate himself presents and *enthrones* Jesus as king."[41] Such enthronement may be anticipatory and await actualization on the cross, but the procurator's statements surely underscore, however ironically, the reality of Jesus's royal status. The logic extends to the soldiers too, their kingly mockery unconsciously revealing Jesus's true royal, christological identity.

The royal imagery operative here may derive from intertextual means. A number of commentators point to the use of the same ἰδοὺ ὁ ἄνθρωπος phrase in 1 Sam 9.17,[42] a context redolent with royal overtones, uttered to distinguish Saul as the first of Israel's kings (1 Sam 9.15–17). The lexical/thematic similarity is certainly notable. There is also the accompanying contextual resonance of 1 Samuel 9 portraying Saul as "king-elect," akin perhaps to the anticipated "enthronement" of the crucifixion scene. However, the allusion demands really quite specific awareness of the Samuel text, and requires more from the reader than the simple Adam/ὁ ἄνθρωπος association. And pointing to Saul—as opposed to David—sits less well with the wider kingship portrayal John unpacks, particularly in respect of the broader glorification context. One wonders, for example, whether John would really want to point to a *failed* king such as Saul.

Alternatively, a case might be made for John 19.5 being an allusion to Zech 6.12 (Ἰδοὺ ἀνήρ), the phrase perhaps thereby functioning as a messianic title.[43] There is broad lexical similarity, and, more importantly, a fair degree of contextual resonance too. The prophet is exhorted to make a crown (Zech 6.11) and to place it on the head of Ἰησοῦς (6.12), providing an attractive symmetry with the imagery of John 19.5. The one so crowned will build the eschatological temple of the Lord (6.13), a fitting co-text for the charge of John 2.19. There is added narratival significance too, in terms of the role Pilate would be seen to play, and specifically in terms of scriptural fulfillment. As with the soldiers' actions in 19.24, and perhaps more significantly, "Pilate is unconsciously showing that the prophecy has been fulfilled, in fact he acts the part of the prophet."[44] But again, this requires somewhat specific knowledge of the Zechariah text, and overlooks the fact that Ἰησοῦς is crowned as high priest, rather than as king (one of the overriding images of the trial scene). And it is difficult to see how/why this phrase functions as a *messianic* title, as Wayne Meeks proposes; messianic imagery may be found in the "Branch" appellation (6.12), but it is not clear why such imagery should necessarily extend to ἀνήρ.

Hence one might suggest that kingly echoes may be operative, but without doing so voluminously, at least not in 19.5 itself, and/or they come more effectively to the fore once the subsequent declaration of 19.14 is made. The alleged royal associations also derive more from Jesus's clothing than from Pilate's proclamation, with the purple robe likely evocative of kingly attire.[45] Jesus's dress shows the "insignia of kingship,"[46] evocative perhaps of the purple robe and a golden crown of 1 Macc 10.20. But lexically at least, Pilate's 19.5 utterance draws attention to Jesus's *human* status, rather than to his royal credentials, and it is not immediately evident as to what motivates his announcement or how (at this in this stage of the trial at least) it impacts on the trial's progression. Parallelism (between 19.5 and 19.14) does not equate to synonymity, and the interpretative significance for the specific inclusion of ἰδοὺ ὁ ἄνθρωπος warrants further consideration, particularly in terms of any intertextual play. The suggestion that the phrase is a metonym for Son of Man[47] is effectively special pleading, or tries to resolve or add to the text in a way that goes beyond the textual witness. Its potential parallel with Jesus's claim to be Son *of God* (19.7) is tempting, it must be said, but the phrase Son of Man would look odd on the lips of Gentile Pilate. Besides, the human/divine tension of 19.5–7 still works without the filial aspect, and "man" is nowhere else used in the Fourth Gospel as an abbreviation for Son of Man.[48] As such, there are no textual grounds to retrospectively add υἱὸς language to 19.5.

Instead, we venture that 19.5 sets out a further creation-orientated echo, and specifically a reference to the figure of Adam—namely *the* man (thereby accounting for the presence/impact of the definite article).[49] The other (royal) scriptural possibilities noted above can, of course, still be part of the scriptural matrix operative within 19.5, and, as we have already seen, there is a characteristic plurality to the intertexts upon which John may draw.[50] As we are finding, it is counter-character to reduce the Fourth Gospel's intertextual engagement to merely one operative lens. But such plurality notwithstanding, and with the already established garden backdrop to the Passion account, the Adamic reference is likely the most prominent one. As Klink helpfully surmises: "in the light of the Genesis-laden context of the Gospel of John and the Genesis lens applied to its interpretive telling of the person and work of Jesus, the connection to Adam is hardly a stretch."[51] And the human and royal lenses are not mutually exclusive, of course, and may even be mutually informing. The putative Adamic echo might also carry (Genesis) Adam's regent or "kingly" function (cf. Gen 1.26, 28), and that may serve to tie the ἰδοὺ ὁ ἄνθρωπος proclamation to the 19.14 equivalent and/or to the royal attire of 19.5.

Several scholars have hence advocated for a significant Adamic texture or flavor to John's Passion.[52] Nicholas Schaser, for example, ventures that "John draws on Genesis 1–3 to present Jesus's judgment and crucifixion as a reversal of humanity's disobedience in the Garden of Eden,"[53] with 19.5 functioning as an echo of Gen 3.22. The lexical similarity is limited, of course—Ἰδοὺ Αδαμ has become ἰδοὺ ὁ ἄνθρωπος—and hence any similarity is more thematic and contextual. There are nonetheless, though, some interesting parallels between the respective accounts, to which Schaser draws attention:[54]

- *Clothing:* In the previous verse (Gen 3.21), Adam and Eve have been attired and are no longer naked. In John 19.2, Jesus is also dressed (in a purple robe) and attention is drawn to the nature of Jesus's clothing as part of the ἰδοὺ bidding (19.5).
- *Goal:* The action spoken of in Gen 3.22 is Adam seeking to live forever, the anticipated goal or vocation of Jesus (cf. 10.10, 3.16).
- *Tree:* The lexical dimension is not exploited by John, but the cross as "tree" (ξύλον—Gen 3.22) links to, or becomes, with quintessential Johannine irony, the tree of life (cf. 10.10).
- *Crown of thorns:* The crown may echo Gen 3.18, reversing the negative connotations of the thistles that resulted from Adam's sinful action.

Pursuing similar ground to Schaser, Litwa extends the intertextual connections more widely, to include putative echoes of *Vita Adae et Evae* 13.3, which manifests the same "Behold the man" phrasing as Gen 3.22. The Adam of *Vita*, however, is a more limited figure, one who is tricked by the devil, a pathetic individual who is forced into hapless existence, "a fallen, reproachful being who cannot avoid the punishment of pain and death."[55] If an intertext is in place with the Adam of *Vita*, then there is a fundamental contrast between the respective figures. John's Jesus is an ironic reversal of the miserable character of *Vita*, presenting him as the very image of God.[56]

Adamic reference does not exhaust the human element of the intertextual reading of John 19.5, and with Litwa, the acclamation evokes "a surplus of meaning which goes beyond any intertextual echo or suggested background."[57] It is possible, for example, that John 19.5 alludes to Num 24.15–17, and to the image therein of Balaam as the man who "truly sees" (24.15). With the concept of seeing so prominent across John's Passion, the association of Jesus with Balaam as one who hears divine oracles and "sees" a divine vision (24.16) is not completely foreign to the evangelist's narration. And more significantly, the ἄνθρωπος that emerges out of Israel (24.17) could conceivably be understood in messianic terms, or even as a messianic title,[58] and hence John 19.5 might be capturing elements of Num 24.15–17 imagery in that way.

But the overall, multi-faceted intertextual associations of Genesis 1–3 make Gen 3.22 the most potent backdrop for 19.5, and one may even wish to push its interpretive significance further. If the Adam/Genesis allusion is indeed operative, and if the wider Genesis 1–3 imagery is so invoked, such imagery may be said to do double duty, or extend in further riddled or reversed form too. That is, assuming the Genesis 1–3 backdrop, its constituent roles are reversed; Pilate becomes cast in Adamic/human terms, with Jesus becoming the divine figure. As Schaser notes, Pilate is afraid (19.8), akin to the fear Adam has when he has heard or encountered God: "whereas Adam hears God's 'sound' (φωνή), Pilate hears a 'word' (λόγος) about Jesus's divinity; the embodied deity who startled Adam now stands as the incarnate Word of God before Pilate."[59] This further reinforces the intertextual backdrop Genesis 1–3 generates (cf. John 1.1–4); Pilate has heard the word of the Word, the "logos" of the Logos, and John thus positions the procurator as a quasi-Adamic figure before the One who is with God at creation (John 1.1).

We suggest therefore that the Genesis 1–3 backdrop serves to make "sense" of the 19.5 declaration and its immediate context. Pilate's to-ing and fro-ing draws attention to the physical location of the trial scene and introduces a further instance of Johannine irony. The avoidance of ritual defilement that precludes the Jewish leaders entering Pilate's (apparently impure) πραιτώριον (18.28) is also turned on its head. The πραιτώριον becomes reconstituted as Eden—that where the divine figure is located—and the area "outside" is just that, merely *outside*. Adam, of course, is cast out of Eden—and the Adamic Jesus is likewise sent to Golgotha—but his ultimate fate is in a new garden, a place that will likewise become the source of new life.

Creation Imagery: John 19.25–27

One further scene contributes to John's evocation of creation imagery, particularly if we have already conceded that Genesis 1–3 and Adamic imagery are operative within John's Passion retelling. The gathering at the cross of the Beloved Disciple and the four women (19.25–27) is unique to the Fourth Gospel. It occasions significant interpretative interest as a result, particularly for its ecclesial and soteriological implications. As we noted in respect of the citation in 19.28, the handing over of his mother to the Beloved Disciple (19.26–27) is the climax of Jesus's work, and that which leads Jesus to know that all was now finished (19.28). Jesus's address to his mother as "woman" intratextually recalls the Cana sign (2.4), and such linkage commends the idea that the crucifixion scene is the moment at which Jesus's hour has fully come (cf. 2.4), commensurate with the *telos* imagery of 19.28–30. If any scene has a claim to being the "focal" one for the Fourth Gospel, then 19.25–27 would surely be a contender.

However, John 19.25–27 initially appears remarkably devoid of explicit appeal to Israel's Scriptures, and the omission is striking bearing in mind the liminal, new era-birthing moment it encapsulates, the apparent founding of the Johannine church along with the confirmation of the authority of the Beloved Disciple (and likely also that of Jesus's mother). The implications of Jesus's actions of 19.26–27 extend into 19.28–30 and his accompanying τετέλεσται declaration, and hence evoke various scriptural reference through the citation of Ps 69.3. But the specific handover itself (19.25–27) is not designated as demonstrating scriptural fulfillment, a surprising lacuna bearing in mind how both the mundanity of 19.24 and the climactic declaration of 19.28 are explicitly said so to do. Instead, at a surface level at least, 19.25–27 sits within an *inclusio* bookended by 19.24 and 19.28, with their respective scriptural warrant only underscoring its apparent omission in 19.25–27.

Some commentators suggest that the absence derives from 19.25–27 being the least scandalous part of the Passion Narrative and hence not requiring scriptural support in the same fashion.[60] But that assessment sits ill both with the implied, seminal nature of the moment and with the apparent need for scriptural fulfillment in the equally "non-scandalous" distribution of Jesus's clothes (19.24). Thus if Scripture is supposedly integral to John's Passion narration, its absence from such a key stage in the Passion account (and potentially of the whole Fourth Gospel enterprise) is striking. If Scripture really is the heartbeat of John's Passion Narrative, then one might have expected 19.25–27 to be pounding with scriptural association.

On initial sight at least, that seems not to be the case, but such a perception may be misplaced, particularly if one considers that the garden/Genesis 1–3 discourse remains operative within 19.25–27. Where the garden allusion tends to function in more negative terms, reminding the reader of the denial scene of Genesis 3, it may also provide a more positive, life-giving intertext, taking the attentive reader to the anticipated human inhabitation of the Garden, one that yields "life." The scenic portrayal of the Beloved Disciple and Jesus's mother captures the prior narrative of Adam and Eve—a "new" Adam and Eve perhaps, a (re-)new(ed) creation episode, whose future now awaits them. On that basis, far from being scripturally silent, 19.25–27 extends the Genesis 1–3 backdrop to John's Passion, espousing a "symbolic depiction of the new Adam and Eve standing beneath the tree, only this time to obey the divine command, and community rather than strife results."[61] The unnamed mother of Jesus (19.25) recalls the former woman named merely as γυνή (Gen 2.23), the same term Jesus uses to address his mother (19.26). When the Genesis woman is named, she is called Ζωή—that is, life, resonant with the purpose and goal of the Fourth Gospel (10.10; 20.31).[62] It is tempting to see Jesus's mother therefore patterned as the one crushing the head of the serpent (Gen 3.15), but that is probably an intertextual overreach, or at least John does not explicitly direct the reader that way. The image could well extend into the resurrection account too, with the resurrected Jesus and Mary Magdalene embodying the Adam/Eve roles.

The liminal moment at which Jesus's mother is welcomed into the Beloved Disciple's home marks the inauguration of a new community, personified by both founding figures. The presence of the four women—in contrast to the four Roman soldiers—may also have gynecological significance, inculcating further birth/life imagery. New life is implicitly birthed at Jesus's death,[63] in a similar pattern to that of the grain which must fall to earth and die before it can bear fruit (12.24). The scene also invokes further intratextual echoes of 16.21, activating the new birthing moment to which 16.21 alludes; the woman's recognition that her "hour has come" resonates with Jesus's previous comment to that effect (2.4) but which is now completed in his moment of death (19.28–30). If so, Isaianic intertextual links may also form part of the scene (Isa 49.20–22; 54.1; 66.7–11),[64] with the mother of Jesus characterized in Zion terms (Isa 66.8),[65] but such connections are allusive at best and require a very competent reader to make them.

The Genesis 1–3 backdrop also extends to the imagery of 19.34. At the climax of the Johannine discourse, Jesus's side (πλευρά) is pierced (19.34), generating the resonant, life-generating outflow.[66] The same language is found within LXX MSS in respect of the Adam figure and the taking of one of their inner parts (2.21). Even if the precise body part may vary, the common terminology harks back to the creation narrative, further instilling the life-giving implications to 19.34. As Schaser surmises: "just as Jesus's pierced side emits life-giving liquids (John 19:34), so Eve—the 'mother of all living' (Gen 3:20 LXX)—emerges from Adam's side (Gen 2:21–22 LXX)."[67] The intertextual Genesis allusions therefore reinforce the prevailing Johannine principle that the moment of Jesus's death is precisely the time at which new life is forthcoming.

* * *

In sum, John's Passion Narrative presents Jesus as the "centre of creation's renewal,"[68] the one whose completed mission restores the created order (19.28; cf. 3.16). To demonstrate such renewal, the Fourth Gospel utilizes the imagery and narrative of the Scripture's Creation story. Hence Scripture is not merely a convenient "tool" or "ingredient" for the Fourth Gospel's intertextual enterprise; it is far more than that. John uses Scripture to speak back to Scripture, and to develop and perfect the claims of Scripture. Even with allusive methodology, the scriptural narrative of Genesis 1–3 is not left unchanged by its encounter with the Johannine Jesus. Instead, there is effectively a retelling or reworking of the Genesis creation narrative, one built around the trial and death of the divine Word become flesh.

OTHER ALLUSION IMAGERY

"Without question, John casts the crucifixion of Jesus in terms of both the Suffering Servant and the sacrifice of the paschal lamb."[69] Such is Gerry Wheaton's confident assessment of the respective contributions of two other scriptural themes to the Johannine portrayal of Jesus's death. Their fusion or integration in 1.29 assumes something of a programmatic function in this regard.[70] Both images are, we suggest, intrinsic to John's Passion narration, and we consider both in turn, beginning first with the Paschal motif.

Passover Imagery in John's Passion Narrative

It is generally agreed that the Fourth Gospel depicts Jesus's ministry in alignment with the fulfillment of Israel's feasts, with Passover prominent amongst that festal list and thus core to John's presentation of Jesus's Passion.[71] Passover imagery in relation to Jesus's death features in other NT texts (cf. 1 Cor 5.7), but to a far more mooted volume than the Fourth Gospel sets forth (even if, unlike Paul, John does not make the Paschal lamb designation explicit). If there is a theme or motif to challenge the primacy of creation within John's Passion scriptural appropriation, then Passover is surely a contender. As we have seen in respect of John 19.36, the composite quotation found therein foregrounds imagery of the Passover Lamb, the one whose bones will not be broken. Through the quotation, whatever its specific *Vorlage*, "a powerful link is established between Jesus's sacrificial death and the Passover."[72] The rhetorical function of the paired quotations of 19.36–37, bringing the Passion Narrative to a stylistic climax, underscores the Paschal significance to John's interpretation of Jesus's death. The scriptural fulfillment motif and the Passover concept so converge, implying the fulfillment not just of Scripture, but vicariously that of Passover itself.[73]

Passover is, of course, a prominent theme across the Jewish Scriptures, with its inception or institutional narrative found in Exodus 12. The Israelites are instructed to slaughter a lamb, and daub its blood on the front of their houses (12.7), thereby avoiding the resulting plague on Egypt's firstborn (12.12). Its events comprise a continuing "day of remembrance" for Israel, an ongoing feast for subsequent generations to celebrate (12.14). Not every scholar has been persuaded of its significance within the Fourth Gospel, however; C. H. Dodd, for example, was hesitant as to its import for John's scriptural unpacking of Jesus's death.[74] After all, John does not *explicitly* connect Jesus's death with the Passover until 19.36, or at least this is the first explicit, unchallenged connection, and even this correlation is derivative rather than specific. Where the *mode* of Jesus's death is explicitly signalled, leaving the audience in no doubt as to its anticipated cruciform nature, the Passover dimension is more deductive, more allusive, more implicit.

But just as with the garden/Genesis association, the frequency of the potential links start to stack up. Hence in more recent times, few commentators would now deny that Passover imagery has significant impact in the Fourth Gospel, and particularly in John's narration of Jesus's Passion and its portrayal as the Passover Lamb *par excellence*.[75] Perhaps the most vocal advocate for Passover's role within the Fourth Gospel, and particularly within its Passion Narrative, has been Stanley Porter.[76] For Porter, Jesus's death is the culmination of John's elucidation of the Passover theme, with 19.36 being the specific climax, and notably so in view of 19.36's claim to scriptural fulfillment: "in the death of Jesus, as climactically defined by the Old Testament quotations, the Old Testament fulfillment motif and the Passover theme converge."[77] Likewise, as Tat Yu Lam avers, the emphatic double fulfillment expressed in the quotations of 19.36–37 attests "the convergence of the fulfillment and Passover motifs of the whole Gospel."[78] The Paschal theme is proclaimed at the gospel's outset with the proclamation of the role of the Lamb (1.29), and is brought to a climax by the fulfillment claim of 19.36–37, bringing the whole plot to its interpretive zenith. And the lamblike portrayal of 19.36 means that Jesus's death as Passover Lamb is in continuity with the prior characterization of his public ministry.[79]

Three related contextualizing points may be made. First, although the framework of the Passover is present within John's Passion Narrative, and while the unpacking of the motif reaches its *telos* therein, the Passover functions as a core element of the *whole* of John and not merely its Passion account. It offers a "unifying concept" for the Fourth Gospel.[80] Daise argues, for example, that Passover provides a formal structure for the Johannine Gospel, and its appeal to festal imagery "clocked the coming of Jesus's 'hour.'"[81] Second, and resultingly, assessing the extent of paschal influence upon the Gospel's portrayal of Jesus's death necessarily requires attention to Johannine material beyond the contours of the Passion. That is, even more than with the creation motif, the evocation of the Passover theme has its origins from earlier on in the Fourth Gospel. The Passion Narrative may provide the full unveiling or narrative climax, but the roots have already been laid, and once again—as with its cited quotations—attending to the Passion Narrative's scriptural usage is necessarily *intra*textual as well as intertextual.

Third, the way in which the allusion is outworked is therefore significant. The very recognition of Passover imagery and its function in the Passion account is contingent upon its prior anticipation and signposting. Even if 19.36 is in some sense "quoting" Exod 12.46, the quotation itself does not explicitly specify Passover or lamb vocabulary, and the reader is expected to make the Paschal connection themselves. Lexical variation is present too, most notably in the appellation of the lamb figure of 1.29 (ἀμνὸς). Exodus 12 uses πρόβατον rather than ἀμνὸς (though cf. Num 28.19), with the use of ἀμνὸς likely driven by the Isaianic association (see later). Once again, it is a thematic rather than lexical allusion that the evangelist seeks to evoke and which the competent reader is assumed to comprehend.

How then does John set about establishing this pervasive Paschal theme? Integral to the unifying aspect of Passover in the Fourth Gospel is the famous declaration of 1.29, reinforced by 1.36, and the Baptist's specific personification of Jesus as the Lamb. From the very outset of his ministry, John's Jesus is programmatically cast in lamblike terms and the Passover expectation set in motion. And more than that, Jesus is *visualized* as such—in both instances it is the *seeing* of Jesus that evokes the Lamb of God appellation. This is tied, one suggests, with the subsequent invitation to "come and see" (1.39, 46), implying therefore that the outworking of Jesus's "lamb-ness" is something to be visualized and anticipating the climactic ocular encounter of 19.37. We might suggest therefore that the "visual" image of the pierced Jesus (19.34–37) is intrinsic to this, the *seeing* of Jesus in his post-crucifixion state is integrally intertwined with the Lamb characterization. The Beloved Disciple's testimony is also to that which they have *seen* (19.35), and the climactic appeal of 19.37 is likewise to focus on the (glorious) implications of what has been visualized (cf. 17.24, also 12.41).

Having been initiated in 1.29, the Passover imagery appears sporadically across the subsequent discourse, its mention teasingly suggestive but without further explication as to the significance of its inclusion. The heavenly feeding of John 6 is timed as near Passover (6.4), alerting the reader to the anticipated association of Passover and Jesus's death, and linking it to his offering of flesh and blood for them (6.52–56). The opening of John's farewell discourse, and Jesus's knowing his hour had come, is tantalizingly timed as before the Passover Festival (13.1). Sometimes, the Passover link is more implicit or nuanced. For example, John's reference to Moses, and his testimony to Jesus (5.36), may conjure Passover resonances, or at least bring the wider exodus narrative to the interpretive table. Similarly, Jesus's claim that the disciples' death—just like his own—could be conceived as a worship offering (λατρείαν προσφέρειν—16.2) may also be said to locate Jesus's death within a Passover framework.[82] If so, it adds further irony of the crucifixion scene. In the light of 16.2, the soldiers' offering (also προσφέρω) of a wine sponge (19.29) becomes λατρεία to Jesus—and in so doing, they participate in the wider fulfillment of Scripture (as they do both in the piercing of Jesus and in the distribution of his clothing). And if 16.2 lurks in the Paschal intratextual background, then Jesus's reminder that his words (i.e., those of 16.2) are to function as a reminder or remembrance (16.4) may also do so; where Passover was "a day of remembrance for the Israelites and hence celebrated as a festival in perpetual memory of God's deliverance," its liberative and memorial aspect is now extended to the fulfillment given by Jesus's death. As Zumstein concludes: "A transfer occurs: the deliverance of God's people is no longer linked to the exodus from Egypt, but to the cross."[83]

Within the Passion Narrative itself, three features are explanatorily significant for underscoring its Passover backdrop:

1. *Passover Timing:* The Fourth Gospel explicitly timetables its Passion narration in terms of contemporary Passover practice. Pilate reports the custom of releasing a prisoner at Passover time (18.39). Those who bring Jesus to Pilate will not enter his headquarters for fear of ritual impurity that would prohibit their eating the Passover (18.28), thus suggesting that the eating was an imminent event. Likewise, the climax of Jesus's trial is specifically noon on the day of preparation for Passover (19.14); the proclamation of Jesus's kingship therein—however ironically—is therefore staged in relation to Passover. The timing of Jesus's death—admittedly a contentious issue within gospel comparisons—is set or coordinated with the afternoon slaughter of the lambs in Temple ahead of the Passover meal on the following day. The removal of Jesus's body from the cross (19.31) and his burial before nightfall (19.42) are both given temporal linkage to the Day of Preparation for Passover, specifically the day on which the Passover lambs are killed. The removal of Jesus's body from the cross—and that it cannot remain until the morning—may also have connection with the need to burn any remnants of the Passover meal (Exod 12.10), rather than leave them for the following day.
2. *Passover Imagery:* The offer of a sponge full of wine on a hyssop branch (a detail absent from the Synoptic accounts), is surely driven by the use of hyssop in Exodus 12.22 to daub the lamb's blood on their doorposts.[84] The scribal correction to javelin—rather than hyssop—testifies to the latter being the harder reading (the capacity of hyssop to bear the wine is implausible bearing in mind its limpness), but equally its inclusion only serves to underscore its role in undergirding the Passover backdrop to the account. Its internarratival symbolism is hard to ignore.[85] As noted earlier, John's use of προσφέρω in respect of the hyssop-sourced offering of the wine (19.29) may also reinforce

the Passover element, as the verb is customarily used in respect of sacrifice.[86] Even if that wrongly implies a cultic aspect to the Passover account, we might still suggest that προσφέρω is not a neutral term, and conveys more than just the physical act of lifting up.

3. *Passover Lamb:* But perhaps the most evocative aspect of the Passover context for Jesus's death is the implied association of Jesus's death and that of the Passover lambs, in preparation for the Passover meal. The connections are implicit rather than explicit, but they are redolent nonetheless, and so enable the conclusion that the quotation of 19.36 pertains to the unbroken bones of a Passover Lamb. The parallels with the accompanying action at the Temple draw the associations acutely. The connection with the Temple and Jesus's body is well-established by John (2.19–22), and, as we will see, there are implications for the Temple's role and function in that respect. The slaughtering of lambs in the Temple would yield blood, and would traditionally replicate the flow of water and blood through two distinct channels and flow out into the Kidron (*m. Mid.* 3.2). Coloe's phrasing of the event is thus deliberate: "As Preparation day drew to a close, quite literally, blood and water would flow from the side of the temple down into the Kidron."[87] That is, the blood and water outflow from Jesus's side (19.34) replicates—fulfills even—the same outflow from the Temple animals,[88] and contributes to the pattern of Jesus, in his death, building a new temple, a temple of his body (2.21). Once again, the Passion Narrative's usage of the Passover theme is as much intratextual and intertextual; both elements are mutually informing, and we will return to this concept in chapter 5.

And if the flow of blood from Jesus's side (19.34) does echo the blood of the Passover lamb, it yields a further instance of Johannine irony. With the piercing of Jesus, the Roman soldier (echoing perhaps Pharaoh's army) is the one who releases and unconsciously enables the *life*-giving work of deliverance of the one they have put to do death. If so, we notice once more how John's intertextual activity is outworked in ironic or reversed form. But more than that, the evangelist stresses the contemporaneity of Jesus's death and that of the Passover Lamb in terms of both timing *and* function—the "narrative chronology and narrative Christology are inseparable."[89]

Why, then, has the evangelist chosen to embed the Passover motif so prominently within the Fourth Gospel, and to find its fulfillment in Jesus's death? The temptation is to default to atonement or soteriological discussions, to conceive of the Passover Lamb as a sacrifice for sin, and a case can be—and has been—made for the soteriological efficacy of Jesus's death as Passover Lamb.[90] Porter, for example, ventures that hyssop "is used to form a connection between the sacrificial victim and those for whom it or Jesus is the sacrifice."[91] However, it is important to recognize that the Passover Lamb, at least in its Exodus portrayal, did not have that sacrificial function. Yes, the blood of the lamb is an integral part of the way in which Israel's liberation is secured, but it does not derive from any specific sacrificial or hamartiological dimension.[92] The assumption that that lamb of 1.29 that "takes away the sin of the world" is easily critiqued on the basis that the blood of Paschal Lamb is not said to have soteriological effect. Although there are obviously significant liberative and salvific resonances to the Exodus itself, the Lamb's role in them is secondary, and hence cautions against reading John 1.29 solely in Passover terms. Indeed, as Wheaton rightly conjectures above, it is the fusion of Isaiah 53 and Passover together in John 1.29 that enables any sacrificially related, intertextual allusion.

Hence Passover imagery may function in the Fourth Gospel for other reasons. Christine Schlund, for example, argues that rather than pertaining to sacrifice for sin, the meaning of the Passover in John takes on a more rounded form. Passover gives communal identity and is used in respect of purity matters—that is, washing, and not entering Pilate's headquarters. Jesus's death is effective in that it will deliver the believer from the evil one (17.15), rather than being a sacrifice for sin.[93] Alternatively, Wheaton, in his discussion of what constitutes the Fourth Evangelist's perspective on the fulfillment of festivals, contends that the Passover imagery—and Jesus's death as Paschal Lamb—is to enable believers to eat the Passover meal. They participate in the meal *of the Lamb*. John's interest in the Jesus's Paschal Lamb characterization is not about ascribing soteriological significance to his death (that aspect is left for Isaiah 53), but rather about participation in the festival feast. Importantly in terms of comparison with the status of Scripture and/or supersessionist discussions, the Passover is fulfilled, but its fulfillment effect is not in respect of atoning efficacy. As Wheaton concludes in his assessment of Jesus's death as Paschal Lamb: "The significance of the sacrifice of Jesus as paschal victim lies not predominantly in any value intrinsic to the sacrifice itself, but rather in its function as provision for the paschal meal, the eating of which is requisite for participation in the covenant community that is restored through the death of Jesus."[94]

But such salvific concerns notwithstanding, a strong case still exists for some form of typological relationship between Jesus's death and the Passover Lamb. In some sense, Jesus "fulfills" the Passover feast.[95] Passover does not exhaust the significance of the Lamb image of 1.29 and there is good reason to see this as one more of John's polyvalent images that draw on a plurality of sources. It is only in combination with Isaiah 53 that the (Passover) Lamb can properly be said to take away the sins of the world (1.29). But bearing in mind the frequency with which Passover imagery is generated, it is hard to overlook the Paschal implications operative within John's Passion retelling, particularly as the Lamb imagery offers such a fitting *inclusio* (1.29 and 19.36–37) to the Johannine discourse of Jesus's death.

And the Passover example may yield further insight on how the reader is expected to make intertextual connections mediated by allusive means. The reader is invited to take up the invitation of 5.39 to search the Scriptures and discern how they speak to Jesus. They are expected to be capable of making the Paschal connections to/within Jesus's Passion, and not need heavy-handed signaling to forge them. The frequent Paschal references steer the reader in the right direction, of course; the repeated asides are present for them to make and reinforce the Passover connection. But the broad familiarity of the Passover event also means that the audience doesn't have to work *too* hard, or bring *too much* prior knowledge to the table, to make that connection.

Suffering Servant Imagery in John's Passion Narrative

Scholars generally aver that John portrays Jesus's death as his exaltation and glorification. The ironic reversal of the lifting up motif (3.14; 8.28; 12.32–34) leads in this direction, and in its cruciform manifestation, the climactic point is reached, the *telos* of John's argument and of Jesus's work. Frey's analysis of Jesus's Passion is therefore fairly uncontroversial, at least for its presentation in the Fourth Gospel: "To be sure, the Johannine passion narrative (like the whole gospel) is portrayed strongly from the perspective of Easter and fundamentally by the means of the interpretive categories of exaltation and glorification."[96] More contentious, though, is Frey's following suggestion, namely that the origins of the exaltation/glorification theme tie back to the fourth Servant Song (Isa 52.13–53.12), and specifically to the glorification/lifting up imagery of Isa 52.13.[97]

Frey's observation is contentious in that, for varying reasons, some scholars dismiss the relationship between the Fourth Servant Song and the Johannine Passion, or at least are very cautious about assuming any connection. Zumstein, for example, contends that, unlike the Synoptics, the Johannine Jesus is not the personification of the Isaianic Suffering Servant because the evangelist does not emphasize the expiatory function of Jesus's death.[98] Similarly, aspects of the *suffering* characterization of Isaiah's Servant 53 sit ill with the implied absence of such suffering in John's Passion rendering. Bultmann, for example, disavows any alleged Isaianic portrayal on the grounds that Jesus *acts* rather than suffers, and is presented as assuming control of the overall situation: "He does not appear in the passion story as the sufferer but as the one who takes the initiative. . . . Whereas in the eyes of the world his opponents have achieved a conquest, in the light of a devastating irony they appear as the conquered."[99] And it must be said that, although we have suggested some possible Isaiah 53 reference in the composite citation of 19.37,[100] there remains no formal, explicit Isaianic citation in John 18–19, at least not in the overt, signaled fulfillment mode the evangelist uses.[101] Bearing in mind the explicit fulfillment imagery used in John 12.38 (Isa 53.1), thereby contextualizing the response to Jesus in terms of the Servant Song, one might well have expected the evangelist to bring the Servant image to its explicit fulfillment precisely at the moment of Jesus's death. The 12.38 citation also relates to *non-belief* in Jesus, and this could equally serve to preclude further reference to the Song in the Passion Narrative itself.[102]

But such matters notwithstanding, it remains the case that John 12.38 does explicitly tie Jesus's death to Isaiah 53, and at a critical turning point in Fourth Gospel's narration. The Baptist's programmatic statement of John 1.29 has already introduced the Servant allusion, and this is solidified by the formal quotation the evangelist makes in 12.38. The appeal to Isa 53.1 likely arises from Jesus's prior reference to being lifted up (12.32; cf. Isa 52.13), indicative of his anticipated mode of death (12.33), and the crowd's misunderstanding of what that "lifting up" (of the Son of Man) might entail (12.34). In particular, they appeal to the Law (12.34)—rather than the Scriptures—to make that point, averring that the Messiah remains forever, and most certainly cannot undergo death, let alone a cruciform one. Rather than Torah, though, John's Jesus has in mind the fate of the Servant, as the one who would be ὑψωθήσεται καὶ δοξασθήσεται (Isa 52.13), and exceedingly so (σφόδρα—Isa 52.13). The crowd have disbelieved the teaching of Jesus (what they have heard (53.1a)) and have failed to see the "revelation" of what Jesus has done (53.1b). Where his opponents seek to invoke Torah, John's Jesus instead instills the Servant Song as the primary scriptural testimony.[103] The correlation between Jesus's death and the Servant Song is therefore firmly established at this point, setting up the subsequent developments in the Passion Narrative, and critically the visual imagery of "lifting up."[104]

John 12.38 addresses the situation of those who have witnessed the signs of Jesus but have not responded with belief (12.37). As McWhirter rightly surmises in respect of the belief/non-belief dimension: "Although John never quotes Isa. 52:13–53:12 with reference to Jesus's death, he *consistently* describes it in terms of Isa. 53:1 LXX."[105] More significantly, as we saw in chapter 2, 12.38 also marks the Fourth Gospel's critical move from scriptural testimony to scriptural *fulfillment*. The evangelist quotes Isa 53.1 (12.38), casting Jerusalem's non-belief in terms of scriptural fulfillment and investing the Servant Song with significant, directive authority in this regard.[106] John rarely acknowledges the specific sources of its quotations, so its attribution to Isaiah here (cf. also 1.23, 12.39) further heightens its function and significance, potentially "reminding" the reader that Isaianic Servant imagery is on its radar and hence to anticipate further reference(s) in the Passion itself. Such reference may ultimately be outworked in unexpected fashion, or in ways that re-calibrate the Servant image in different form, akin to the re-calibration or reconfiguring of scriptural imagery the Fourth Gospel enacts elsewhere (and which we have seen in the ironic rendering of kingship, for example).[107] But nonetheless, the Song's inclusion establishes it as an integral part of the scriptural framework for narrating the events leading up to Jesus's death.

The Isaianic dimension to John 12—albeit not explicitly pertaining to the Servant—continues with the subsequent citation of Isa 6.10 (John 12.39), and John's declaration that Isaiah saw his glory (John 12.41). The identity of the αὐτοῦ (12.41) is left undefined, but, bearing in mind that it is their δόξα that Isaiah witnesses, it seems likely that John still has in mind the scene of the Servant's exaltation/glorification, and thus combines the respective visions of Isaiah 6 and Isaiah 53 to speak prophetically of the anticipated crucifixion scene. Indeed, Frey contends that, for the evangelist, Isaiah actually sees Jesus's glory in the Song—and in effect transfers that onto the Passion account: "If Isaiah spoke about Jesus, he thus prophesized the exaltation and glorification of the servant (i.e., of Jesus, the crucified one)."[108] Jonathan Lett's summary of the combined effect of the Isaianic citations is likewise apposite: "With Isa 52:13–53:12 and Isa 6, John delivers the most startling news: the divine and holy Jesus sits on the temple throne because he also hangs on a cross—scorned, disfigured, steeped in shame—and because he hangs there forsaken, he also presides gloriously over all the earth in his heavenly temple."[109]

In sum, then, we might say that John 12.37–41 functions as an anticipatory precursor of the Isaiah-sourced revelation of Jesus's glory to be unveiled in the Passion retelling. *Prior* to the Passion Narrative, John uses Isaiah 53 (combined with Isaiah 6) to set the parameters for what chapters 18–19 will ultimately manifest. On that basis, Lett rightly surmises that "the Servant Song seems paradigmatic for the entire Gospel, even at a cursory level."[110]

What, then, of the Passion scene itself? If 12.37–41 anticipates the agency of Isaiah 53, to what degree and how does John extend its imagery to the Passion retelling? Pursuing Hays's "echo" language and approach, we might hear several possible Servant echoes or resonances across John's Passion retelling:[111]

- *John 18.13, 28; 19.4, 13, 15/Isa 53.7–8:* The Fourth Gospel's repeated ἄγω language, climaxing with its repetition in 19.15, may echo the similar leading (ἄγω) of the Servant/lamb to their destiny.
- *John 18.38; 19.4, 6/Isa 53:9:* Pilate's repeated declarations of Jesus's innocence echoes or confirms the lack of deceit that comes from the Servant's (i.e., Jesus's) mouth.

- *John 19.5/Isa 53.3b:* Pilate's statement of John 19.5 may have some ironic reference to Isa 53.3b, particularly in the wider context of Jesus's mockery (19.1–3),[112] but, as suggested earlier, this may be secondary to the Adamic dimension. At the same time, if John 19.5 does indeed echo Isa 53.3, then Pilate's *"ecce homo"* pronouncement may extend to proclaim the anticipated achievement of Jesus as the (ironic) Servant figure.[113]
- *John 19.15/Isa 53.8:* The Jews' repeated response to Pilate—"away with him" (ἆρον)—picks up the same verb (αἴρω) used of the Lamb's action (1.29), but may also echo the Servant's experience of 53.8, where αἴρω is again used twice.[114]
- *John 19.18/Isa 53.12:* Jesus's crucifixion between two other figures may be an echo of Isa 53.12, and the Servant's numbering with/among other transgressors. John makes no subsequent reference to these figures other than that their bones were subsequently broken to expedite their death and remove them from their cross. Their role is incidental, and might otherwise not merit mention bearing in mind the overall brevity of John's account. Their inclusion, however, sustains the Isaiah 53 backdrop.
- *John 19.19–22/Isa 52.15:* The proclamation of the Jesus's kingship—reproduced in other languages—may allude to Isaiah's prophecy that kings, presumably of other nations, would shut their mouths because of the Servant/Jesus.
- *John 19.38–42/Isa 53.9:* Jesus's burial—in a tomb and with an abundance of spices—may recall the Servant's burial with the wicked and the rich. Indeed, Köstenberger surmises that the burial discourse functions as an explicit fulfillment of Scripture, akin to the preceding fulfillment discourse.[115]

Furthermore, once one "concedes" that Isaiah 53 is to some degree on the radar of John's Passion Narrative, once one concedes it may be operative, other potential associations or links may be seen to be at work:

- The slaughtered lamb makes no noise (Isa 53.7), and hence that may correlate with the absence of cruciform pain/suffering and to Jesus's (relative) silence on the cross.
- We note the importance of παραδίδωμι language within the Fourth Gospel—climactically so in the Passion Narrative at Jesus's arrest (18.2, 5, 30, 35–36; 19.16) and in Jesus handing over his Spirit (19.30). This language potentially references YWHH laying sins onto the Servant

(παραδίδωμι—Isa 53.6) or the Servant being handed over to death for sin (παραδίδωμι—Isa 53.12).[116]

- Although the wording is different, the imagery of the wounded servant is not dissimilar to John's portrayal of a pierced figure (19.34), and particularly the invocation to visualize him (19.37).[117]
- Juel recognizes that the notion of the rebuilding of the Temple was added to targumic interpretation of Isa 53.5—that is, the Messiah would rebuild the Temple.[118] In view of the Temple/body imagery that pervades John's account of Jesus, that may offer a further link to the Servant Song.
- Language from the broader context of the Servant Song may bleed over into the Johannine account. For example, the universal declaration that all the ends of earth will see the salvation of God (Is 52.10) may be alluded to by the multi-lingual titulus inscription (19.21).

Instead of direct citation of Isa 52.13–53.12, then, John's Passion Narrative evokes a series of echoes and allusions, which though not explicit in tenor, still reverberate back to the Fourth Servant Song, and to the Isaianic imagery established by John 12.37–41. This underscores what we noted in respect of Fourth Gospel's use of quotations, namely the diversity of John's strategy in terms of its appeal to the Scriptures. Fulfillment can be found in/by direct specified citation, as it is in Ps 22.18/John 19.24. But equally, as with the creation and Passover motifs, it may be evoked by more indirect allusion or echo, by more subtle rendering of texts already on John's horizon. Isaiah 53 is not a "new" text to John; it is already on the audience's radar, and they are prepared—expectant even—for its material to bleed over into Passion retelling.

Related to this, we also note we might say that although we have made a strong case for John's scriptural usage to be generally applied in retrospect (cf. John 19.28/Ps 69.3 recalling the Temple incident (John 2.19/Ps 69.9)), the Fourth Gospel's use of the fourth Servant Song points in the other direction. Where the Passion Narrative might normally be the starting point for John's scriptural usage and everything else work backwards from that point (particularly, as we shall see, 19.28 and its claims to perfect Scripture), the use of Isaiah 53 points to a more diachronic narration. The Servant Song shapes the (subsequent) patterning of John's Passion narration, rather than the Passion account generating the customary retrospective scriptural interpretation. The Passion Narrative-Scripture interchange thus becomes more dialogical, more two-way, backward *and* forward.

VERBAL ALLUSIONS AND ECHOES

Thus far, our analysis has prioritized thematic allusions, as these motifs evoke the majority of the Passion's intertextual analysis. Although they remain the primary means by which the Passion Narrative allusively evokes Israel's Scriptures, it may also contain several other potential scriptural echoes that shape its narration of Jesus's death. Two in particular warrant further discussion:

John 18.10–11—Isa 49.2

The Synoptic Passion Narratives include the cutting off of the ear of one of High Priest's slaves (Matt 26.51, Mark 14.47, Luke 22.50), but draw different implications from the event to John. Luke's Jesus—unsurprisingly perhaps—heals the ear (Luke 22.51). John, however, names the sword-bearer as Peter, and the wounded slave as Malchus.[119] Jesus chastises Peter for his action (similarly so, Matt 26.52) and instructs Peter to put the sword back in its sheath. John 18.11 may thereby yield a subtle echo of Isa 49.2 and the patterning of the Servant's mouth as a sharp sword (ὡσεὶ μάχαιραν ὀξεῖαν). The only shared word is μάχαιρα, and that is hardly a firm basis on which to pronounce on the existence of an echo, but there are several other factors which might commend some form of intertextual link. Revelation 1.16 is also generally thought to allude to Isa 49.2 (the ὀξεῖα terminology is shared, as is the reference to mouths), but Isaiah's μάχαιρα has become Revelation's ρομφαία, so lexical similarity is not the sole criterion for confirming the echo's existence. But the Apocalypse's appeal to Isa 49.2 in 1.16 would evidence the latter's presence within early Christian scriptural reflection.

There are other notable resonances with John 18.11 too, notably the association with matters oral. Peter's μάχαιρα is to be sheaved, and instead, Jesus is to drink the cup/fate set before him (18.11). Rather than needing physical defense, Jesus welcomes the arrest. The cup which he is to drink (cf. 19.28–30) testifies to Jesus's announced willingness to lay down his life (10.18; 12.27).[120] An echo to Isa 49.2 would resonate with this declaration. That which Jesus imbibes is not a physical μάχαιρα, but his mouth is metaphorically patterned in such terms, and in the context of the Servant's declaration that he will be the one in whom YHWH is glorified (Isa 49.3; cf. John 12.28). The imagery of the cup may itself also draw on scriptural imagery, reprising the cup of God's wrath (e.g., Ps 75.8; Jer 49.12),[121] with Jesus's conscious decision to drink from it thereby showing his willing embrace of such a fate.

John 18.12—Genesis 22

A further echo may be found in the subsequent verse. Jesus's arrest is completed, and his opponents bind him and take him away (18.12). John does not dwell on the binding action (δέω), but he subsequently reminds the reader of Jesus's "bound" status (18.24) ahead of his dispatch to Caiaphas. Such imagery possibly opens up parallels with the binding of Isaac in Genesis 22. Again, there is some lexical dissimilarity (Gen 22.9 uses συμποδίζω in respect of the binding action, presumably to emphasize its podal dimension), but the prevailing sense of the respective actions seems consistent. In both incidences, the binding is in anticipation of death. And the father/son imagery that characterizes the *Akedah* may be said to mirror the paternal/filial dimension implicit in the Passion account (e.g., 18.11). Moreover, John 18.14 reminds the reader of Caiaphas's "prophecy" in respect of Jesus's death (11.49–53), namely that it was better for εἷς ἄνθρωπος to die for the people, similar in tone perhaps with Isaac's status as Abraham's only son (Gen 22.2, 12; cf. John 3.16). There is also the strange mention of the other (unnamed) disciple who accompanies Jesus before Annas (18.15–16); Peter does not go. The pairing of the (bound) Jesus with this other disciple may have resonance with Abraham and Isaac headed together toward Isaac's mortem fate. The unnamed disciple is sometimes identified as Judas, but such identification can only be guesswork,[122] and more importantly, overlooks John's habitual use of unnamed characters as generally positive figures (the man born blind, for example). It may instead offer a positive embrace of participation in Jesus's death—or, akin to Abraham, at least not standing in its way. It may also be a (more positive) means of inviting the reader to participate and vicariously enter into the trial scene, enhancing its witness/testimony dimensions.

Jesus's carrying of his own cross (19.17) has resonance of Isaac carrying the wood (Gen 22.6), and likewise of Isaac's willingness to go to his death.[123] Although it was standard practice for the condemned figure to carry their own cross, that need not rule out John using—or framing—such usage against the Genesis 22 backdrop for intertextual effect,[124] (or indeed, for the reader to make that connection, even if it is not necessarily John's own intention to develop it). John's use of the dative ἑαυτῷ is intriguing and does double duty, namely stressing that Jesus carries the cross both *by* himself and *for* himself.[125] Such tradition is found in early Christian discourse, but it remains the case that the Fourth Gospel itself does not really signal or exploit the *Akedah* association (though 3.16 may be seen to at least echo its sentiment). It is *post*-biblical interpreters, rather than the NT authors, who seem to have exploited the connection.[126] Or at least—and perhaps consistent with its other use of scriptural imagery—the connection is more subtle, inviting the reader to forge their own connections accordingly. We might therefore say that Genesis 22 is a less prominent text than might be expected for John's Passion Narration, but it is still "present," still embedded within John's scriptural mapping. And for an alert reader, the potential is there for this network of influences to be drawn.

CONCLUSION: SCRIPTURAL ALLUSIONS IN JOHN'S PASSION NARRATIVE

In our previous chapter, we drew some initial, tentative conclusions in respect of quotational usage in John's Passion Narrative. We now do the same in respect of John's intertextual allusions:

1. Allusions operate across all three constituent elements of the Passion triptych: arrest, trial, and crucifixion. If quotations were John's only intertextual mode, then our claim that the Passion Narrative is dependent upon Scripture could not be sustained, for, as we demonstrated in the previous chapter, they are located only in the triptych's third scene. Allusions, however, have a much broader scope. They operate across the full Passion terrain, and function to bind the three parts of the triptych together in terms of scriptural warrant. The garden motif in particular runs as a theme throughout the Passion Narrative and bookends the account accordingly.
2. Allusions also tie the Passion account to the rest of the Fourth Gospel. This happened to a limited extent in terms of the Johannine quotations, in that the Passion's characteristic fulfillment function is set in place well in advance of chapters 18–19. But it is far more prominent in terms of John's Passion allusions, and indeed, it is integral to their overall function within the Gospel account. The Passover motif, for example, is set up by 1.29, reoccurs at several points across the main body of the Gospel, and reaches its resolution and climax in the Passion Narrative. The same is the case for the Suffering Servant imagery, running as a thread across the evangelistic witness. In both instances, John's Passion is the place in which the respective themes come to their conclusion, further embedding the relationship between Jesus's death and Israel's Scriptures.
3. Just as we saw in terms of John's use of composite quotations, the evangelist is able to intertwine allusive themes together, and their combined effect is enhanced accordingly. We have argued that 1.29 programmatically fuses the Passover and Suffering Servant images, placing the respective themes in mutual relationship together. What we termed the operative "Creation" motif within the Passion retelling is actually

a somewhat broad definition, incorporating a number of images from across Genesis 1–3 (Adam, garden, betrayal, serpent, woman), each working together to strengthen the allusion's overall effect. There is an inherent plurality to John's use of allusions—the evangelist's intertextuality is very far from monochrome.

* * *

Allusions, we have seen, are potent intertexts. They evoke wider scriptural narratives, broader textual landscapes upon which John can unpack the significance of Jesus's death. They offer the evangelist a veritable intertextual tapestry to bring together the stories of Israel's Scriptures—whether of the Suffering Servant or the Passover Lamb, or of a renewed Adam or quasi-Isaac figure—and to place them in conversation with the story of Jesus's Passion. In so doing, these allusions make the pressing case for Scripture being the heartbeat of the Johannine Passion.

NOTES

1. Coutts, "Exodus," 269.
2. Hays, *Echoes-Gospels*, 284, emphasis original. We also note, however, that such an assessment should not preclude the application of first-century exegetical techniques to enable the Fourth Gospel's christological rendering of such images and figures (cf. McWhirter, "Messianic," 128–29). John's complex intertextual grid resists application of merely one way or feature of rendering its usage of Israel's Scriptures.
3. This would seem conversant too with, as we have seen, the Fourth Gospel's embrace of, and even preference for, composite quotations.
4. W. Gil Shin, "Internarrativity and *ecce homo*: A Masterplot Underlying Zechariah 6.9–15 and 1 Samuel 9.1–11.15 and its Function in John 19.1–16," *JSNT* 43 (2020): 196, drawing particularly on the work of Ziva Ben-Porat.
5. Catrin H. Williams, "Persuasion through Allusion: Evocations of 'Shepherd(s)' and their Rhetorical Impact in John 10," in *Come and Read: Interpretive Approaches to the Gospel of John*, ed. Alicia D. Myers and Lindsey S. Jodrey (Lanham, MD: Fortress Academic, 2019), 112–14.
6. Cp. Michael R. Whitenton, *Configuring Nicodemus: An Interdisciplinary Approach to Complex Characterization*, LNTS 549 (London: T&T Clark, 2019).
7. Dorothy Lee, "Creation, Ethics, and the Gospel of John," in *Johannine Ethics: The Moral World of the Gospel and Epistles of John*, ed. Sherri Brown and Christopher W. Skinner (Minneapolis: Fortress, 2017), 247 rightly avers: "The presence of creation allusions in the Fourth Gospel has long been conceded."
8. See further Anthony M. Moore, *Signs of Salvation: The Theme of Creation in John's Gospel* (Cambridge, UK: James Clarke, 2013).
9. Michael A. Daise, "Quotations with 'Remembrance' Formulae in the Fourth Gospel," in *Abiding Words: The Use of Scripture in the Gospel of John*, ed. Alicia

D. Myers and Bruce G. Schuchard, SBLRBS 81(Atlanta: SBL, 2015), 88–90. For a robust articulation of the Fourth Gospel's employment of creation imagery, see Hengel, "Old Testament," 19–41, particularly 33–34.

10. Genesis 2.1–2 uses συντελέω rather than τελέω (John 19.30), but the climactic end/zenith moment is consistent across both narratives.

11. N. T. Wright, "Pictures, Stories, and the Cross: Where Do the Echoes Lead?," *JTI* 11 (2017): 58. So also Hengel, "Old Testament," 34 in respect of Jesus's cruciform action: "This means that the Son 'finishes' the work of God's Creation, which had been upset, indeed destroyed, by human sin."

12. Daly-Denton, *John*, 210.

13. Brown, *Gospel According to John*, 806: "nothing in John suggests the same garden is involved in both episodes."

14. Lieu, "Scripture," 235.

15. Moore, *Signs*, 62.

16. Jeannine K. Brown, "Creation's Renewal in the Gospel of John," *CBQ* 72 (2010): 275–90.

17. Cf. Keener, *Gospel*, 1077: "the proposed allusion . . . lacks adequate additional support to be clear" (1077); Francis J. Moloney, *The Gospel of John*, SP 4 (Collegeville: Liturgical, 1998), 484 terms it "a valuable reflection but not part of Johannine thought" (484). Others are more positive of the assessment—see Edwyn Clement Hoskyns, *The Fourth Gospel* (London: Faber and Faber, 1947), 509; Zimmermann, "Symbolic," 221–35.

18. E. C. Hoskyns, "Genesis I—III and St John's Gospel," *JTS* 21 (1920): 214 notes that the words can be used synonymously (cf. Eccl 2:5 LXX; Sir 24:23–34), and that both Aquila and Theodotion employ κῆπος in Genesis 2–3.

19. As we suggested in chapter 1, even if the allusion is not intentional, the reader may still make the intertextual connection, and fruitfully so.

20. Zimmermann, "Symbolic," 227.

21. So Brown, "Creation's Renewal," 279: "Although any one of these may not be persuasive in itself, the cumulative effect of these numerous connections with Genesis argues for their inclusion in John's communicative intention."

22. Coloe, *John*, 474. Coloe connects this further to the portrayal of the Wisdom as the Tree of Life in Prov 3.18. She avers: "The placement of the cross in the middle of the garden means that the creative activity of Wisdom/Sophia is present at Golgotha."

23. It is probably the John 20 connections that tip the balance in favor of Genesis 1–3 garden imagery being operative, but that would be a further instance of John working backwards, so to speak, resurrection lenses shaping scriptural memory and symbolic association. On the John 20/Genesis 2–3 interaction, see Mariusz Rosik, "Discovering the Secrets of God's Gardens. Resurrection as New Creation (Gen 2:4b–3:24; Jn 20:1–18)," *LASBF* 58 (2008): 81–98.

24. So Daly-Denton, *John*, 203.

25. So Richard Bauckham, *Jesus and the God of Israel: God Crucified and Other Studies on the New Testament's Christology of Divine Identity* (Grand Rapids, MI: Eerdmans, 2009), 40. Jobes, *John*, 266 further observes that "an allusion to

the Old Testament divine name echoes loudly in the otherwise common response," thereby also reinforcing the scriptural context to Jesus's response.

26. John Suggit, "Jesus the Gardener: The Atonement in the Fourth Gospel as Re-Creation," *Neot* 33 (1999): 166.

27. On the basis of the lexical difference, Keener, *Gospel*, 1077 is skeptical as to the validity of the allusion, also arguing that "John nowhere else uses any explicit Adam Christology." So also Carlos Raúl Sosa Siliezar, *Creation Imagery in the Gospel of John*, LNTS 546 (London: Bloomsbury, 2015), 179–90. Mark W. G. Stibbe, *John* (Sheffield, UK: JSOT Press, 1993), 182 proposes that the garden parallel is intratextual rather than intertextual, namely to John 10.1–5, and the going in/out of the sheepfold. This is a perfectly plausible suggestion, but bearing in mind the Fourth Gospel's capacity for multivalent connections, links to John 10 and Genesis 1–3 are not mutually exclusive.

28. On such matters, see Zimmermann, "Symbolic," 221–35.

29. So also T. Francis Glasson, "Davidic Links with the Betrayal of Jesus," *ExpTim* 85 (1974): 118–19.

30. Christos Karakolis, "'Across the Kidron Brook, Where There Was a Garden' (John 18.1): Two Old Testament Allusions and the Theme of the Heavenly King in the Johannine Passion Narrative," in *The Death of Jesus in the Fourth Gospel*, ed. Gilbert van Belle (Leuven: Leuven University Press, 2007), 751–60.

31. The allusion is certainly plausible bearing in mind the subsequent Davidic patterning in John's Passion Narrative, along with the use of (Davidic) righteous sufferer psalms, but it is not one that is forced on the reader. Cf. also Daly-Denton, *John*, 201: "an alert audience would notice that he is retracing the journey of David, forced to leave his royal city." If picked up, this would then be the first of several potential Davidic references within the Passion Narrative: "whether through resemblances or contrasts, it is the crossing of the Kidron by the shepherd-king about to lay down his life for the sheep that identifies him as the promised 'one shepherd' of 'one flock' that in Ezekiel's prophecies God names as 'my servant David'" (202).

32. Karakolis also observes that the Davidic connection explains John's silence in terms of the Gethsemane nomenclature. The latter would not have carried the royal/Davidic implications of the Kidron/garden combination.

33. Brown, *Gospel According to John*, 960.

34. Cf. Green, *Death of Jesus*, 131: "We can be certain . . . that he [i.e., the Fourth evangelist] knew the tradition of Jesus's troubled, submissive prayer."

35. A. J. M. Wedderburn, *The Death of Jesus: Some Reflections on Jesus-Traditions and Paul*, WUNT 299 (Tübingen: Mohr Siebeck, 2013), 91.

36. On the John 17/Gethsemane relationship, see Marianus Pale Hera, *Christology and Discipleship in John 17*, WUNT 342 (Tübingen: Mohr Siebeck, 2013), 9–11.

37. Harold W. Attridge, "Giving Voice to Jesus: Use of the Psalms in the New Testament," in *Psalms in Community: Jewish and Christian Textual, Liturgical, and Artistic Traditions*, ed. Harold W. Attridge and Margot E. Fassler, Society of Biblical Literature Symposium Series 25 (Atlanta: SBL, 2003), 106.

38. Lindars, *The Gospel of John*, 566.

39. Johannes Beutler, *A Commentary on the Gospel of John* (Grand Rapids: Eerdmans, 2017), 472.

40. On the different intertextual possibilities arising in respect of 19.5, see Adam Kubiś, "The Old Testament Background of 'Ecce Homo' in John 19:5," *Biblica et Patristica Thoruniensia* 11 (2018): 495–519.

41. Shin, "Internarrativity," 206n23, emphasis added.

42. So Dieter Böhler, "'Ecce homo!' (Joh 19,5): ein Zitat aus dem Alten Testament," *BZ* 39 (1995): 104–8; also Ford, *The Gospel of John*, 371; Lincoln, *Gospel*, 466.

43. Wayne A. Meeks, *The Prophet-King: Moses Traditions and the Johannine Christology*, NovTSupp 14 (Leiden: Brill, 1967), 71.

44. Lindars, *The Gospel of John*, 566.

45. Brown, *Death*, 865.

46. Feník, "Clothing Symbolism," 63.

47. For example, Moloney, *Gospel of John (Sp)*, 499; Stibbe, *John*, 191.

48. Lincoln, *Gospel*, 466.

49. M. David Litwa, "Behold Adam: A Reading of John 19:5," *HBT* 32 (2010): 135.

50. This is the thrust of Shin, "Internarrativity," 194–213. An internarrival reading of 19.5 brings together the wider narratives of both Zech 6.12 and 1 Sam 9.17, and resists the allusion being reduced to merely one scriptural source—"an exclusive pinpointing of one alluded-to passage may not be the best interpretive decision" (210).

51. Klink, *John*, 778.

52. See in particular Nicholas J. Schaser, "Inverting Eden: The Reversal of Genesis 1–3 in John's Passion," *WW* 40 (2020): 263–70; Litwa, "Behold," 129–43.

53. Schaser, "Inverting," 263.

54. Schaser, "Inverting," 263–70.

55. Litwa, "Behold," 141.

56. Cf. Litwa, "Behold," 141: "'Behold the man!' is not really a statement meant to excite pity or ridicule, but a statement expressing Jesus's divine sovereignty over his whole trial."

57. Litwa, "Behold," 135.

58. So Meeks, *Prophet-King*, 71–72 who points to Num 24.17 as further evidence for the mooted Zech 6.12 allusion. Philo seems to read the phrase in that way too (*Praem.* 95).

59. Schaser, "Inverting," 267.

60. Ben Witherington, *John's Wisdom: A Commentary on the Fourth Gospel* (Cambridge, UK: Lutterworth, 1995), 308.

61. Witherington, *John's Wisdom*, 308.

62. Lieu, "Scripture," 232–33.

63. In respect of 19.34, Adele Reinhartz, *Cast Out of the Covenant: Jews and Anti-Judaism in the Gospel of John* (Lanham, MD: Fortress Academic, 2018), 41 notes that "[an] outpouring of water is unusual in a wound such as piercing, but it is inevitable during childbirth." Hence "the rebirth of believers can only occur with Jesus's death" (41).

64. Senior, *Passion in John*, 111–12.

65. Bampfylde, "John XIX 28," 259.

66. Coloe, *John*, 493.

67. Schaser, "Inverting," 264. Such connections reinforce the Adam connections proposed earlier in the chapter. Schaser subsequently avers: "The interplay . . . between the life-giving sides of Jesus and Adam offers a compelling case of Adamic Christology in John's Passion" (265).

68. Brown, "Creation's Renewal," 282.

69. Gerry Wheaton, *The Role of Jewish Feasts in John's Gospel*, SNTSMS 162 (Cambridge, UK: Cambridge University Press, 2015), 91. See also Nielsen, "Lamb of God," 217–56.

70. On the interpretation of 1.29, see Nielsen, "Lamb of God," 225–26. He lists a dozen or so different assessments of the Lamb of 1.29, only one of which is specifically the Passover Lamb. As such, he proposes that a new "Lamb" concept is established, Passover or otherwise, one composed of the two traditions of Isaiah 53 and Passover.

71. See *inter alia* Schuchard, "Temple," 381–95.

72. Köstenberger, "Exodus in John," 106.

73. Cf. Stanley E. Porter, *John, His Gospel and Jesus: In Pursuit of the Johannine Voice* (Grand Rapids, MI: Eerdmans, 2015), 224: The scriptural quotations make the "sacrificial Passover not only specific but virtually undeniable."

74. Dodd, *Interpretation*, 424: "Nowhere in the discourses is it adduced in explication, or even illustration, of the meaning of Christ's death." Such hesitancy may derive from caution as to the soteriological implications of applying Passover Lamb imagery to Jesus's death, rather than to the allusional validity of the Paschal imagery.

75. W. R. G. Loader, "Revisiting Tensions in Johannine Christology," in *The Death of Jesus in the Fourth Gospel*, ed. Gilbert van Belle (Leuven: Leuven University Press, 2007), 457–67 represents the emerging consensus, perhaps. He admits to being initially skeptical of the capacity for the Passover imagery to carry forth into the Passion Narrative, but has come to a different view now, venturing that the "Passover motif is important in John's passion. 1.29 allows itself to be read proleptically as an allusion to this" (462).

76. See Stanley E. Porter, *Sacred Tradition in the New Testament: Tracing Old Testament Themes in the Gospels and Epistles* (Grand Rapids, MI: Baker Academic, 2016). He finds seven passages or instances where this is outworked.

77. Porter, *John, His Gospel and Jesus*, 200.

78. Tat Yu Lam, "The Effusion of Blood and Water for Purity and Sanctity: Jesus's Body, the Passover Lamb, and the Red Heifer in Johannine Temple Christology," in Stanley E. Porter and Andrew W. Pitts (eds.), *Johannine Christology* (Leiden: Brill, 2020), 210.

79. Charles H. Talbert, *Reading John: A Literary and Theological Commentary on the Fourth Gospel and the Johannine Epistles* (London: Smith & Helwys, 2005), 254.

80. Porter, *John, His Gospel and Jesus*, 198–224, especially 198n2. Porter is the most prominent voice for advocating how the Passover theme develops across the whole gospel rather than just featuring at the Fourth Gospel's beginning and end. Cf. for example, Stanley E. Porter, "Can Traditional Exegesis Enlighten Literary Analysis of the Fourth Gospel? An Examination of the Old Testament Fulfillment Motif," in

The Gospels and the Scriptures of Israel, ed. Craig A. Evans and W. Richard Stegner (London: T&T Clark, 1994), 396–428, which sets out a critique of Stibbe and Davies for not working through the theme in sufficient detail (397–401).

81. Michael A. Daise, *Feasts in John: Jewish Festivals and Jesus' "Hour" in the Fourth Gospel*, WUNT 2/229 (Tübingen: Mohr Siebeck, 2007), 172.

82. Cf. Lam, "Effusion," 212: "Jesus implies that he will be persecuted first by being killed as offering Passover service" (15.20). Lam continues: "the blood of Jesus, which is the Paschal blood, sets apart God's people, so that fellowship between them becomes possible."

83. Zumstein, "Purpose," 343.

84. The "correction" to καλάμῳ in the manuscript tradition (cf. Mk 15.36) testifies to the practical oddity—impossibility even—of hyssop functioning in this way, and makes ὑσσώπῳ the *lectio difficilior*. It would seem to concur that hyssop's Passover association, rather than its functional efficacy, drives its inclusion in 19.39.

85. There may also be echoes here of Heb 9.18–20, and the covenant-sealing sprinkling of blood with hyssop.

86. Lam, "Effusion," 211.

87. Coloe, *John*, 493.

88. Cf. Hoskins, "Deliverance," 296: "The blood flowing out from his side also points to his fulfillment of the Passover lamb, whose blood is poured out." One wonders, though, whether the association is necessarily as explicit or clear as Hoskins implies.

89. Stibbe, *John*, 196.

90. Hoskins, "Deliverance," 285: "deliverance from death and sin is a significant element of the Passover typology of the Gospel of John."

91. Porter, *Sacred Tradition*, 146.

92. And there is a well-established literary discourse that recognizes this, and which therefore notes the need to nuance the Lamb of God (1.29) through the lens of the Servant imagery.

93. Christine Schlund, *"Kein Knochen soll gebrochen werden": Studien zu Bedeutung und Funktion des Pesachfests in Texten des frühen Judentums und im Johannesevangelium* (Neukirchen-Vluyn: Neukirchener Verlag, 2005).

94. Wheaton, *Role*, 88.

95. Alan Kerr, *The Temple of Jesus' Body: The Temple Theme in the Gospel of John*, JSNTSupp 220 (London: Bloomsbury, 2002), 374: "Jesus . . . fulfils the Jewish Passover by becoming the Passover Lamb himself."

96. Frey, *Glory*, 210. Likewise, Bauckham, *Gospel of Glory*, 54: "Whereas the more common early Christian way of thinking envisaged humiliation followed by exaltation, suffering followed by glory, John sees exaltation and glory in the humiliation and death."

97. Frey, *Glory*, 210n63.

98. Zumstein, "Purpose," 341.

99. Bultmann, *John*, 633.

100. See the discussion in chapter 2.

101. NA28 offers no formal citation of, or reference to, the Servant Song in John 18–19.

102. See discussion in Michel Gourgues, "Mort pour nos péchés selon Les Écritures," in *The Death of Jesus in the Fourth Gospel*, ed. Gilbert van Belle (Leuven: Leuven University Press, 2007), 181–97. Gourgues sees Isa 52.13–53.12 as the primary passage attested to by the NT writers in respect of Jesus's cruciform death (184). On the tendency both to overstate and underestimate the role of the Servant Songs in the Passion Narratives, see Moo, *Old Testament*, 162–72.

103. Cp. the similar usage of Isaiah 53 in respect of unbelief in Rom 10.16—citing Isa 53.1.

104. Catrin H. Williams, "Isaiah in John's Gospel," in *Isaiah in the New Testament*, ed. Steve Moyise and M. J. J. Menken (London: T&T Clark, 2005), 115: "Where Isaiah speaks of the future exaltation and glorification of the Servant (53:12) before giving account of his humiliation and death (52:14– 53:12), John interprets the exaltation and glorification of Jesus as evident in, rather than following, his humiliation and death." Hence for Williams, "Jesus's death, for John, is the supreme disclosure of his divine glory."

105. McWhirter, "Messianic," 133.

106. Cf. Johannes Beutler, "Greeks Come to See Jesus (John 12:20f)," *Bib* 71 (1990): 337: "The first quotation, our text from Isa 53:1 in John 12:38, bears considerable weight. The very fact that it introduces the passion of Christ, makes it very probable that its origin from the fourth Song of the Suffering Servant is not accidental."

107. On the notion of John "reconfiguring" Scripture, see Judith M. Lieu, "Text and Authority in John and Apocalyptic," in *John's Gospel and Intimations of Apocalyptic*, ed. Christopher Rowland and Catrin H. Williams (London: Bloomsbury, 2013), 247–48.

108. Frey, *Theology*, 165. Speaking of Isa 6.10, Evans, "Quotation," 82 ventures: "This Isaiah text became the foundational Old Testament text for the evangelist and set the theological tempo for the passion narrative." Evans' analysis is valid/helpful, but we suggest rather that it is the *combination* of Isa 6.10 and Isa 53.1 that sets the Passion Narrative's theological tempo—i.e., bringing together the images of glory, vision and (un)belief. So also Lett, "Divine Identity," 159–73, who notes the lack of attention to the wider force of Isaiah 53 in John 12, and is critical of those commentators who restrict discussion Israel's blindness to just Isaiah 6, and not chapter 53. Isaiah 53 must be allowed to share the explanatory burden, and this reinforces the notion that 12.37–41 anticipates the events and responses of John 18–19.

109. Lett, "Divine Identity," 172.

110. Lett, "Divine Identity," 165. Lett points, for example, to the rejection implied by John 1.11 as symptomatic of the experience of Jesus/the Servant. He continues: "the background narrative of the Servant Song forces the reader to contemplate Jesus as the humiliated and exalted figure in his crucifixion" (166).

111. See further the helpful discussion/examples in Wheaton, *Role*, 90n24.

112. So Anthony Tyrrell Hanson, *The Prophetic Gospel: A Study of John and the Old Testament* (Edinburgh: T&T Clark, 1991). The mockery discourse may equally reflect or echo Isa 50.6 (so Moo, *Old Testament*, 139–40).

113. So Kubiś, "Ecce Homo," 501: "A competent reader of the Johannine Gospel would detect the irony that this seemingly helpless human Jesus is in fact to be identified with the almighty God (Jn 1:18; 20:28), enacting at this very moment his salvific act."

114. So Ford, *The Gospel of John*, 374. He continues: "At this time when Passover lambs are being killed, the same verb *airein* . . . is used for doing away with Jesus as it has been for doing away with sin."

115. Köstenberger, "John," 506.

116. Keener, *Gospel*, 1148.

117. Cf. Ridderbos, *John*, 623 on 19.34–37: a "figure strongly reminiscent of the man of sorrows in Isaiah 53."

118. Donald H. Juel, *Messiah and Temple: The Trial of Jesus in the Gospel of Mark* (SBLDS 31; Missoula, MT: Scholars, 1977), 202.

119. John does not expand on the Malchus nomenclature, and his naming may be merely a further appeal to eye-witness testimony. But the "king" meaning behind the name is intriguing bearing mind the Passion Narrative's subsequent discourse around Jesus's kingship.

120. Moloney, *Gospel of John (Sp)*, 484: "the Johannine passion story begins because Jesus allows it to begin."

121. Jobes, *John*, 267. There is also the contrast with the Synoptic Gethsemane tradition in which Jesus raises the possibility of not drinking from such a cup (Matt 26.39; Mk 14.36; Luke 22.42).

122. If it were Judas, why not merely identify him as such? That would surely only increase the desired (negative) effect.

123. Brown, *Death*, 1442.

124. Keener, *Gospel* suggests that the "historical" practice negates the need for or function of the Genesis 22 imagery, but the options are surely not mutually exclusive.

125. See further Brown, *Death*, 917. The inclusion of ἑαυτῷ may suggest that John is aware of the Synoptic Simon of Cyrene testimony and wishes to set aside any suggestion of his crucifer participation.

126. Cf. Brown, *Death*, 1435–44; so also Moo, *Old Testament*, 162–72.

Chapter 4

The Implications of Scriptural Usage in John's Passion Narrative (1)

For Israel's Scriptures

Our two previous chapters have considered different ways in which John's Passion Narrative appeals to Israel's Scriptures. Whether mediated through signaled fulfillment quotations, through verbal allusions to the Old Testament, or through the evocation of fundamental scriptural themes such as Creation or Passover, we have argued that scriptural appeal is core to John's Passion retelling. This is particularly the case for the third part of the Passion triptych (John 19.16b–42), with its abundance of scripturally sourced material. John's cruciform portrayal is brief enough as it is, and were its engagement with Israel's Scriptures removed, one would be left with very little indeed. We have also elucidated other features of John's scriptural appeal—the ironic dimension to Scripture's fulfillment or the way in which it is outworked in both intertextual and intratextual fashion. Although the volume of scriptural reference is not consistent across John's Passion retelling—the trial scene still remains comparatively "undercooked" in terms of intertextual reference—the first element of our core thesis stands. Scripture is a primary ingredient of John's Passion and provides the heartbeat of the Johannine retelling.

But this is only one side of the discussion we are undertaking. We turn now to assess the consequences of John's scriptural usage, and specifically to its impact on the concept of Scripture itself, the second element of our overall thesis. What happens to Scripture—at least in the evangelist's conception—through its participation and usage within the Johannine Passion Narrative? As we have seen in respect of John's quotational usage, there is general agreement that Scripture is somehow completed or fulfilled by this process (cf. 19.28–30), but less attention is given as to what that actually means for

Scripture itself, for its status, authority, or ongoing role. Some have pointed to the *telos* aspect implied by such fulfillment, and to the accompanying christological consequences, and within a canonical assessment, particularly for the modern reader, such insights are valid, rightly drawing out the way by which John's christological perspective is outworked. However, such discussion still tends to portray the matter in purely christological fashion and/or in terms of the status of the Fourth Gospel itself, or without necessarily considering the specific fate of the Jewish Scriptures. This chapter seeks to address this lacuna,[1] proposing that Israel's Scriptures do not emerge unscathed or untouched by their Johaninne encounter.

"SCRIPTURE" IN THE FOURTH GOSPEL

Assessing the character and function of the Fourth Gospel's scriptural usage, Anthony Hanson concluded that "Scripture, far from being used merely as illustrative material in his work, is part of its very woof and warp."[2] As such, and as we ourselves have sought to demonstrate, Hanson sees Scripture as directing John's evangelistic narration, exhibiting a prevailing Johannine concern to demonstrate Jesus's fulfillment of prophetic expectation. For Hanson, the Fourth Gospel's content and argument are essentially conditioned and shaped by Scripture, and the Gospel essentially becomes a story of Jesus built out of, or created from, scriptural texts. He so avers: "John only inserts teaching, conversations, and incidents in his historical tradition if he believes he has justification in scripture for doing so."[3] Hanson's restriction of Johannine content *solely* to that permitted or predetermined by Scripture likely goes beyond the textual testimony, however, and, instead, the reverse appears to be the case. That is, the Christ-event is the determinative factor for an event's inclusion, with Scripture ultimately in the service of the presentation of Jesus, not vice-versa. However, Hanson's claim for the fundamental embeddedness of the scriptural warrant within the Fourth Gospel is surely valid and worthy of consideration, particularly in light of the Passion Narrative discourse. Lieu similarly opines that Scripture gives the "indispensable reference point and scaffolding for the argument and the thought of John,"[4] and, in the light of the preceding chapters, it is hard to dissent from this foundational statement. For the evangelist, as we have seen, Jesus's actions demonstrably fulfil Scripture, and Scripture acts in service of such christological fulfillment.[5] Along with the Beloved Disciple's eye-witness testimony (cf. 19.35; 21.24–25), Scripture is John's primary authoritative source, and even a cursory or surface reading of the Johaninne Passion Narrative testifies to Scripture's internal, structural, and underlying function.[6]

But one might equally suggest that the converse of Lieu's statement also has verisimilitude. That is, even if just within its own testimony or parameters, the Fourth Gospel *provides a scaffolding for elucidating the thought or function of Scripture.* Scripture is both an essential ingredient or component for evaluating Jesus's death *and* an entity whose status and function is (through Johannine spectacles) transformed by the intertextual encounter. Brawley, for example, draws attention to the tension presented within the Johannine account and the resulting impact on Scripture's status: "the narrator recognizes a temporal differentiation—whatever scripture meant, it can be augmented, supplemented, completed . . . John 19.28–29 violates the boundaries of ἡ γραφή at same time that it values them."[7] That is, through its appeal *to* Scripture, John effects something in respect *of* Scripture; it is not a neutral encounter for either party.

This is evident from the outset of the gospel account. John's opening Ἐν ἀρχῇ declaration avowedly locates its narrative within the scriptural world. Such language anticipates a rhetorical, climactic end,[8] one that doesn't merely use Scripture instrumentally, but rather one that implies resulting consequences for the very essence or status of the Scriptures themselves. Hence John is more than "retelling Scripture" (to use Sheridan's titular term),[9] although it is, of course, at least still doing that. Beyond such retelling, particularly in/through its Passion Narrative, the Fourth Gospel is adjudicating on Scripture's status and function, and the essential character of "Scripture"—both Jewish and Christian—is changed by the intertextual Passion encounter. This will be the key proposition we seek to explore in this chapter.

JOHN 19.28–30 AND ITS IMPACT ON "SCRIPTURE"

As we have seen, one of the most striking aspects of John's Passion Narrative—perhaps *the* most striking feature—is its explicit, avowed declaration that Jesus's cruciform death *fulfills* Scripture.[10] In particular, its claim that all was now finished (τετέλεσται) in order that Scripture might be fulfilled/completed (τελειωθῇ—19.28)[11] has significant implications for the status of Scripture, at least in terms of the Fourth Gospel's conception. Of course, John's commentary on Scripture's fate is not limited to the Passion, and key principles as to Scripture's character and ethos are elucidated outside of the Passion account.[12] Scripture cannot be annulled (10.35), for example, and, prior to that, the evangelist evaluates the claims of scriptural testimony in respect of messianic origins (7.42). But both the intensification of fulfillment language within the Passion account, and the synchronicity of Jesus's death and its alleged scriptural warrant (19.28–30), surely give the Passion Narrative a particular prominence in this regard.

Furthermore, Scripture does not determine Jesus's *public* ministry in the same way that is does for Jesus's death. Scripture informs it, shapes it, is embedded within John's narration, and is the most authoritative of the retinue of witnesses John marshals to testify to Jesus (5.45–47 or 9.28–29, for example). But it is not the *defining* factor that it proves to be within the Passion account,[13] nor does it anticipate the fulfillment lens that permeates the second half of John's scriptural usage. In the Signs discourse, there is no sense that the Scriptures necessarily warrant fulfillment or that such fulfillment is essential for belief in Jesus (cf. 20.31). Yet in the second half, this new characteristic or dimension is perceived within Scripture—the prevailing, fundamental necessity for its ultimate fulfillment. Hence, purely at a rhetorical level, the Fourth Gospel presents scriptural engagement in two discrete, complimentary forms, demonstrating an internal evolution in Scripture's role. In the first of these, to use Obermann's helpful distinction, Scripture forms the interpretational background (in his terms, the *Deutehintergrund*) of the Christ-event, whereas in the second, the Christ-event is the explicit fulfillment (*explizite Erfüllung*) of Scripture.[14] Once again, in the latter, the Gospel of John is doing something *to*, as well as *with*, Scripture.

In our discussion of the scriptural quotation found in 19.28, we commented on the unusual—but not unprecedented (cf. 19.31)—"front-loading"[15] of the ἵνα clause, placed ahead of the main verb λέγει. Furthermore, we proposed that the ἵνα τελειωθῇ ἡ γραφή clause operated in Janus form, enabling both the specific intertextual engagement with Ps 69.3 (*inter alia*), while also postulating a far more substantive claim in respect of the overall fulfillment of Scripture itself. In chapter 2, we focused primarily on the former aspect, the more "micro" statement in respect of scriptural fulfillment, without fully addressing the "macro" implications of the latter claim. To this more significant statement we now turn. Although 19.28 functions as a specific allusion to a series of thirst-related antecedent texts, and while these texts combine to produce an "upward" trend in scriptural fulfillment, there remains an accompanying, and indeed somewhat more significant, "meta-teleiosis" of Scripture, one that is evoked because ἤδη πάντα τετέλεσται (19.30). What is the significance of this claim, and how does it inform John's perception of Israel's Scriptures?

Some initial, comparative comment may help in this regard. In other instances of the NT's scriptural usage, we see a text of Scripture changed in its new milieu, but discussion about such matters tend to be restricted to matters of interpretation or meaning. Compare the usage of fulfillment language in Matthew 2, for example. Space precludes an expansive engagement with such matters, but we could say (overcritically, perhaps) that Matthew is merely proof texting or working the Scriptures to its own way of thinking,[16] or rather that the evangelist finds resonance between what was said in the scriptural texts and what is now encountered in the Jesus event. Some of these associations are more creative than others. For example, Matthew amends—reverses even—its Mic 5.2 citation (Matt 2.6) to reshape the portrayal of Bethlehem, and the attribution of fulfillment to Hos 11.1 (Matt 2.15) is likewise hermeneutically innovative. Equally, unpacking the Jer 31.15 citation (Matt 2.18) is a notoriously complex task, and one must set one's interpretative lens widely to assess how Matthew might perceive it being fulfilled.[17] However, the *status* or ontology of the received text is not changed by Matthew, or at least the emphasis remains on the Jesus event and on the accompanying fulfillment that is occasioned or happens therein. Either way, and even taking Matt 5.17 into account, Matthew remains unconcerned, ambivalent even, about the implications for the ontological status of the antecedent texts. John, then, is distinctive for the specific focus it places on the fulfillment of Scripture *qua*-Scripture, and for the interpretative outworking that entails. And in particular, it associates such explicit fulfillment with the moment of Jesus's death; the rhetorical play on finishing (the *tel*-language of 19.28, 30) serves to underscore the association.

Let us turn then again to the testimony of John 19.28, and to the crux issue of the τελειωθῇ claim. Jesus's knowledge that "all is finished" (19.28) heightens the narrative moment, and anticipates some form of completion—or τέλος—to Jesus's work and ministry. Jesus announces such completion (τετέλεσται—19.30) after drinking the proffered wine, and then gives up his spirit (or Spirit) and dies (19.30). The specific verbal usage to express the fulfillment action—the shift from πληρόω (19.24) to τελειόω (19.28)—accentuates this, presenting 19.28–30 as effectively the climax of the Gospel account, and evidenced as such by the macro-fulfillment of Scripture. The τελειόω form therefore seemingly represents an upgrade from or heightening of the previous πληρόω usage.[18] In view of such linguistic heightening, its juxtaposition between the two τετέλεσται appeals (19.28–30), and their resonance with the end or goal of Jesus's work (τέλος—13.1), τελειωθῇ surely bears a significant interpretative burden in assessing the overall impact of John's use of Scripture. Some manuscripts still render πληρόω in 19.28, but on *lectio difficilior* reasons, τελειόω is surely the most likely—and evocative—reading. What then is the significance of 19.28's τελειόω claim? What is distinctive about it?

For a start, the verbal usage does seem deliberate and/or effective on John's part. Chennattu, for example, points to a potential chiasm operative within 19.24–36, or at least a verbal patterning that underscores the centrality of the 19.28b claim:

A) 19.24—πληρόω
 B) 19.28a—τελέω
  C) 19.28b—τελειόω
 B') 19.30—τελέω
A') 19.36—πληρόω[19]

This serves, at a literary level at least, to direct attention to the specific choice of τελειόω, and to place 19.28b at the very heart of the Passion Narrative's claims for "completion" in terms of Jesus's death. And alongside the differentiation of τελειωθῇ, its resonance with τελέω, of which is it likely a cognate form, further acknowledges the distinctiveness of Jesus's self-controlled death. It evinces something different to mere (πληρόω-type) fulfillment (important as that concept is), either going beyond its claims, or simply implying something ontologically different and with much greater significance. After all, John's Passion Narrative still anticipates *subsequent* fulfillment of individual scriptural texts, and necessarily/significantly so (19.36–37). The latter passage still serves to function as an *inclusio* with 12.38–40, and remains in broad continuity with the preceding fulfillment discourse. John 19.28 (and 19.28–30 as a unit) has therefore completed something, but it hasn't *completely* completed Scripture, at least not in terms of ending Scripture's πληρωθῇ capacity or vocation. Instead, John 19.28 seems to be drawing out something different, tying something more explicit to the outcome of Jesus's death. That is, at his mortem moment, the combined *telos* of Jesus's mission and that of Scripture is achieved. Quite simply, τελειόω is to be understood and rendered *differently* to πληρόω.[20]

If τελειόω is distinct from πληρόω, how does it relate to τελέω (19.28)? Are they broadly synonymous terms, with the invocation of τελειόω at the critical moment being merely stylistic variation from τελέω and/or reinforcing the essential *telos* conception of the mortem event? Some have ventured as such, and, of course, the phonetic resonance of the *tel-* moment explicitly associates the teleiosis of Scripture with Jesus's pronouncement and action (19.28, 30). There is good, rhetorical basis for the lexical similarity. But at the same time, such auditory correspondence need not imply synonymity or equivalence; that is, we suggest the evangelist's usage of τελειόω is specific and does more than merely restate the completion implied by τελέω. Teleiosis is at least fulfillment or completion, but its referent for John's Passion Narrative, we argue, goes beyond that, beyond merely pronouncing on the completion of the task. It also ascribes a qualitative dimension to that achievement. It denotes the impact of the task's completion, rather than just that "it is finished." The verbs are clearly related, but in terms of their 19.28–30 function, their respective meanings are somewhat different; for τελειόω, "the focus is on making perfect, and in the case of τελέω on the idea of ending, finishing."[21] To put it more bluntly, τελειόω is more than fulfillment, more even than completion. Jesus's *tetelestai* of his task generates a related—but ontologically distinct—"teleiosis" of Scripture.

How is this distinctiveness outworked and how then might one best render τελειόω? Bearing in mind the significance of the verbal idea in 19.28, clarity as to implied meaning and function would seem imperative, even if that is not an easy assessment to make.[22] John has used τελειόω four times previously (John 4.34, 5.36, 17.4, 17.23), and in each instance, it is applied to the teleiosis of the divine vocation with which Jesus has been charged. Its use in 19.28 is both similar to and distinct from such previous instances. On the one hand, as we have suggested, its proximity to John's τετέλεσται language, and its location specifically in respect of Jesus's death, vicariously juxtaposes it with the completion of the paternally prescribed vocation, and underscores the way in which Jesus's death forms the *telos* of that task. As Brown succinctly surmises: "John relates the finishing of Jesus's work and life to the completion of God's preordained plan given in Scripture."[23] But on the other hand, key differences exist between 19.28 and the previous Johannine examples. John 17.23 is the only other instance where, like 19.28, the passive voice is used. In the other three cases, Jesus is the active agent of the *teleiosis*, but 17.23 addresses its effect on the disciples, and 19.28 on Scripture. Use of the passive voice might therefore be the means by which the reader's attention is drawn to assess the outcome of the teleiosis, rather than merely to confirm that it has "happened."

What kind of teleiosis, then, does 17.23 anticipate? It expresses the unity of Father-Son-Disciples, and raises its status to the goal of perfection, something akin almost to *theosis*. It attests to the essence or internal character of the completion process, not merely the fact that it has happened. Hence one suggests that 19.28 might warrant a similar sense in terms of the *teleiosis* of the Scriptures; yes, the task/goal or function of the Scriptures is fulfilled in terms of their anticipation of the death of Jesus (and that is entirely consistent with John's christological hermeneutic). But equally it extends beyond that, manifesting a more qualitative assessment, a maturing, a coming of age, so to speak. We might therefore say that the teleiosis of John 19.28 incorporates two integral dimensions—completion and change.

Teleiosis as Completion

As a minimum, and in accordance with its τελέω cognate, τελειόω denotes the completion of the prescribed task. In this way, teleiosis mirrors the fulfillment demonstrated by John's prior (and subsequent) πληρόω claims, and hence the nature of what such fulfillment implies. But it does so in representative fashion, capturing the essence of the *whole* of Scripture as ultimately fulfilled by Jesus. Scripture is not the only thing to which John ascribes christological fulfillment; it is also attributed to concepts such as the Temple (2.19–22),[24] or the true vine (15.1) perhaps. But in none of these is the fulfillment dimension expressed so explicitly. How is such completion outworked? In terms of the Janus character of 19.28, it functions looking both backward and forward:

Looking Backward

As noted in chapter 2, some commentators propose that τελειόω functions in respect only of 19.28a and excludes reference to Jesus's actions in 19.28b–30. This demarks the overall effect of Jesus's death as that which demonstrates scriptural fulfillment. Such an assessment of scriptural teleiosis is valid, and rightly underscores the christological function and purpose John sees as intrinsic to the Scriptures of Israel. It draws attention to the burden and purpose of the Scriptures in service of christological vindication. The Scriptures find their *telos* in the completion of the christological task—their vocation is that of the Word. Chennattu asserts with similar focus, drawing attention to the way in which the John's purposes are telicly aligned with those of Scripture: "The fourth evangelist aims at convincing his readers that in Jesus Christ one can find the definitive fulfillment of the christological prophecy of the entire Scripture."[25] John's Passion account inextricably combines the fulfillment of Scripture with the fulfillment of Jesus's salvific work—"in the very moment of Jesus's death, both fulfillments find their realization."[26] Even if the scriptural teleiosis of 19.28 is unrelated to Jesus's subsequent thirsty declaration, it nonetheless still underscores, strengthens even, the association between Jesus's Passion as the completion of his life/ministry (τετέλεσται—19.28) and its outworking as scriptural fulfillment.[27]

Looking Forward

But as we have seen, τελειωθῇ also refers to what follows it—the appeal to Jesus's thirst (διψῶ) and the explicit fulfillment of the quotation he voices (Ps 69.3). We might further suggest, therefore, that the fulfillment introductory formula functions not just in terms of the succeeding scriptural lemma, but extends to the subsequent actions Jesus's utterance yields, namely the offering of the wine and Jesus's drinking of it. The latter occasions the climactic τετέλεσται declaration, signalling both the completion of Jesus's work (cf. 4.34, 5.36) and the simultaneous "finishing" of Scripture. That is, in 19.28–30, the entirety of Scripture is fulfilled or completed in/through Jesus's *action*, with Jesus himself dictating the moment of completion. Scripture speaks of/to Jesus and his purposes, and Jesus's exalted death brings to completion the goal or *telos* of Scripture's function. And critically, it is Jesus himself enacting that teleiosis. Avowing that the ἵνα clause of

19.28 addresses both διψῶ and πάντα τετέλεσται, Obermann concludes: "die Schrift kommt als Ganze zu ihrem τέλος im umfassenden Sinn von 'Ziel' und 'Ende.' Mit der Verwirklichung (dem 'Zum-Ziel- Kommen') des Heilswillens Gottes kommen auch die Verheißungen der Schrift zu ihrem Ziel im Sinne einer Vollendung."[28] The combination of both elements—the macro and the micro—are effectively mutually informing, and so "beschreibt . . . den Zielpunkt des Evangeliums schlechthin: Gottes Werk ist vollende."[29]

Tabb arrives at not dissimilar conclusions, though does so by different means. He ventures that the fulfillment of Scripture is achieved by Jesus's *conscious* fulfillment of Psalm 69; Jesus "willingly drinks the Father's cup of judgment (18.11) and it is precisely in his death that he provides the gift of the Spirit (19.30) to slake believers' thirst (7.37–39)."[30] The τελειόω fulfillment language resonates with the completion imagery elsewhere in the Fourth Gospel, particularly Jesus's task to make his followers completely one (τελειόω—17.23). Such fulfillment is done through the agency of Psalm 69, however; the Psalm bears the burden in representative fashion, and enables the combined intertextual-intratextual exchange. John 19.28 thereby carries a pivotal role for explicating Scripture's vocation, namely how the latter is ultimately in service of christological fulfillment. For the Fourth Evangelist, Scripture has been tasked with this goal, and the τελειόω claim encapsulates it, bringing to a focused, nuanced climax the previous πληρόω fulfillment. The events of the Passion, and particularly the actions of 19.28–30, are "divinely revealed scriptural events that are unfolding according to divine purpose. It is more than simply that they have 'fulfilled scriptural prophecies,' but that the events themselves to which they refer—and by extension all of the events of the passion section—are depicted as fulfilling divine purpose and revelation."[31]

With the declarative statement of 19.28, the Fourth Gospel's fulfillment motif therefore reaches its zenith. The concept has been premeditated and signalled by the previous πληρόω quotations, but the fulfillment remains anticipatory until its actualization in the moment of Jesus's death. We suggest, therefore, that, as it is avowedly the narrative of Jesus's death, the *entire* Passion account is—in and of itself—"fulfilling" Scripture; John's Passion Narrative actively "encapsulates" or enacts such fulfillment. The individual fulfillment texts alluded to previously find their *telos* through its narrated action. John 13.18 is a case in point. It announces an impending betrayal or raising of the heel against Jesus, and may implicitly identify Judas as the agent in this regard. But 13.19 is clear that the citation of the Psalm is anticipatory; it is/will be fulfilled, but it still awaits that fulfillment moment. John 19.28–30, with its combination of scriptural teleiosis and Jesus's *tetelestai* cry, provides the pivotal point for the fulfillment realization.

Christological Fulfillment

Whatever Scripture's macro-fulfillment encapsulates, for the Fourth Gospel, it is fundamentally christological in orientation. As Thompson opines: "John does not draw scriptural texts into his narrative as much as pull the person and narrative of Jesus back into the Scriptures."[32] Consider 19.37 as a case in point. It is not that the Fourth Gospel merely finds a correspondence or parallel between the piercing of Jesus's side and the Zechariah testimony. It remains at least that, of course, the different verbal forms in 19.34 and 19.37 notwithstanding, but the relationship is far more profound. That is, the piercing of Jesus's side "realizes" Zech 12.10, it encapsulates and embodies it. Such realization, such actualization, such fulfillment action is more than mere testimony or witness; it underlines Jesus's authority and ultimately legitimates Jesus's actions. As we noted in chapter 2, John's interest in 19.34/19.37 attends more to what comes out from Jesus's side than from the piercing action itself. The evangelist focuses on what Jesus himself visually displays, reinforcing the notion that Jesus is the one actuating Scripture's fulfillment, even in his postmortem state. And such fulfillment equally extends to what is *not* said about Jesus's death. As we have noted, John's Passion makes no reference, for example, to any pain Jesus endured. The soldiers participate in the fulfillment, of course, but do so vicariously, and under the ultimate authority of Jesus. And the same may be said for the reader too, as the one who is led to belief through what they "see" of the pierced Jesus (19.37; cf. 20.31). In that sense too, the audience's faithful response to the Fourth Gospel's christological purpose is also "in itself part of the ongoing fulfillment of Scripture."[33]

Several further points may be made in respect of this christologically focused fulfillment. First, the sheer brevity of the 19.28 statement warrants comment. With the whole scope of scriptural testimony plausibly available to John, the *telos* moment comes not from extended theological justification to that effect, but rather from a sharp, pithy statement in respect of Jesus's physical need. It seems somewhat appropriate that the pinnacle of the journey to Scripture's fulfillment comes with such brevity and precision, thereby commending Jesus's absolute capacity to pronounce on such fulfillment. John's Jesus is *consciously* fulfilling Scripture, consciously seeking after its fulfillment, and controlling events accordingly. Second, although, as we have observed, Jesus's thirst is more likely occasioned by the need for *scriptural* fulfillment, it remains the case that such thirst appears to be of a physical nature, hence the offer of the ὄξος. John associates the achievement of scriptural teleiosis not just with Jesus's divine nature, but, at this specific moment, with his humanity. The διψῶ declaration expresses fleshly need, and the attentive reader might hear accompanying intratextual resonances of John 1.14.

Third, scriptural fulfillment is not demonstrated by an unquestioned, explicit Scripture citation to that effect; or at least it is presented in a textual form not obviously recognizable as a verbatim quotation. One word bears a weighty burden on behalf of the totality of Scripture. We tentatively suggest that such formatting points to fulfillment being more than just text or word, important as those aspects or dimensions are. Rather, the "inexact" citation represents what we might call the very essence of Scripture, a more ontological appeal to its very nature.

Fourth, and perhaps most significantly, the fulfillment statement is voiced by Jesus himself as the first-person subject of the action. Jesus has implicitly "voiced" previous citations—notably 19.24—but such incidences do not require Jesus to "do" the specified activity. Particularly when, as we shall see, the very words of Jesus likewise assume scriptural status (or more maybe, that Scripture has become equivalent in status/authority to Jesus's words—a "pulling up" of Scripture's status), we demonstrably have Jesus speaking a (non-specific) citation such that it somehow "becomes" Scripture, and assumes the full weight of scriptural authority accordingly. This is not to deny that 19.28 is, in some form, a scriptural quotation, as we discussed in chapter 2. But rather, it is to draw attention to the paradoxical nature of διψῶ (19.28), that it can be both "Scripture" and "made even more Scripture" through Jesus's authoritative, christological declaration.

One further textual example seems pertinent in this regard. Although technically outside of our Passion Narrative scope, we suggest that the gift of the Paraclete in 20.22 is integrally linked to the fulfillment achievement claimed within 19.28–30. The lack of explicit scriptural warrant for 20.22 is striking—it receives neither γραφή confirmation nor any particular indication that the event is the intratextual climax for the Fourth Gospel. The gift just "happens," and its narrative context is somewhat muted bearing in mind the prior climactic teleiosis claims of 19.28–30. Of course, the Gen 2.7 resonances in John 20.22 are prominent, and important for underscoring Jesus's divine/creator credentials, but these are allusive rather than explicitly signalled. The precise, climactic fulfillment reference one might have expected from 20.22 remains noticeably absent. In the light of such signalled scriptural lacuna, we suggest that 19.28–30 bears that function by extension. The gift of the Spirit is both that which enables the ongoing/future work of Jesus, and also that which is anticipated by the actions of 19.30. Jesus's τετέλεσται cry inaugurates the proleptic fulfillment of the gift of 20.22 (with Jesus the agent of both actions). John 19.30 is the scripturally sourced "fulfillment" of the gift of the Paraclete, and hence the Fourth Gospel needs no further scriptural appeal within the 20.19–23 discourse.

Why so? First, John describes Jesus's death as the giving up (παραδίδωμι) of his s/Spirit (πνεῦμα). The juxtaposition of the handing over of his/the Spirit, at the very, self-identified moment when all is done and Scripture fulfilled, ties the gift of the Paraclete into the process of scriptural fulfillment. Commentators have commonly assessed the pneumatological aspects of 19.30, and its relationship to the (subsequent) gift of the Spirit-Paraclete (20.22), and it is fair to say that they arrive at contrasting conclusions.[34] Although it is initially tempting to associate 19.30 and 20.22, there is no explicit linkage between the two events, and 19.30 may be merely similar vocabulary and nothing more. But at the same time, 19.30 is the sole Johannine instance of Jesus as the agent of παραδίδωμι (even if, as we suggested in the previous chapter, the Fourth Gospel draws on the παραδίδωμι imagery of Isa 53.12 and intertextually applies it to Jesus). Bearing in mind the rhetorical significance of παραδίδωμι across the Passion Narrative, whether in respect of Judas (18.2, 18.5), Pilate (18.16) or the Jews (18.30, 18.35), Jesus's (sole) action of the verbal idea seems somewhat suggestive. The handing over (παραδίδωμι) of the Spirit accompanies and marks the completion of Jesus's own, self-enacted handover (παραδίδωμι).[35]

Second, the Spirit-Paraclete is the one who will remind the disciples of what Jesus had said (14.26), and lead them into all truth (16.13), and, as the ongoing presence of Jesus with the disciples, enables the ongoing efficacy of their work. Because of the teleiosis/completion of his own scripturally endorsed task, Jesus can hand over (παραδίδωμι) the Spirit. But the work/function of the Paraclete can only be initiated once the Scriptures which point to Jesus are fulfilled, and as Jesus pronounces on their teleiosis. The gift of the Paraclete is therefore tied to the fate of the Scriptures, its function inextricably linked with their post-teleiosis status.[36] The Paraclete continues the work of Jesus, the one to whom Scripture points, and who pronounces authoritatively as to their fulfillment. And if Jesus's words are to assume scriptural status (as we shall suggest in chapter 5), and if the Paraclete is to remind the disciples of what Jesus has said (14.26), then the Paraclete's testimony bears effective γραφή authority by extension.

The prevailing christological fulfillment focus reinforces the notion that, for the Fourth Gospel, the Scriptures are ultimately about Jesus.[37] Simply put, Scripture is in service of Jesus. And the Passion Narrative's appeal to Israel's Scriptures personifies that principle. Hays assesses John's scriptural perspective precisely on that basis, concluding: "John summons the reader to recognize the way in which *Israel's Scripture has always been mysteriously suffused with the presence of Jesus*, the figure who steps clearly into the light in the Gospel narrative."[38] Suzanne Luther contends likewise:

The quotations present Jesus's crucifixion and death as events that are predetermined by Scripture. In the Johannine narrative, they become events in space and time as the concretization and fulfillment of Scripture. Thus, in the perception of those standing under the cross as well as of the reader, Scripture comes to pass.[39]

The "what" and the "why" of the Fourth Gospel's concern for scriptural fulfillment are thus integrally connected. Because the Scriptures ultimately speak of Jesus, their christological outworking necessarily leads to their fulfillment. John's Passion discourse engages with the very concept of Scripture, with its very DNA; scriptural texts are more than just mere ingredients for christological fulfillment, their very essence is integral to John's narration. What Scripture *is*, and what it becomes in the light of Jesus's death, is indelibly tied to John's Passion retelling.

And vice versa, we might say, as the process is dialogical and mutually informing. Scripture is (supremely) fulfilled by the Christ-event, and specifically Jesus's death. The latter unveils Scripture's very purpose, and Scripture's character and status are impacted by the process. But at the same time, John's portrayal of Jesus is fulfilled, demonstrated, conditioned even, by Scripture and the Fourth Gospel's scriptural hermeneutic. It is not that Scripture "governs" Jesus—the reverse is surely the case—but Scripture's "assent" to Jesus and his death is a necessary prerequisite for the Fourth Gospel (and its implied audience). A Christology lacking profound scriptural fulfillment or integrity could not possibly be a Johannine Christology.

This begs the question, though, as to what John means by "Scripture." What is within the purview of ἡ γραφή? One must, of course, recognize that Scripture is itself a slippery term. It is not yet a canonical body of texts, nor a fixed constituency in that regard,[40] and the precise contours of what comprised ἡ γραφή for John is not clear. Likewise, as the extensive work on the Fourth Gospel's quotational *Vorlage* shows, textual pluriformity and fluidity meant the evangelist could draw on and rework scriptural texts for kerygmatic purposes, and do so without undermining their authority or authenticity.[41] But at the same time, even if the Hebrew canon was not yet closed, there is still a broad textual tradition to which John attributes the term "Scripture." The Fourth Gospel is still speaking of *something*—and something really quite important—when it makes scriptural connections or association. The glass is surely more than half full, even if it is not completely so, and ἡ γραφή represents a portfolio of material whose individual elements and corporate identity ascribe it status and authority *as Scripture*, and capable of offering testimony to Jesus accordingly. Indeed, one might even suggest that, in view of the Fourth Gospel's suffusive christological lens, it is a text's capacity to attest to Jesus that actually qualifies or accredits it as *Scripture*. And of course, for evangelistic communication to fruitfully occur, what the Fourth Gospel designates as ἡ γραφή must have been broadly recognized as such (in terms of textual form and authority) by its interlocutors.[42]

In our discussion of the Passion Narrative's quotational usage, we reviewed the question of whether John is interested more in the fulfillment of Scripture as a whole, rather than in that of individual passages or texts. We suggested that both aspects were at play, both fulfillment *qua*-Scripture and fulfillment *qua*-text, but the former has tended to become the default perspective in Johannine scholarship, and not without some justification. Hengel rightly notes that γραφή is generally in the singular,[43] perhaps indicative of the inherent unity of Scripture (and that accords with other one-ness or unbroken-ness images of the Fourth Gospel, such as Jesus's body or the net of 21.11).[44] The way in which John embeds scriptural allusion across the warp and woof of its account, the more limited appeal to direct quotation (at least compared to the Synoptic accounts), the limited identification of a citation's location, and particularly just the very deliberate, specific use of the γραφή term is indicative of this. Generally speaking, it does seem to be the status of a text *qua*-Scripture that generates the evangelist's interest. Ed Gerber opines: "it is clear from the *prima facie* evidence that the FE was directly engaged with the 'whole' story of scripture, as it interacts with the 'whole' story of Jesus."[45] The *telos* of Jesus's mission and *telos* of (the essence of the whole of) Scripture are in dialogical interplay.

But at the same time, as we concluded in chapter 2, it remains critical that the Fourth Gospel invokes individual passages of Scripture, and that the particular context of those texts "matter" for John, if only so that the necessary intertextual baggage might accompany the citation. Whether it is Psalm 22 or Psalm 69, Isaiah 53 or Zechariah 12–13, their constituent imagery and foreshadowing are integral to John's argument. Although the citation in John 19.36, for instance, is merely identified as ἡ γραφή (i.e., undefined and singular), we have argued that its usage necessarily requires attention to its plurality/compositeness and to its defined remit in terms of the Passover Lamb, the Righteous Sufferer and the Isaianic Servant. The very complexity and multiplicity of the Johannine quotations,[46] and the degree to which they invite ongoing examination and consideration, warrants against limiting John's conception of γραφή—and its fulfillment—to merely undefined or general terms. The Fourth Gospel can find scriptural fulfillment both in the general *and* in the specific, and in ways that are mutually informing and complementary. Scripture is therefore both a micro and macro entity, both the full picture and the proverbial jigsaw pieces of which it is composed.

Moreover, the composite nature of the quotations/allusions within John's Passion Narrative contributes to the increased status and capacity for Scripture. Of course, other NT authors and Second Temple interpreters utilize this mode of bringing together scriptural texts—John is far from unique in this regard. But at the same time, it is notable that such combination or composition comes to a fore at a key—the key—point in the Fourth Gospel's Passion retelling (19.36–37), so as to evince the Passover/sufferer perspectives of the Passion Narrative. Scripture is 'able' to do this, is capable of doing so; by association with Jesus, its *multiple* voices are combined, and the assembled scriptural choir is able to address Jesus in this way. To pursue the choral imagery further, John's Passion Narrative's scriptural offering invokes solos, duets and trios, as well as performances of the whole choir, as different elements of Scripture are combined together for kerygmatic effect.

Teleiosis as Change

Scripture's fulfillment of its christologically orientated task does not leave it unaffected by the experience. There is a qualitative dimension to the teleiosis of Scripture; it is *changed* by/through the process. It is part of Jesus's "work" to engage Israel's Scriptures; the teleiosis of the divine charge is inextricably linked, comprises even, the teleiosis of Scripture itself. But rather than—as some have suggested—scriptural teleiosis effectively yielding its redundancy or retirement,[47] we venture that the argument of the second half of the Gospel renders its fate in more positive terms. It is not that John's christological hermeneutic has ended Scripture's role or function, nor reduced its efficacy, but rather, the Passion Narrative raises the authority of the text higher, advancing its reputation. Scripture is pulled *up*—rather than pulled down—by its encounter with the Johannine Jesus. Because their fulfillment is inextricably linked with his exaltation and with the completion of the divine charge undertaken by the Word becoming flesh, the Scriptures are vindicated, brought to their maturity. Jesus's death therefore does not signal the end or demise of the Scriptures, but rather their very moment, their very coming of age, their renewal rather than their end. Rather than merely offering a prophetic forward-looking orientation, or testimonial function in respect of Jesus, the Scriptures are now present in a new way. Rather than being what was said (1.23) or written (6.51), indicative perhaps of a restricted or background function, they now *speak*, actively, and in the present (cf. 19.37).[48]

To put it another way, it is only through the death (and resurrection) of Jesus that the essence and role of the Scriptures come properly to the fore and are fully understood. This is partly operative in narrative terms, through the intensification of scriptural citation and imagery found within John's Passion Narrative, and in the crucifixion scene in particular. This is Scripture's "moment," its *telos*, the point in the John's narration when quotational fulfillment is voiced most loudly, and when the Fourth Gospel's exploration of scriptural images such as creation or Passover comes to the fore. But it is also manifest in temporal fashion. John is clear that the meaning and interpretation of the Scriptures was a post-Easter phenomenon; the disciples generally do not understand the (unspecified) Scripture regarding Jesus's resurrection (20.9) and they remember and re-understand Jesus's citation in the light of Jesus.[49] And it is not just the meaning of the Scriptures that has been impacted by the Passion, it is their very essence, their very being. To this end, we suggest that a better rendering for τελειόω might be "perfected"[50]—that is, not just functional characterization in terms of a role achieved and fulfilled (though that is of course absolutely foundational for John), but also a qualitative statement as a new status assumed by the Jewish Scriptures in the light of Jesus's death. How might this be so?

At the risk of getting into historical testimony, it is likely that the final, written form of the gospel postdates the fall of the Temple.[51] John inextricably links the fate of the Temple with Jesus—indeed 2.17 may be suggested as a programmatic statement for the gospel's purpose, particularly for how it relates the Temple and Jesus's bodily resurrection (2.18–21). Another text inextricably tied to the fate of the Temple is the Epistle to the Hebrews, and one wonders whether there are some helpful parallels between the Fourth Gospel and Hebrews at this point, particularly in their respective positions on teleiosis. We might say that John and Hebrews are on same page in terms of the crucifixion scene—their focus on Jesus's death and self-offering, the backdrop of Psalm 22, and the language of teleiosis/perfection being found in both texts.[52] For Hebrews, perfection is the goal of the divine salvation project and is made possible by Jesus's sufferings (2.10); the law could not achieve such perfection (Heb 7.19) nor could sacrifice (Heb 10.1). Only Christ's offering can ultimately achieve perfection (Heb 10.14). Jesus is both perfected by his cruciform suffering (Heb 2.10, 5.9, 7.28) and also the one who perfects the faithfulness of others (Heb 12.2). There is a parallel with John perhaps too in that Hebrews' *Beispielreihen* are paraded before the reader, and affirmed for their faithful actions, but still await "perfection" (Heb 11.39–40). And such perfection does not mean an end to their activity; the righteous spirits made perfect now hold authority and significance, but in a qualitatively different role. Perfection is thus an "outcome"—it is an end game, but not an *end*.

But perhaps the most significant aspect of Hebrews' portrayal of teleiosis is the fact that Jesus the high priest was himself perfected (τελειωθείς—5.9), with such teleiosis taking place during his suffering and cruciform death. Such teleiosis did not indicate that his previous state was deficient or incomplete, nor that something was missing; Hebrews' Jesus is the precise imprint of God's very being (Heb 1.3). Rather perfection is the process of coming of age, of reaching one's vocational purpose. Perfection does not mean an end to work or function, or to completion in that sense; rather, perfection is forward-looking, a necessary status or preparation for the forthcoming task. It is both function *and* quality; and it is the perfected Jesus, the perfected high priest, who enters into the heavenly arena (Heb 9.24). And there is still work to be done *post*-perfection, or on the basis of the perfected state having been achieved.[53]

To what extent does Hebrews' perspective on teleiosis matter for the Fourth Gospel? Once Scripture is fulfilled, once it has undergone teleiosis, once it has reached its *telos* or purpose in terms of the revelation of Jesus's identity and mission, does the Johannine evangelist ascribe it any further, ongoing function? If John and Hebrews are on common ground, then the implications of this are significant. Rather than their perfection being the end of their role or function, the converse is the case. Scripture—in its perfected state—is now prepared for further work and business. It is "job to do" as well as "job done." The same may be said for the teleiosis of 17.23, and the unity of Father, Son and believer(s); rather than this merely signalling an end or completion of the task, it sets forth a new life, a new way of being, a new overall "oneness."

It is possible, of course, that the Fourth Gospel differs from Hebrews, and teleiosis relegates Scripture, and/or denudes its authority, and some commentators have come to that conclusion. For Jaime Clark-Soles, the testimony of the Fourth Gospel deems that Scripture no longer has power or authority;[54] once someone "believes," there is no concept of Scripture left, as its role has effectively been fulfilled. Scripture remains a witness, but no more than that; its "completion" in John's Passion ends up reverting it back to the former testimonial function operative in the first half of the gospel. The arrival of Jesus has divested Scripture of its "remaining power";[55] its proverbial day is done. The absence of formal quotation in the resurrection accounts—chapters 20 and 21—might be said to point in this direction, and it is certainly the case that Scripture's character is "different" here, likely because of the prior *teleiosis*. But equally Scripture is not absent from the resurrection accounts, quite the reverse. There is still some aspect of scriptural warrant in that (20.9), and importantly so. Scripture—in some form—anticipates the resurrection, and likewise, the (belated) understanding testifies to Scripture having ongoing function beyond even the resurrection (cf. also 2.22). Sheridan hence points to 20.9 as primary evidence of the ongoing impact of scriptural interest and fulfillment—Scripture's efficacy is far from done.[56] The ongoing fulfillment testimony of 19.36–37 likewise accords with such an assessment. Post-teleiosis, Scripture still speaks; 19.37 renders a present tense (λέγει), indicative of ongoing, continuous action, suggestive of Scripture actually *increasing* in status, rather than it being lost or silenced.

In contrast, Moloney comes close to affirming a renewed status for Scripture in the light of its christological fulfillment. Recognizing the double meaning present within τελειόω—conveying both the "end" moment and the perfect completion of the task—he contends that the Scriptures have been brought "to their 'perfect end,' their *telos*."⁵⁷ Such a change or development sounds positive—"perfect" even—and seems to ascribe a qualitative (i.e., perfect) dimension to the task's achievement." But one suggests the verdict still remains limited. That is, Moloney's characterization retains the terminology of "perfect end"; even with the language of "perfect," the focus is still—at least in Anglophone terms—on Scripture's "end." It implies a terminus to their operation, albeit an excellent one, and leads to the conclusion that, having come to their perfect fulfillment, Scripture's role comes to a finish.

Hence neither assessment—Clark-Soles nor Moloney—quite does justice to the perfection implied by τελειόω, particularly in the light of the Hebrews' comparison, and limits the qualitative, christologically authorized change the Fourth Gospel ascribes to Israel's Scriptures. Of course, it is right to associate Scripture with the end or *telos* of the christological task, and their critical role in achieving that. But at the same time, it is to confuse their identity with their task, and/or overlook their distinction in that light. The teleiosis of Scripture, its inherent perfection, does not signal an end to the role/function of Scripture, but instead enables Scripture to function with new authority. Jesus does not replace the Scriptures in John's eyes; they may function in his service, but "replacement" is the wrong language to use. The Scriptures become even more part of the divine w/Word, are brought even further into the divine identity. It may be an argument from silence, but it is notable how Jesus's τετέλεσται claim (19.30) does not receive scriptural fulfillment designation (that is left instead to the διψῶ claim). Jesus says two things on the cross, but the evangelist only relates one—his thirst—specifically to scriptural fulfillment. This likely derives from John's desire to distinguish between the fulfillment of the task and the fulfillment of the Scripture. The two concepts are inextricably linked, but, in typical Johannine paradoxical character, they are also *dis*associated, so to avoid the implications of finality in respect of the Scriptures. Jesus's work is finished. But the Scriptures are not. Their work is only beginning, as, in their perfected state, they operate under new measures.

How does this sit, then, with the evangelist's characterization of Scripture as unable to be annulled or broken (λυθῆναι—10.35)? One suggests it fits it very well. Although the Passion Narrative does not use λύω, the latter's implications remain prominent across John's account. Various elements remain unbroken, and critically so: Jesus's body (19.31–33, 19.36), Jesus's tunic (19.23–24), or the Johannine community (18.9—very different to Mark 14.27). In the same way, Scripture, in its perfected state, might similarly be characterized as unbroken. Indeed, the assertion of 10.35 may derive—with post-resurrection lenses—from the memory of Jesus's own cruciform unbrokenness. If the one whose death brought about the teleiosis of Scripture was unbroken, then such unbrokenness vicariously extends to Scripture itself, particularly when/as such Scripture both testifies to that unbrokenness (19.36) and is perfected (τελειόω—19.28) at that point. This would seem entirely conversant with the statement of 10.35 that Scripture is "everlasting in its authority and applicability"[58]—it is not "ended" by teleiosis, but rather its status is only enhanced.

Scripture—that is, ἡ γραφή—is thus to be distinguished from other similar terms in the Fourth Gospel because of the distinctive "upgrade" it receives. A particular case is νόμος, often treated (erroneously) as synonymous to γραφή.[59] John's Passion Narrative utilizes νόμος terminology when adjudicating on Jewish (in)ability to put someone to death (18.31) and for explicating the mortal fate that befalls someone claiming to be the Son of God (19.7). Although both claims are predicated on the testimony of Torah, John does not present them as *scripturally* endorsed claims; their context and premise are legal as opposed to scriptural (so also 7.19, 7.51, 8.5). Elsewhere, the Prologue seems to distance Jesus from the Law (1.17), or to use νόμος in more of an "othering" or differentiating sense. That is, νόμος becomes more polemical, pertaining to contested *interpretation* of the Law rather than just the Law as concept, an assessment of the implications of the scriptural/legal text (cf. 12.34), not the text itself. Jesus's reference to *your* (10.34) or *their* (15.25) Law (surely it is his Law too?) concern interpretative matters rather than those of internal authority.

John 15.25 is the case in point. Unlike the other fulfillment quotations either side of it (13.18, 19.24), 15.25's introductory formula announces the fulfillment (still πληρόω) of ὁ λόγος ὁ ἐν τῷ νόμῳ αὐτῶν—not Scripture, or at least not ἡ γραφή. The evangelist's choice of language is significant, one suggests, and distinguishes 15.25 from the other "scriptural" fulfillment discourse in which the Fourth Gospel is engaged.[60] Scripture is different from νόμος; it is γραφή, it is the Jewish entity that Jesus's death explicitly fulfills. It is true that John 15.25 still warrants fulfillment, of course, but it is not so directly linked with Jesus's Passion. Or it might provocatively suggest that his opponents' actions remain "according to the Law" rather than "according to the Scriptures," and/or are, by implication, *inimical* to Scripture. They have failed to understand how their own γραφή (Ps 69.4)[61] vindicates the righteous figure whom they oppose, and on that basis, they have effectively reduced the γραφή to (mere) νόμος. Such reduction is even more telling in view of Psalm 69's usage elsewhere in the Fourth Gospel. It is both the written γραφή that the disciples remember Jesus speaking in respect of the Temple clearance (2.17) and subsequently apply to his resurrection (2.22; 20.9), and, of course, it is the very phrase that Jesus "quotes" to pronounce the teleiosis of Scripture (19.28). Their reduction (i.e., to νόμος) of a Psalm so intrinsic to John's christological reading of Scripture, so tied to its portrayal of Jesus's death and resurrection, and the implied rejection of Jesus as Messiah, are thus mutually informing. Jaime Clark-Soles takes the argument further, contending that Jesus's opponents therefore become not law *breakers*—but rather law *fulfillers*.⁶² Scripture (and particularly its interpretation) thus ends up functioning as a marker of sectarian identity, of demarking those who properly understand its γραφή character.

The converse of νόμος fulfillment is also the case. Israel's νόμος cannot lead to Jesus's crucifixion—indeed, Jewish νόμος precluded Jews putting Jesus to death (18.31). One might say likewise of the Jews' invocation of Torah in John 19.7, where νόμος (perhaps Lev 24.16), rather than γραφή, is the basis for the petition. If the appeal were to γραφή, then it might follow that Scripture endorsed the claims of Lev 24.16 for Jesus's death, implying that Jesus was a blasphemer, something of course entirely inimical to the Johannine project. Hence John does not present the Jews pursuing a γραφή-driven argument. Their demand is instead premised on νόμος foundations, and contributes to the more ambivalent terms in which John portrays the Law. Torah can be queried or questioned by the Fourth Gospel (cf. 1.17), and/or be used to articulate misunderstanding or misuse of Scripture (cf. 15.25). This is not so for γραφή—the latter is effectively "holy writ."

JOHN AND SCRIPTURE— HERMENEUTICAL QUESTIONS

Let us briefly address one further, related matter. The Fourth Gospel's engagement with the concept of γραφή raises a question prominent within the broader study of the NT authors' use of Scripture, namely the degree to which their interpretation of the received text is essentially continuous with that found in its prior context.⁶³ When a NT author invokes a scriptural text, are they doing so such that they bring out its anticipated full meaning? Or, to put the counter view, is the original sense hidden from, or foreign to, the original authors, and/or only properly understood retrospectively by the NT authors "reading backwards" (to use Hays's titular label)? Moo and Naselli use the terms *sensus praegnans* and *sensus occultus* to distinguish between these contrasting perspectives,⁶⁴ and somewhat binary or dualistic arguments so ensue. Related theological questions also emerge, such as how God (the "author" of Scripture) might be heard in the process, or whether the meaning of the scriptural text can change—in a radical way—from its earlier context without undermining the text's theological integrity. It also has ramifications for the language we use here. Does the Johannine claim for the teleiosis of Scripture imply that the latter is somehow deficient or incomplete in its pre-Jesus state? Or is it suggestive—to the contrary—that Scripture is on a journey to a fuller sense or depth in the Johannine Passion, what is often termed a *sensus plenior*?

We might suggest that the Fourth Gospel resists such binary application. That is, just like 19.28 demonstrates *in nuce*, John appropriates a further Janus-style *modus operandi*, embracing both *"sensi"*:

- *Sensus occultus:* Scripture is completely re-worked in the light of the Christ-event. John's lens is fundamentally christological, and Jesus is the supreme interpreter of the Scriptures; they point to Jesus in ways that are purely christologically orientated—for example, Isaiah seeing and speaking of Jesus (12.41). Likewise the capacity for Jesus to be the agent of fulfillment, as the Passion Narrative attests; Jesus is the one controlling the fate and content of the scriptural testimony (19.28–30). Scripture's teleiosis is ironic, surprising, strange—challenging the portrayal that may be found in a scriptural text's prior form or context. Its re-orientation or re-presentation is not a parody, but it remains unexpected and unanticipated. This is not superseding or limiting Scripture's status, but it is at least transformational—scriptural images are viewed afresh or *differently* in the light of Johannine testimony.
- *Sensus praegnans:* But at the same time, the very essence of Scripture is upheld, fulfilled, perfected. The purpose of Scripture—as divine revelation—is set forth, and, as we have argued, reaches its zenith, its goal, within the Passion narration. It may be that the significance is hidden from the original human author (so in that sense some element of *sensus occultus* inevitably remains). But if, as we shall suggest in chapter 5, the Fourth Gospel is itself γραφή, the fate of Israel's Scripture is endorsed by Scripture itself. John's Passion Narrative offers a self-avowed, self-declared commentary on what Scripture is and does.

This is akin perhaps to the assessment of the Epistle to the Hebrews in respect of its explication of a New Covenant (cf. Heb 7–10). Just as with their respective perspectives on teleiosis, Hebrews and the Fourth Gospel are on common ground. Although the unpacking of the New Covenant is ultimately founded on the sacerdotal actions of Jesus the great high priest, and is avowedly christological in that sense, Hebrews appeals to Scripture's own *internal* testimony to new covenantal expectation (particularly Jer 31.31–34; Heb 8.7–13). Hebrews' hermeneutical approach is both continuity and change, old and new—*sensus occultus* AND *sensus praegnans*,[65] and the Fourth Gospel's scriptural appropriation is likewise dually-faceted.

CONCLUSION—THE STATUS OF SCRIPTURE IN THE PASSION NARRATIVE

Scripture—ἡ γραφὴ—is without doubt a prominent concept within the Fourth Gospel. The term occurs twelve times across the Gospel, the same amount of times in total across its three Synoptic counterparts.[66] It is the primary ingredient in terms of its contribution to John's kerygma, fundamental to its evangelistic enterprise, and specifically in respect of John's depiction of Jesus's death. But even more than this, Scripture's very identity is inextricably caught up with the portrayal of Jesus's Passion. As Michael Labahn concludes, Scripture "realizes its meaning by being understood in relation to the deeds and words of Jesus, which are recorded in John's Gospel and which lead to belief in Jesus as the God-sent son."[67]

To put it another way, existing "scripture" becomes "Scripture" in/through John's Passion retelling. In the light of the Johannine Jesus's Passion, the very conception and function of (existing) scripture is changed. It is not just completed—it is *perfected*, and undergoes an ontological process of teleiosis. It comes of age in the advent of Jesus's death, and its overall status and authority is increased rather than decreased. Rather than pronouncing the *end* to scriptural usage, its Johannine teleiosis advocates for ongoing consideration of Scripture's function. Because the whole of Scripture is fulfilled by Jesus (19.28), the reader is given encouragement to make other Jesus-Scripture connections, both in the Passion Narrative and across the rest of the Johannine account. The reader is invited to search the Scriptures (5.39) for further incidence of how they have been "perfected" or proved to speak to/for Jesus.

In short, the second element of our core thesis stands. Scripture is the heartbeat of John's Passion retelling, but that metaphorical heartbeat changes as a result of the encounter. The Fourth Gospel has brought a new type of heartbeat into being.

NOTES

1. We must note that it is not an absolute lacuna, and that several works have sought to explore in detail the Fourth Gospel's conception of Scripture. In particular, one notes the extensive discussion of John's scriptural understanding in Obermann, *Erfüllung*, or the various contributions of Francis Moloney, notably Francis J. Moloney, "The Gospel of John: The 'End' of Scripture," *Int* 63 (2009): 356–66. Our discussion builds particularly on their respective insights.

2. A. T. Hanson, "John's Use of Scripture," in *The Gospels and the Scriptures of Israel*, ed. Craig A. Evans and W. Richard Stegner (London: T&T Clark, 1994), 370.

3. Hanson, *Prophetic*, 245.

4. Lieu, "Narrative," 143. Cf. the similar assessment in Lieu, "Text and Authority in John and Apocalyptic," 247: "it is incontrovertible that John's conceptual and textual world is created by Scripture and by the refashioning of Scripture."

5. Cf. Coutts, "Exodus," 269: "John reads Israel's Scriptures explicitly in light of one dominant feature of his own context, namely the climactic event of Jesus."

6. Hence it is hard to accept Bultmann's contention that the Fourth Gospel "does not have a primary concern for proof from Scripture" (Bultmann, *John*, 671). He concedes that "occasionally he does give it [Scripture] room" (671), but the sheer abundance of scriptural appeal found in the Passion account, and the raising of intensity in terms of scriptural fulfillment, surely warrants against such a minimalistic assessment.

7. Brawley, "Absent," 433.

8. Hengel, "Old Testament," 33–34.

9. Sheridan, *Retelling*. We recognize that Sheridan uses "retelling" in a very particular sense, one that rightly draws attention to the rhetorical and ideological dimensions of the evangelist's re-narration of Scripture.

10. So Vistar Jr, *Cross-and-Resurrection*, 193: "The first thing to notice with the evangelist's understanding and portrayal of Jesus's death is the overwhelming emphasis on the fact that the crucifixion took place in explicit fulfillment of the Scriptures." John's focus on scriptural fulfillment is generally well recognized within scholarship, particularly in respect of its association with Jesus's death—cf. Moloney, "End," 356–366.; Brian J. Tabb, "Johannine Fulfillment of Scripture: Continuity and Escalation," *BBR* 21 (2011): 495–505; Tabb, "Thirst," 338–51.

11. We query whether either of these is the best translation for τελειόω in 19.28; see later.

12. Cf. the Mosaic (1.45; 5.45–46) or Isaianic (12.41) testimony to Jesus, for example.

13. Lieu, "Narrative," 154–55.

14. Obermann, *Erfüllung*, 93, 218.

15. Tabb, "Thirst," 340.

16. S. Vernon McCasland, "Matthew Twists the Scriptures," *JBL* 80 (1961): 143–48.

17. On such matters, see Steve Moyise, *Was the Birth of Jesus According to Scripture?* (London: SPCK, 2013).

18. Cf. Hengel, "Old Testament," 33: "Only here in the entire gospel does the Evangelist speak of a teleioun of the Scriptures, an increase over the previous formulaic pleroun, which expresses the 'ultimate fulfillment' of all christological prophecy in the Scriptures, which in turn reach their goal in the death of Jesus."

19. Chennattu, "Scripture," 179–80.

20. Obermann, *Erfüllung*, 88: "Gegenüber πληρόω ist daher bei τελειόω das Moment des Zieles und endgültigen Höhepunktes beton."

21. Kubiś, *Book of Zechariah*, 215.

22. Bampfylde, "John XIX 28," 252 rightly observes: "It is now plain that τελειόω is not easy to translate." He suggests "bring to fruition" as the best English translation,

but such a rendering lacks the qualitative and perfective aspects John 19.28 seems to imply.

23. Brown, *Gospel According to John*, 2.908—he points to similar examples of this in Acts 13.29 or Luke 22.37. Likewise Moloney, "End," 360: "the revelation of the glory of God in and through the death of Jesus, as told in the story of the Gospel of John, is the 'end,' the fulfillment, of the biblical story."

24. Paul M. Hoskins, *Jesus as the Fulfillment of the Temple in the Gospel of John* (Milton Keynes: Paternoster, 2006).

25. Chennattu, "Scripture," 178.

26. Kubiś, *Book of Zechariah*, 215.

27. Tabb, "Thirst," 340 rightly opines that the front-loading of the ἵνα clause and Jesus's knowledge that all was now finished, "accentuate[s] Jesus's conscious scriptural fulfillment."

28. Obermann, *Erfüllung*, 355–56.

29. Obermann, *Erfüllung*, 356.

30. Tabb, "Thirst," 351. He concludes: "According to the evangelist, Jesus declares his thirst in order consciously and willingly to bring the Scripture—Psalm 69 specifically but in some respects the entirety of the Old Testament—to its τέλος as a witness to him" (345–46).

31. Stanley E. Porter, "The Linguistic Function of Biblical Citations in John's Gospel," in *Biblical Interpretation in Early Christian Gospels. Volume 4: The Gospel of John*, ed. Thomas R. Hatina (Library of New Testament Studies, 613; London: T&T Clark, 2020), 136.

32. Marianne Meye Thompson, "Hearing Voices: Reading the Gospels in the Echo Chamber of Scripture," *JTI* 11 (2017): 45–46.

33. Polinski, *Scriptures*, 137.

34. For a positive assessment of the 19.30/20.22 association, see Moloney, *Gospel of John (Sp)*, 508–09; Bampfylde, "John XIX 28," 247–60; Zumstein, "Purpose," 345. For a more cautious one, cf. Sheridan, "Pierced," 191n2; Senior, *Passion in John*, 119: "The phrase 'hand over his spirit' . . . refers to the moment of death itself and the focus is on Jesus's return to God." In view of the "handing over" language of 19.30, and the accompanying fulfillment this occasions, one suggests the burden of proof lies with the negative assessment. *Pace* Sheridan/Senior, it would seem appropriately Johannine for s/Spirit to be a functional *double entendre*; the two concepts/senses are entirely complementary. The Spirit is to be given when Jesus is glorified (7.39), and this "completion" moment (19.30) and the lifting up it manifests (12.32–33) would seem to be the exemplary instance of Jesus's glorification. And to reduce 19.30 to *just* Jesus's enacting his death is to miss the force of the final statement—cf. Gary M. Burge, *The Anointed Community: The Holy Spirit in the Johannine Tradition* (Grand Rapids: Eerdmans, 1987), 134: "Nowhere in Greek literature is παραδίδωμι τὸ πνεῦμα used as a description of death."

35. The presence of Jesus's mother at the critical Spirit-παραδίδωμι moment, and her implied absence from the Pentecost scene of 20.22, ascribes further significance to 19.30's Paraclete-inaugurating status. Were there not some proleptic aspect to the handing of Jesus's s/Spirit, she would not be explicitly portrayed as in "receipt" of it.

36. Miller, "They Saw His Glory," 131 seems to arrive at a similar conclusion, but from a different starting point: "The true meaning of Scripture cannot be found within the text itself, but only in its fulfillment in Jesus and in the sending of the Spirit."

37. Cf. Thompson, "Hearing," 45–46: "John does not draw scriptural texts into his narrative as much as pull the person and narrative of Jesus back into the Scriptures."

38. Hays, *Echoes-Gospels*, 289.

39. Luther, "Authentication," 161.

40. On the formation of the Hebrew canon, see Timothy H. Lim, *The Formation of the Jewish Canon* (New Haven, CT: Yale University Press, 2013).

41. See also Sheridan, *Retelling*, 22–24.

42. So Schuchard, "Form Versus Function," 27n15: "the evangelist only cites those texts that both the synagogue and the earliest church of his day would have readily recognized as Scripture."

43. Hengel, "Old Testament," 28.

44. The exception is John 5.39—and that may pertain more to the interpretation that accompanies the Scriptures, rather than to ἡ γραφή *per se*.

45. Edward H. Gerber, *The Scriptural Tale in the Fourth Gospel: With Particular Reference to the Prologue and a Syncretic (Oral and Written) Poetics*, BibInt 147 (Leiden: Brill, 2017), 12–13.

46. As Hays, *Echoes-Gospels*, 284 observes, the quotations bear "proportionately greater gravity as a pointer to Jesus's identity."

47. Cf. Miller, "They Saw His Glory," 131: Scripture is "completed, superseded, and even replaced by the living words of Jesus."

48. This may parallel how John depicts the future of Israel's festivals. These are not said to "end" with Jesus. Instead, they find their true meaning in the light of the Christ-event, and become even more significant in this way. See further Wheaton, *Role*.

49. So Frey, *Glory*, 243: "It is the Johannine Easter experience that prompted the witnesses to recognize the glorified one in the crucified one."

50. So also Myers, *Characterizing Jesus*, 168n92, but she does not explore the significance of such a rendering.

51. See Kerr, *Temple*, who links it specifically to that event: "the Johannine Jesus replaces and fulfills the Jerusalem Temple and its cultic activity" (2).

52. On the concept of perfection in Hebrews, see David Peterson, *Hebrews and Perfection*, SNTSMS 47 (Cambridge, UK: Cambridge University Press, 1982).

53. See David M. Moffitt, "'If Another Priest Arises': Jesus' Resurrection and the High Priestly Christology of Hebrews," in *A Cloud of Witnesses: The Theology of Hebrews in Its Ancient Contexts*, ed. Richard Bauckham, et al. (London: Bloomsbury, 2008), 74–76.

54. Clark-Soles, *Scripture*, 323.

55. Clark-Soles, *Scripture*, 323.

56. Sheridan, *Retelling*, 36.

57. Moloney, "End," 360.

58. Klink, *John*, 482.

59. Cf. Hengel, "Old Testament," 28: Law is "practically identical with the expression 'graphe.'"

60. Hanson, *Prophetic*, 186 calls 15.25 "an unusually explicit reference to the fulfillment of scripture," but that is effectively not the case. John 15.25 makes no γραφή assertion.

61. The citation source may instead be Ps 35.19, which shares the same lexical form as Ps 69.4. A further righteous sufferer psalm, it has elements that might form parts of the Fourth Gospel's intertextual matrix (35.4, 11, 16). However, the prominence of Psalm 69 across the Gospel, and the opponents' apparent misuse of it, makes it the more likely source.

62. Jaime Clark-Soles, "Scripture Cannot Be Broken: The Social Function of the Use of Scripture in the Fourth Gospel," in *Abiding Words: The Use of Scripture in the Gospel of John*, ed. Alicia D. Myers and Bruce G. Schuchard (SBLRBS 81; Atlanta, 2015): "they have indeed fulfilled *their* law, but in the most tragic of ways."

63. See the discussion in Keefer, "Context," 85–95.

64. Douglas J. Moo and Andrew David Naselli, "The Problem of the New Testament's Use of the Old Testament," in *The Enduring Authority of the Christian Scriptures*, ed. D. A. Carson (Grand Rapids, MI: Eerdmans, 2016), 736.

65. See further Graham Hughes, *Hebrews and Hermeneutics* (SNTSMS 36; Cambridge, UK: Cambridge University Press, 1979).

66. Obermann, *Erfüllung*, 38.

67. Labahn, "Scripture," 150.

Chapter 5

The Implications of Scriptural Usage in John's Passion Narrative (2)

For the Fourth Gospel

Thus far in our analysis we have drawn out the first two elements of our core thesis. We have argued for the primacy of John's appeal to Israel's Scriptures when the evangelist recounts the events of Jesus's death. Mediated in a variety of intertextual forms, Scripture provides the heartbeat for the Fourth Gospel's Passion Narrative. And alongside this, we have contended that Scripture's status, at least in terms of its Johannine portrayal, is impacted by such cardial function. Scripture's overall character is fulfilled—it undergoes a process of perfection, of teleiosis, of upgrade to its ultimate purpose.

But a third, related element to our enquiry still remains. That is, if Scripture is so central to the Johannine project, and if it is so changed by its encounter with John's narration, does the same logic somehow extend to John too? What is the impact on the Fourth Gospel *itself* in terms of its encounter with Israel's Scriptures? We suggest that John's authoritative claim to fulfill Scripture directly relates to a declaration of its own scriptural credentials, and hence the Fourth Gospel is produced avowedly *qua*-Scripture. It perceives itself as effective γραφή. Our three-part thesis is thus mutually reinforcing or informing. John's self-conception as Scripture qualifies it both to draw so foundationally on Israel's Scriptures and, in so doing, simultaneously pronounce on their fundamental teleiosis.

We turn to such matters in this chapter, considering the impact the Fourth Gospel's use of Scripture, and specifically in its Passion Narrative, has on its own status and self-conception as γραφή. We will do so in three ways. First, and primarily, we shall consider John's own scriptural credentials, its claim to be written *qua*-Scripture, and the degree to which its Passion Narrative attests this. We have already drawn attention, for example, to the intriguing claims of John 18.9 and 18.32, texts avowing the same πληρόω fulfillment character the evangelist ascribes to scriptural quotations, but where no such text from Israel's Scriptures is cited. Jesus's word, rather than a scriptural γραφή, is said to be fulfilled. What is the implication of such claims? Second, we will press the logic of John's scriptural claim beyond the Passion Narrative to consider its impact on other parts of the Gospel testimony. We have frequently drawn attention to how the use of Israel's Scriptures in John's Passion Narrative has intratextual as well as intertextual resonance, and the same (intratextual) logic extends to the Fourth Gospel's own scriptural self-perception. That is, we will want to draw out how the Passion Narrative's appeal to "Scripture" becomes a bi-focal one, external *and* internal, embracing reference to both Israel's Scriptures *and* to the Scripture/γραφή exhibited by the Fourth Gospel itself. We will use John 19.34 as an example of such scriptural bi-focality. And third, we will consider a short case study in this light. Recognizing the anti-Jewish perspective often ascribed to the Fourth Gospel, and particularly to its Passion retelling, to what extent is its use of Israel's Scriptures complicit in this?

THE FOURTH GOSPEL AS SCRIPTURE

If Scripture is changed by the experience of its teleiosis, is there a similar impact onto the Johannine text which makes such teleiosis claims? We suggest that there is, namely that its appeal to scriptural teleiosis demonstrates, vindicates even, the Fourth Gospel's own status *qua*-Scripture, and as authoritative, divine testimony to the life and teaching of Jesus.[1]

Commentators have grappled with this question, and with the resulting implications for John's alleged scriptural self-perception. Some scholars remain unpersuaded by the claim, or at least are cautious about specifically identifying the Fourth Gospel as γραφή. Beutler, for example, concedes that the sayings of the Johannine Jesus assume an "authority comparable with that of 'scripture,'" yet at the same time maintains that nowhere do they "become formally part of the scripture."[2] A clear distinction thus remains between the authority of Jesus's teaching and its ontological γραφή status. Other commentators demonstrate similar restraint. Chris Keith, for example, acknowledges that the Fourth Gospel is "on a par with those written texts [i.e., Israel's Scriptures] since it can lead to life,"[3] yet falls short of ascribing it formal γραφή status. Keener is perhaps more positive, but still manifests caution: "Because he is inspired by the Paraclete . . . the author may quietly suggest that his work belongs in the same category with the Scriptures of old."[4] For such commentators, the Fourth Gospel is an authoritative text, surely, but its *full scriptural* credentials remain ambiguous or await later confirmation.[5]

Others, though, are more persuaded of the Fourth Gospel's self-avowed γραφή character. One of its most recent prominent advocates is Obermann, unsurprisingly in view of his overall characterization of the evangelist as a *Schriftteologe*, and his conclusions have been resultingly influential for many. Obermann concludes that the Gospel functioned as Scripture for its readers, effectively a kind of new holy writ,[6] assuming equivalent purpose to the Scriptures of Israel, and operating as the authoritative writing of the Johannine Community.[7] Just as Israel's Scriptures were thought to be the source of life (5.39), those same Scriptures now witness to Jesus and to his testimony declared within the Fourth Gospel, written as authoritative γραφή (20.31). Some caution, though, perhaps still remains within Obermann's analysis, at least in terms of its full outworking. Although affirming that John's own record of Jesus assumes γραφή status, Obermann concedes that some distinction still remains between the Scriptures of Israel and the narrative presented by John such that: *"rückt auch das Joh von seiner Anlage und seinem Anspruch her selbst in die Nähe der als heilig anerkannten Schriften."*[8] That is, the Fourth Gospel is *in die Nähe* in respect of Israel's Scriptures, rather than absolutely united with them. But one is eventually arguing over fine points of difference here. To all intents and purposes, Obermann contends that John presents its narrative as γραφή, demonstrated by the authority it shows in respect of the teleiosis of Israel's Scriptures.

Others have taken Obermann's work forward, and done so with even greater confidence as to the Fourth Gospel's avowed, internal scriptural status, though arriving at that verdict in different ways. Appealing to the presence of scriptural allusions at the beginning and end of the Gospel,[9] to the post-Easter vantage perspective the evangelist adopts, and to the authoritative testimony of the Beloved Disciple, Menken avers that John presents itself as "a new Holy Scripture, fulfilling and exceeding the old Scriptures."[10] Interestingly, though, Menken gives relatively little weight to the Fourth Gospel's authority to fulfill Scripture as the grounds for making this judgment. Instead, he concludes: "because the Scriptures testify to Jesus, and Jesus is represented by the Gospel of John, the Scriptures indirectly testify to John's Gospel, and the authority of this Gospel is correspondingly greater than the authority of the Scriptures."[11] Chennattu likewise advocates for the Fourth Gospel's γραφή status, but does so assuming a more theological lens: "John's Gospel is presented as a Scripture for the new/covenant eschatological community, as normative and authoritative revelation of God in Jesus Christ for the redemption of humanity."[12] Others arrive at the same conclusion, but with more emphasis placed upon the process of Scripture's completion and its associated implications for the Fourth Gospel's own status, hence pursuing the same posture we have adopted thus far. Sheridan, for example, proposes that John is "re-telling" Scripture, re-working the biblical narrative to its own perspective, and the Fourth Gospel is necessarily claiming γραφή status for itself.[13] Julia Lindenlaub's insightful study of the Beloved Disciple's function in respect of scriptural fulfillment likewise draws attention to "a guiding trajectory throughout the πληρωθῇ citations that progressively erodes differentiation between scriptural text and gospel text."[14] Wolfgang Kraus, following Obermann's contention that John is a *"neue Schrift,"* similarly avows that the authority that was once the preserve of Israel's Scripture is now extended to the scriptural witness of the Fourth Gospel, with the latter's authority resultingly even greater.[15]

But perhaps the strongest advocate for the Fourth Gospel's self-demonstrated scriptural status is Francis Moloney, who contends: "The use of 'fulfillment' language in the second half of the Gospel, culminating in 19:28–30, shows that the author claims to have brought the story of Israel's Scripture to an end. As this is the case, *the story the evangelist tells, heard and read by later generations, is ἡ γραφή*: the completion of Israel's Scripture."[16]

John's claims for scriptural fulfillment testify to an avowed sense of its own status as Scripture. Israel's Scriptures have reached their teleiosis because the agent of that teleiosis assumes the essential scriptural character for itself. In our previous chapter, we queried Moloney's portrayal of scriptural teleiosis in that it could be understood to imply an *end* to Scripture's function, but his position on John's own scriptural/γραφή, and the basis for it, is the one that we seek to advocate and unpack.

Before doing that, we must note one particular feature of Moloney's argument, namely his contention that the γραφή of 20.9 applies to the Gospel of John itself, rather than to Israel's Scriptures, thereby explicitly designating the former as Scripture. Positively, this addresses the apparent tension within 20.8–9, that the Beloved Disciple can believe but do so without understanding the γραφή that Jesus would rise from the dead. On Moloney's reading, the Beloved Disciple is not part of those who fail to understand the γραφή that anticipated Jesus's resurrection, because he is the agent of that Scripture and fully comprehends the Gospel's claim that Jesus would rise from the dead. Those who do not understand the γραφή, however, are those who have not yet had access to it, who have not yet appropriated the Fourth Gospel (i.e., representatively 20.9) and embraced its evangelistic claims.

Commentators have generally been skeptical as Moloney's argument,[17] and it is fair to say it requires a significant redefinition of the use of γραφή within the Fourth Gospel, a shift from being Israel's Scripture to being that of the Fourth Gospel itself. However, such a redefinition is entirely what the preceding Passion Narrative has achieved in respect of γραφή/Scripture (as per the claim of 19.28–30), and hence it is plausible at least to acknowledge the ambiguity of the term, and to include within 20.9 some form of reference to Fourth Gospel. It would be quintessentially Johannine to retain such ambiguity. There is no explicit subject for ᾔδεισαν, and it possible that 20.9 has a parenthetical rather than causal association. If so, and recognising the intertextual plurality John evokes, the γραφή of 20.9 incorporates, as with 19.28, the dual micro/macro rendering of both a specific LXX text (such as Ps 16.10–Ps 15.10 LXX) and the broader curvature of Scripture as a whole (cf. 1 Cor 15.4).[18] But at the same time, unlike 19.28, in the light of the Beloved Disciple's visual testimony (19.35) subsequently formulated in the Fourth Gospel, it extends (for the later reader) to include the γραφή manifest by the Gospel of John. The future evangelistic claim of the gospel—written to believe—draws a further association between 20.9 and 20.30–31, blurring the distinction between the perspective of the first disciples and the later ones. The first ones did not have the formal Scripture and depend on Jesus's words rather than textual γραφή; but the later reader of the Gospel has the γραφή testimony of the Gospel itself that testifies to Jesus's (verbal) anticipation of the resurrection (cf. 2.19–20).

Assessing John's γραφή Status

The initial datum for John's γραφή identity, and the one to which most advocates for John's scriptural status refer, is that the Fourth Evangelist accords Jesus's words at least the same authority as that manifest by Israel's Scriptures. The disciples' scriptural recollection (John 2.17; Ps. 69.9) and their resultant belief in the Scripture (2.22), is equated with Jesus's prediction of the destruction and "rebuilding" of the Temple (2.19), anticipating the resurrection of his temple/body (2.21). The disciples believe both the Scripture *and* Jesus's words (2.22); both entities manifest the same perceived authority and capacity for fulfillment. Jesus's prediction is at least on the same footing as Scripture, and likely even more than that. To believe the Scripture, therefore, is to believe Jesus's word, and vice versa. It may even be that the καί of John 2.22 is functioning epexegetically, thereby rendering the phrase "the scripture, i.e., the word that Jesus had spoken."[19] If that is the case, then Jesus's λόγος does not merely have the same status as γραφή—it *is* γραφή. And it possesses that designation well in advance of any Passion teleiosis in respect of Israel's Scriptures, even if it takes the Passion events for that to be retrospectively realized.

Such characterization extends to several of Jesus's subsequent λόγοι within John's Passion retelling (18.9, 18.32). These statements receive the same πληρωθῇ designation or introductory formula accorded to the fulfillment quotations, and, although generally not classified as quotations, thereby assume the same authority as their textually endorsed equivalents. The fulfilled γραφή of 17.12 likely also points in this direction as no recognizable text from Israel's Scripture is cited. John 18.9 restates the same premise as 17.12 (i.e., that Jesus would not lose anyone), but presents it as a λόγος of Jesus (cf. 6.39) rather than as scriptural γραφή. The statements make the same point and, in the absence of a scriptural citation, 17.12 is best understood as Jesus's 6.39 logion re-presented as γραφή.[20] John 18.32, also credited with fulfillment, likely refers back to 12.32–33, and to the fulfillment of Jesus's prediction of his mode of death. In all three instances (i.e., 17.12, 18.9, 18.32), the rhetorical effect implied by the introductory formula when no *scriptural* quotation is present is resultingly all the stronger, drawing further attention to Jesus's own πληρόω capacity, both to fulfill Scripture and also be fulfilled in what he has spoken.

It is also fitting that each λόγος awaiting fulfillment (18.9, 32) is uttered by the one who is ὁ Λόγος enfleshed. The fulfillment of the spoken word accompanies the fulfillment of the task given to the Word—just like the divine words of the Jewish Scriptures, the word of the Word is likewise fulfilled. With this authoritative equivalency between Jesus's words and scriptural warrant, with their increased coalescence as the Fourth Gospel progresses, and with their combined πληρωθῇ dimension present in John's Passion Narrative, one might well conclude that "the Johannine crucifixion narrative is [simultaneously] the fulfillment of ἡ γραφή and ὁ λόγος."[21] Although not absolutely synonymous, because of and through Scripture's christological teleiosis, γραφή and λόγος (of Jesus) become almost interchangeable terms. The word(s) of Jesus have assumed γραφή status and authority.

This has implications, one suggests, for other parts of John's intertextual Passion narration. Consider, for example, the absence of any reference—explicit at least—to Scripture during Jesus's trial before Pilate. Bearing in mind the testimonial authority the Fourth Gospel ascribes to the Scriptures, and to the fact that Jesus's (Jewish) opponents contribute to the trial scene, one might well have expected the trial to yield some expression of γραφή fulfillment. After all, as we have seen, Scripture is deployed in 19.24 in service of Jesus's kingly identity, drawing on the Davidic/kingship imagery of Psalm 22. And John 19.2–3 may also resonate with Psalm 22, or Psalm 69, in that regard, though any connection is more subtle. But just as we have observed of several other units, John's intertextual silence is somewhat loud. Hence the lack of explicit reference to Israel's Scriptures might instead point to the way in which Jesus's *own* words assume that authority, and effectively function as γραφή. The previous instance of πληρόω fulfillment (18.32) has been ascribed to Jesus's λόγος, and its logic plausibly extends across the rest of the trial scene. When Jesus addresses Pilate during the trial scene, his λόγοι effectually assume scriptural status; "Scripture" is spoken.

The quotation of 19.28 points in a similar direction. As noted earlier, when Jesus voices διψῶ, he alludes to Scripture, assuming/personifying the voice of the psalmist. The limited nature of the scriptural element gives further weight to Jesus's own voice and to his λόγος utterance, in this case his declaration of thirst. That is, it suits John's purposes to make the διψῶ intertext sufficiently strong to enable the Psalm 69 intertextual play (it remains a scriptural citation), but at the same time sufficiently minimal to preserve the focus on Jesus's speaking of it. The διψῶ utterance can bear the significant *pars pro toto* burden for scriptural fulfillment precisely because its particular lexical formulation, and thereby its scriptural "character," is endorsed, vindicated even, by Jesus himself. John's Jesus makes διψῶ "Scripture" even if it were not previously or otherwise so; he endorses it as a scriptural quotation to be fulfilled. The Word of God speaks the word of God, and the word(s) of the Word become scriptural.

Granting Jesus's words scriptural authority is hugely significant, but it remains one stage further to determine whether the Fourth Gospel *as a whole* thinks of itself as Scripture. One cannot be definitive either way, but we suggest that the Fourth Gospel does indeed perceive of itself as such, and avowedly so. As Ford rightly surmises, the Gospel's opening discourse claims a status in respect of Scripture (Gen 1.1/John 1.1), and such positioning sets the prevailing scriptural context for its subsequent narration of Jesus's ministry.[22] Likewise, John 20's closing statement, that the Gospel is written (ταῦτα . . . γέγραπται, 20.31) with the prescribed kerygmatic purpose, establishes a γραφή inclusio to the Johannine text. The Beloved Disciple has recorded (γράφω—21.24γράψας) the Gospel material and its potential content would exceed a myriad of books (τὰ γραφόμενα βιβλία—21.25). Such repetition of γράφω language would seem to place the evangelist's narration on the same level as the γραφή of Israel's Scripture. And more than that, the Fourth Gospel's claim—and particularly that of its Passion Narrative—to be able to pronounce definitively on the fulfillment of Scripture is testimony to its self-assessed scriptural understanding. The perfection of Scripture that Jesus's death enacts is simultaneous with the manifestation of the Fourth Gospel's own (scriptural) authority. Its authoritative narration of Scripture's teleiosis is intertwined with the same declaration in respect of John's own scriptural status. Only "Scripture" can fulfill Scripture in that way. Only "Scripture" can bring other forms of Scripture to their maturity. The pronouncement of the new, perfected state to which Israel's Scriptures are brought can only be made by that which has the equivalent, or even greater, authority to make such a pronouncement. Because the very entity that comprises Scripture is being fulfilled, the Fourth Gospel must necessarily conceive of itself as Scripture. The relationship is dialogical and mutually informing; the Johannine claim to fulfill the totality of Israel's Scriptures acts in service of installing the Fourth Gospel as γραφή.

Coupled with this is the testimony of the Beloved Disciple, who articulates the authority of the Johannine gospel (21.24–25), and whose witness to the piercing scene (19.35), along with its juxtaposition to 19.37's climactic fulfillment claims in respect of Jesus's divine identity, underscores the Fourth Gospel's fundamental verisimilitude. The alignment of the Disciple's visual witness with Scripture's teleiosis also brings both aspects into mutual relationship. The precise extent of the Beloved Disciple's testimony in 19.35 is perhaps ambiguous, whether just to the event of 19.34, or to the Fourth Gospel more widely, but we might at least say that the fulfillment of Scripture is verified and accompanies the Fourth Gospel's—or the Beloved Disciple's—own declaration of the authority of its testimony, in self-fulfilling style.

The epilogue function of John 21 may have some explanatory significance here. The Gospel's prevailing narrative has finished at 20.31, but a new or subsequent stage in the life of the Johannine Community is still to be recounted. The Johannine story is thus both finished and unfinished, both over and not over, both done and also demanding a sequel or follow-up. The Paraclete has been handed over (20.22) and brought insight one suggests, but there is still work to be done, still a place for further narration. This has implications for the role of "Scripture" in the Fourth Gospel post-Passion and in the light of its experienced teleiosis. There is no formal intertextual citation in John 21, but that may be because the prior work of *Israel's* Scripture is done. Instead, there is significant *intratextual* references made in John 21, and the reader is encouraged to make those connections accordingly as its new scriptural/γραφή links. The Sea of Tiberias location (21.1) recalls prior miraculous feeding of the 5000 (6.1). Nathanael's Cana origins takes the reader back to the first sign and the abundant wine (2.1–11; cf. also 4.46–54). The place of Peter's restoration, the charcoal fire (21.9), takes the reader back to the same location of his denial (18.18). Jesus's pastoral charge to Peter (21.15–19) recalls Jesus's own shepherding vocation (10.11–16). The language of "fulfillment" may have gone, but John 21 models an equivalent process to that undertaken by the Passion Narrative. It establishes its discourse on the authority of Scripture, but sets out its case through the γραφή attested within the Fourth Gospel itself rather than that of Israel.

This returns, then, to the question we started to probe in chapter 4, namely the ongoing function of the Scriptures, whether those of Israel or, in the light of its own γραφή status, the particular instance of the Fourth Gospel. Chennatu contends that "John understands and presents his story of Jesus as a Scripture, which is not merely a continuation of the Old Testament but its completion and fulfillment (19.28–30)."[23] Her argument is correct for identifying the Fourth Gospel's own self-perception as Scripture, and for the drawing out the continuity of one overall scriptural story. But at the same time, her proposal seems to imply, that the Scriptures of the Old Testament are completed but in such a way as to end (for John at least) their ongoing function. We suggest that, for the Fourth Gospel, the reverse is true, that rather the expansion of what Scripture *is*—the "combination" of Israel's Scripture and that articulated by the Fourth Gospel—continues to live and evolve. We might say then that this blurs the division between its own testimony and the testimony of Scripture precisely because John thinks of itself "as Scripture." The Old Testament texts and images get incorporated into this new "entity" that is Johannine Scripture.

"SCRIPTURAL" USAGE IN JOHN 19.34

The John 21 example earlier, and the Fourth Gospel's self-perception as γραφή, have implications for assessing scriptural usage in the Passion Narrative itself. Although our core focus has hitherto been on the evangelist's intertextual (i.e., external) evocation of Israel's Scriptures therein, the notion that John understands itself as Scripture theoretically extends the parameters of our enquiry to include the Gospel's use of its own content (*qua*-Scripture), in intratextual (i.e., internal) mode. In our analysis of John's use of scriptural quotations and allusions, we drew attention to the intratextual dimension to their usage and to the corresponding interpretive implications. Hence even without having resource to the Gospel's γραφή self-characterization, consideration of the wider Gospel content was already within our scope. But if the Fourth Gospel is indeed γραφή, if it is in and of itself Scripture, the scriptural interaction within John's Passion becomes even more in-depth; the scriptural heartbeat to John's Passion potentially beats even faster.

Let us turn to John 19.34 to illustrate this phenomenon. The verse conveys one of the most evocative images of NT discourse, let alone of the Fourth Gospel. The scene's inclusion, and its accompanying need for testimonial confirmation (19.35), seemingly renders it remarkable, extraordinary even. It is presented as a "real" event,[24] one that can be visualized and attested by the Beloved Disciple. But equally, it is one whose very oddity requires authoritative confirmation, particularly in view of the water's presence.[25] It seemingly evidences something more profound than just Jesus's mortem state, and one is reluctant to enter into discussion of its interpretation and "tantalizingly imprecise"[26] symbolism. The very ambiguity of the image, its implicit dualism for example, and the sheer variety of interpretation it has occasioned (literary, theological, medical, rhetorical) cautions against interpretative confidence or surety. Instead, the converse would seem to be the case; the event's ambiguity or imprecision is something to acknowledged, underlined, celebrated even, resisting attempts to pronounce once and for all on merely one interpretive solution.

But such caution noted, John 19.34 nonetheless offers a nuanced case of how the Fourth Gospel's γραφή self-perception is outworked in practice, how the full gamut of scriptural interaction is outworked *after* the teleiosis of Israel's Scriptures and in the light of John's own self-claimed scriptural identity. It provides a concrete example of the Fourth Gospel's bi-focal scriptural usage, how the Passion Narrative attests to the fulfillment both of Israel's Scriptures *and* of its own Scriptural testimony. John 19.34's γραφή evocation is intertextual *and* intratextual.

One question immediately presents itself, however, as to the nature of 19.34's scriptural engagement. In a pericope so invested with scriptural fulfillment, at times of apparently mundane matters (cp. 19.24), and with 19.34's implied import, why does the evangelist not make *explicit* scriptural comment in respect of the flow of blood and water? The non-breaking of legs receives such mention (19.36), as do the respective acts of piercing and seeing (19.37), but the blood and water outpouring is neither *explicitly* associated with the respective citations,[27] nor does it receive its own scriptural proof or formal vindication. John draws an association between the fluid outflow of 19.34 and the 19.37 quotation, and we began to explore the latter's relationship to 19.34 in chapter 2, but we noted there how 19.37 gravitates more to the visualization of the piercing's outcome, rather than to the significance of the evulsion's content. And if the citations in 19.36–37 attest that Israel's Scriptures still have post-teleiosis warrant or function, why does 19.34 not receive similar fulfillment attribution? On initial reading, as with the trial scene instance noted above, 19.34's scriptural silence again seems somewhat loud.

But the surprising absence of (explicit) scriptural proof may be a datum in and of itself. It widens our assessment to a more comprehensive hermeneutical assessment of how John's Passion Narrative—and, by extension, the Fourth Gospel as a whole—utilizes Scripture in the light of the enacted teleiosis of 19.28–30. John 19.34 offers a case study for how scriptural allusions might be operative *after* the completion of Scripture, and in a way that, different to 19.36–37, also incorporates an intratextual, internal scriptural lens.

How so? On the one hand, John 19.34 follows on from the climactic fulfillment of Scripture, the latter's constituent teleiosis or perfection (19.28–30). On the other hand, it precedes the accompanying, definitive scriptural interpretation of Jesus's death (19.36–37) and the Beloved Disciple's authoritative testimony to the event's verisimilitude (19.35) which will ultimately receive γραφή status (cf. 20.31). As Vanhoozer opines of 19.34's narration: "The episode . . . takes place *in a framework of scriptural fulfillment*. The evangelist describes what happens to the body of Jesus from the perspective of the broader canonical context. In order to be competent interpreters, we must do no less."[28] We thus suggest that, in a quasi-intercalated form, juxtaposed between two scripturally endorsed units, 19.34 bridges together the respective concepts of completion (that of Scripture and of Jesus's ministry—19.28–30) and the accompanying testimonial/evangelistic role the reformulated γραφή consequently undertakes (19.35–37). That is, 19.34 functions, partly through vicarious proximity to such perfection, and partly through its future-facing, evangelistic role, as a pivotal example for how Johannine combined γραφή usage might function.

John 19.34 and Israel's Scriptures

What association from Israel's Scriptures might then be found in or generated by 19.34? We take each element in turn (including the blood and water as a combined entity) and consider the respective intertextual and intratextual links they evoke.

John 19.34 — Blood

Intertextual: The presence of the effusive blood evokes a number of potential scriptural intertexts. It might echo the salvific red cloth found at Rahab's window (Josh 2.18), but more likely, it extends the Passion Narrative's invocation of Passover Lamb imagery, the blood this time from Jesus's side.[29] As we have seen, 19.36 reinforces the Paschal imagery, and the blood motif in the Passover is critical to Israel's deliverance. Klink, for example, posits a clear Passover association to 19.34, and "the image of blood . . . serves to declare Jesus as the Passover Lamb par excellence and therefore the fulfillment of Passover."[30] But even here, with 19.36 still yet to come, the intertextual assessment of blood in paschal terms still functions on an *intra*textual basis—that is, the prior embedding of Passover imagery in the Fourth Gospel rather than on the verbatim citational testimony. As we saw with both John's Passion quotations and allusions, their interpretation requires intratextual as well as intertextual outworking, and the same is true here in respect of the blood intertext.

The blood imagery likely also extends beyond Paschal parameters, particularly in its capacity to manifest or yield life (a feature also shared by the accompanying water—the water that is living—cf. 7.37). Blood was a sign in the Exodus Passover (Exod 12.13), and it retains that semiotic dimension in the Fourth Gospel outflowing. But the "life-giving" function of blood seems to point elsewhere, particularly in terms of scriptural association, and to the wider context of the sacrificial system (the Passover Lamb is not a sacrificial offering in that sense). Moffitt, for example, draws attention to the way in which the Pentateuch commonly equates blood and life (Lev 17:14; Gen 9:4;

Deut 12:23–25), and following Sklar, notes that "the life in the blood is the agent that has the power to redeem and purify."[31] John has already drawn connections between blood and birth (1.13), albeit not within the ritualistic context, and drinking of Jesus's blood is to be the source of life (6.53–56). We suggested in the chapter three that the presence of the four women at the Cross also has life/gynecological associations and the blood outflow may have new birth implications too. Such life-giving—and purifying—imagery is resonant with the Temple context, and bearing in mind the association John draws between Jesus's death and the fate of the Temple (cf. 2.17–22), cultic or ritual purification symbolism likely compromises intertextual aspects of 19.34's blood imagery too.[32]

Specific purification language may be relatively limited overall in the Fourth Gospel,[33] but purity themes remain reasonably foregrounded in its Passion Narrative. The Jews will not enter Pilate's quarters for fear of ritual impurity (18.28), and the removal of Jesus's body is motivated by ritual cleanliness factors (19.31). One might conjecture therefore that visualization of the blood is life-giving, but also effects cleansing of a Temple, in this case the one of Jesus's body. John might therefore be offering a dual commentary, both on the "impurity" of the present Temple, exemplified by 2.14–16, and the resultant need for its purification, via the offering of blood. After all, the Temple incident is located at Passover (2.13) and that serves to link 19.34—along with references to Jesus's body—back to the Temple milieu. In this light, "the effusion of the blood and water in the New Temple is closely related to the purity and sanctity of God's people in John,"[34] and so contributes to the wider concept of the Johannine Temple Christology.

Intratextual: The blood of 19.34 also draws on the Fourth Gospel's own internal, "scriptural" testimony. This is most explicit in terms of John 6.52–59 and the drinking of Jesus's blood, evoking eucharistic overtones which 19.34 can be said to re-play. Even if the sacramental aspect to this can be overstated, 19.34 is still the awaited clarification of that to which 6.53–55 alludes, but which it leaves unresolved, ambiguous, and difficult to understand (cf. the disputed response of 6.52). As the subsequent literature on 19.34 testifies, elements of that ambiguity still remain in terms of how the flow of blood from Jesus's side should be understood, but 19.34 brings completion—or fulfillment, even—to the 6.53–55 discourse. Applying the same teleiosis/perfection perspective we proposed for Scripture in our previous chapter, and the way that perfection is enacted to enable rather than terminate scriptural function, we might say that the 19.34 effects the *teleiosis* of the earlier blood-drinking material. John 19.34 "perfects" 6.53–55, in anticipation perhaps of forthcoming eucharistic practice. Post-teleiosis of 19.28, John uses its own γραφή to interpret and thereby perfect other (pre-19.28, and so as yet "unperfected") Scripture.

John 19.34 — Water

Intertextual: Where the blood outflow is expected, confirming Jesus's physical death and symbolizing the forthcoming life it yields, the presence of the water is contrastingly *un*anticipated. It is the "anomaly" of the 19.34 imagery,[35] the element that invites particular scrutiny, intertextually or otherwise. As mentioned in chapter two, it seems likely that the hydrous emission from Jesus's side resonates with Zech 13.1's fountain of water, particularly in view of the subsequent Zech 12.10 quotation (John 19.37). The outflow benefits the house of David (Zech 13.1), and the prior appeal to Ps 22.18 has likewise patterned Jesus in Davidic/royal terms. The living waters of Zech 14.8, flowing out of Jerusalem, may also form part of the 19.37-resourced intertextual play, with living water texts such as Isa 55.1 or Jer 2.13 also potentially operative.[36] The evangelist may also have Num 20.11 in mind, particularly as John has already made use of an earlier Numbers episode in respect of informing Jesus's death (3.14–15; Num 21.5–9).

Intratextual: But as with the blood motif, the water's "scriptural" reference is likely mediated as much by intratextual as by intertextual means, by internal rather than external Scripture. It reawakens the Fourth Gospel's other, prior reference to a significant liquid outpouring, namely Jesus's declaration of the outflow of living water (7.37–38), and particularly to the γραφή evidence to that fact (7.38). By implication, the γραφή is drawn from Israel's Scriptures, but the cited lemma lacks a known LXX *Vorlage*. This suggests that the evangelist has a more intratextual γραφή in mind, namely the testimony visualized in the water outflow of 19.34.

The associations between 7.37–39 and the Passion scene are vivid.[37] Both events are timed in respect of a great day (7.37, 19.31—μεγάλη ἡμέρα). Both scenes include matters of thirst and its satiation, one by means of living water (7.37–38), the other, ironically so, with sour wine, potentially poisonous and death-enhancing (19.28–30). The Tabernacles association with the Temple outflow further embeds the association of Jesus's cruciform body and the Temple (cf. 2.21–22). Likewise, the flow of living water is accompanied by the promised receipt of the Spirit (7.39), the anticipated gift that awaits Jesus's glorification, namely his death. We suggested in the previous chapter that Jesus's τετέλεσται declaration and the handing over of his s/Spirit (19.30) manifested proleptic declaration of scriptural fulfillment for the gift of the Holy Spirit (20.22). The 7.38/19.34 association compounds this view, namely that the overall teleiosis of Scripture—and the theoretical "fulfillment" of the individual γραφή of 7.38—is enacted by the proleptic handing over of the Spirit upon Jesus's death (19.30). Its full release by Jesus and the reception by the disciples still awaits (20.22),[38] but 19.34—in the light of both the immediately preceding completion of Scripture and the handing over of the Spirit—effectively pronounces its arrival. Where 7.39 avers that there was no Spirit, John 19.30—and the visually demonstrative evulsion of 19.34—responds that there now *is*.

John 7.38–39 is infamous for its interpretative ambiguity, particularly as to the respective sources of both the living water and the specific Scripture Jesus cites in support of his invitation. In terms of the latter, 7.38 appeals to ἡ γραφή, but does so citing a text-form otherwise unknown from Israel's Scriptures (at least in explicit *Vorlage* terms) and for that reason 7.38 is commonly removed from the list of the Fourth Gospel's quotations.[39] At the same time, there are a number of scriptural resonances or allusions that may be operative in 7.38, particularly when aligned with 19.34 and with other scriptural intertexts that have been operative across the Passion Narrative. Moo ventures, for example: "The γραφή to which Jesus refers in 7.38 is difficult to determine, but it is difficult to deny that Zech 14.8 was not at least one of them."[40] Bearing in mind the wider significance that Zechariah 9–14—and especially Zechariah 12–14—has for John's Passion, and the similar fountain imagery of Zech 13.1, such association seems perfectly plausible. John 7.38/19.34 reinforce the Zech 12.10/John 19.37 citation, in that they enable the intertextual bridge to Zech 13.1 and make that association more prominent.

Nonetheless, the *precise* Vorlage for the 7.38 γραφή remains contested. Alternative texts from Israel's Scriptures may contribute to its backdrop, and the multiplicity of operative intertexts may explain the lack of a clear-cut scriptural *Vorlage*. The ritual itself, as enacted at the Temple, has connections with the giving of water from the wilderness rock (Exod 17.6; Num 20.8), and it seems likely that such imagery still remains operative in John's perspective, particularly as the event assumes eschatological connotations, "an anticipation of God's coming work expected at the end of the age."[41] It could be, then, that the Fourth Gospel draws on Isa 28.16 combined with the rock of Exod 17.6,[42] and if so, it would also be a further instance of the strange connection that Paul makes in respect of the wilderness rock being Christ (1 Cor 10.4). Psalm 22.14 imagery, the Psalmist outpouring like water, may also function here, particularly in view of the John 19.24/Ps 22.18 citation. Likewise, there may be an echo of Isa 58.11, particularly as the Isaianic waters address the needs of both thirst and bones (cf. also Isa 32.2), and/or a reference to the life-giving river or fountain of Ps 36.8–9, with its invitation to drink from it (cf. John 7.38). The editorial comment that the γραφή relates to the giving of the Spirit also suggests a patterning after the prophecy of Ezekiel, whether the water/Spirit promise of 36.25–27 or the water/river of life flowing out from the Temple (47.1–12—cf. the similar water/Spirit parallel in John 3.5).

Hence whereas it is difficult to adjudicate precisely on the question of 7.38's *Vorlage*, it seems plausible to suggest instead that it might form part of the broader intertextual/intratextual jigsaw which comes to fruition in 19.34. As we have seen elsewhere, the Fourth Gospel may use a matrix or amalgam of intertexts, rendering a composite quotation, rather than relying merely on one specific example.[43] But at the same time, the scene of 19.34 becomes the primary manifestation of the scene 7.37–39 anticipates, and we might conclude that (in rhetorical rather than lexical terms), 19.34 effectively provides the γραφή cited by Jesus in 7.38. The absence of a prior, "attested" *Vorlage* from Israel's Scriptures is therefore integral in this regard. John 7.38 signals an anticipated scriptural warrant, but delays the specific presentation of the γραφή until the Passion account, and particularly its third triptych, which we have seen to be particularly significant in terms of the relationship between Scripture and Jesus's death.

The testimony of 19.34 might also resolve the other ambiguity of 7.38, namely the source of the living water. On first glance, the parallels between 7.38 and 19.34—and the interpretative value this yields—causes us to read the ambiguous αὐτοῦ (7.38) as pertaining initially to Jesus's κοιλία rather than that of the believer. It is surely christologically focused—as John's hermeneutic repeatedly is—and the 7.38/19.34 axis is informing in this regard. But the identity of the αὐτοῦ is an infamous crux within Johannine scholarship,[44] and there are equally good reasons to read it as referring to the believer—the parallel with 4.14 or the subsequent link with the reception of the Spirit (7.39).

Both options may be possible, and they are not mutually exclusive, particularly bearing in mind how frequently Jesus and the Johannine Community are blurred; the Fourth Gospel's rendering may indeed be deliberately ambiguous.[45] If it were the believer's κοιλία (and that image perhaps has "blood" connotations too), then the evangelist presents Jesus as the ultimate believer, the one who embodies true/proper belief, with the Beloved Disciple's subsequent witness (19.35) also held up in similar consummate fashion. Such exemplary function, and the intimacy of the Beloved Disciple's location, draws the reader into visualization of the scene,[46] and explains the odd insertion of 19.35—not as a parenthesis, but as an essential part of the Gospel's re-narration and argument.[47] Those who (will) look on the scene of 19.34—however vicariously—and believe will be in receipt of the living water generated by Jesus's piercing (cf. 4.11).

Some of the crowd react positively to Jesus's 7.37–38 statement with the response that "this is the Messiah" (7.41). Even if their understanding is misplaced or still to be properly outworked, the nature of the response is notable, and might also hint at some form of messianic exegesis being at work in Jesus's prior announcement. A subsequent quotation is then made in respect of the Messiah origins (7.42), retaining the christological context to the discourse. In some sense, therefore, 7.37–42 captures questions around Jesus's messianic identity and Scripture's attestation to that, but they are left unresolved until the scene of 19.34, with the latter implicitly offering its fulfillment.

On this reading, 7.38 becomes a *scriptural* prophecy because it is voiced by the Johannine Jesus whose Passion vocation is the perfection of Scripture (19.28). But at the same time, John 19.34's manifestation of the 7.38 Johannine γραφή is shaped or informed by other, intertextual/external scriptural imagery cut from similar cloth and which feed or shape the visual portrayal of 19.34. Even as 19.34 lacks explicit scriptural fulfillment language, it is nonetheless riddled with scriptural fulfillment significance—of both Jewish and Johannine Scripture. John 19.34 manifests the bi-focal scriptural hermeneutic, combining the two scriptural "voices" in the Fourth Gospel, the Jewish Scriptures of Israel and the "now Scriptural" voice of Jesus himself,[48] fused together with an enhanced, perfected scriptural identity. The association is made early in the Gospel—2.22—but the two forms are distinguished and require post-Easter reflection for their synonymity to be understood. By 19.34, however, they have—in practice—become indistinguishable, fused together. Post-teleiosis, the evangelist uses Scripture—both internal and external—to fulfill Scripture. The testimony of Jesus and the testimony of Israel's Scripture combine in the new scriptural entity that is the Fourth Gospel. In this critical sense, John's Passion Narrative is scripturally *self*-fulfilling.

John 19.34 — Blood and Water Together

Intertextual: Brown proposes that the water/blood outflow offers an umbrella symbol to attest to way in which the gift of the Spirit permeates the whole Fourth Gospel passion/death/resurrection/ascension discourse.[49] Both images address the theme of new life, and their combination gives further emphasis to that theme. It may therefore be that their amalgamation also carries scriptural warrant, or draws on scriptural imagery where *both* blood and water are found in tandem. Exodus Rabbah 3.13, for example, has both water and blood as coming from the rock struck by Moses, thus going beyond the purely hydrous outpouring found in the wilderness account. Likewise, Lindars notes that Targum Pseudo-Jonathan associates the water of Num 20.11 with the blood of Exod 4.9, stressing Moses' operative capacity in each instance.[50] Such imagery may lurk in the Passion Narrative's background—particularly in view of Mosaic comparison elsewhere in the Gospel—but it is at best only implicit, and, in terms of dating, it is unclear whether such tradition was known to John. There may equally be elements of the Exod 7.20–24 plague, where water is turned to blood, but that image seems unlikely bearing in mind its negative character and the "life-giving" implications of John 19.34.

Therefore, it seems better to consider the respective intratextual and intertextual connections conveyed by blood and water as separate, distinctive images. Although there are key connections in terms of Temple and Jesus's body, generally speaking, the respective motifs are either one element or the other, blood or water, but not combined. There is no blood in 7.38-39, for example, and the life-giving capacity of the blood, drawn from Passover and other sacrifice imagery, is not dependent on water. Likewise, the blood discourse of 6.53-55 has no particular water reference to it. Rather it is the powerful combination of blood and water *together*, a composite image that retains the symbolism of both constituent elements without losing their individual function, and intensifies the scene's life-giving, salvific dimension. Both images, in their different ways, evoke intertextual and intratextual imagery of "life," and the combination of both concepts in 19.34 deepens the life-giving significance and symbolism of the Passion occasion. Just as John drew intertexts together in terms of composite quotations from Israel's Scriptures, it likewise combines intratexts drawn from its own scriptural portfolio to portray the efficacious achievement of Jesus's death. At the very moment at which Jesus's piercing confirms his death, the visual image of the outflow of water and blood confirms the (ironic) gift of new life that death yields. For John, Scripture, both that of Israel and that of the Fourth Gospel itself, confirms that the ultimate moment of death proves to be the quintessential moment of giving life.[51]

John 19:34 Summary

John 19.34 evokes a scriptural backdrop of new life, of a new birth moment. With characteristic Johannine reversal, the scene of Jesus's cruciform death (19.30) is simultaneously the source of new life. The evocation is not explicitly signaled, at least not in terms of the fulfillment quotations, but the verses are still steeped in Scripture, that of both Israel *and* the Fourth Gospel itself. Such usage therefore models how John continues to deploy Scripture post-teleiosis, particularly in bringing to completion that which is left unresolved from earlier in the Gospel account.

JOHN'S PASSION NARRATIVE, SCRIPTURE, AND THE FOURTH GOSPEL'S ANTI-JUDAISM

One of the long-standing issues surrounding the Fourth Gospel is its purported anti-Jewish character, and particularly its negative portrayal of οἱ Ἰουδαῖοι, normally translated as "the Jews."[52] John's Passion Narrative is commonly seen—and with some reason—as presenting a prime locus for this alleged anti-Judaism, particularly for its "othering" of the Jews and underlining their complicity in Jesus's demise. The extended trial scene portrays the Jews seeking after Jesus's death (18.31); the chief priests and police petition for Jesus's crucifixion (19.6), and the Jews appeal to their Law to demand his death (19.7). Again, it is the Jews who seek to override Pilate's wish to release Jesus (19.12), and Pilate's "Here is your King" proclamation receives a negative assessment, yielding further bated demands for Jesus's cruciform death (19.15). With their claim that they have no king but Caesar (19.15), the Fourth Gospel's Passion Narrative draws out the dishonesty and lack of integrity on the part of the chief priests, and stresses their connivance with the powers of Rome.

Although not explicitly named as such until 18.31, it is οἱ Ἰουδαῖοι who hand over (παραδίδωμι) Jesus to Pilate (18.30), and the procurator uses similar terms to stress that the nation and chief priests (i.e., of the Jews) have handed Jesus over to him (18.35). Jesus likewise speaks, in fairly binary terms, of being handed over (again, παραδίδωμι) to the Jews (18.36). Pilate's "I am not a Jew" pronouncement (18.35) only serves to emphasize the Jews' responsibility for the trial even happening in the first place. Even though crucified on a Roman cross by Roman soldiers (19.23), even though it is Pilate who ultimately hands Jesus over to be crucified (19.16), it is to the Jews that Jesus is actually handed over (παραδίδωμι—19.16) and they assume *de facto* responsibility for his cruciform death.[53] It is the Jews who seek the removal of the crucified bodies from the cross (19.31), and Jesus's burial according to the custom of the Jews (19.40) further implies Jewish—as much as Roman—responsibility for Jesus's death. If there is an endemic anti-Jewishness within the Fourth Gospel, the Passion account seems an integral contributor to its formulation.

What role does Scripture play within this? At the very least, Scripture may be a contributory factor in the Fourth Gospel's alleged anti-Jewishness. Sheridan, for example, ventures that this is the case, averring that John's scriptural usage is complicit in establishing the anti-Jewish portrayal. She contends: "Until we grasp this *rhetorical* relationship between the Gospel's presentation of 'the Jews' and its citation of Scripture, we cannot properly understand how or why the Gospel is at once so 'Jewish' and 'anti-Jewish.'"[54] Even without pronouncing on their fulfillment, the evangelist may be seen as utilizing Israel's Scriptures to undermine its opponents (5.45–47), or as a focal means of identifying difference (8.37). Equally, John claims that it is fulfillment of Scripture that occasions those in Jerusalem rejecting Jesus (12.37–41), and likewise the position of Jesus's opponents is justified on the basis that it fulfills their νόμος (15.24–25). As we have seen, the "historicity" of the Passion scene, both trial scene and crucifixion, has likely also been accommodated to the demands of demonstrating scriptural fulfillment,[55] and some interpreters understandably perceive this as the weaponization of Scripture.[56] It becomes used as a tool—a polemical one—both to defend Jesus (19.24), but also a means by which focal aspects of Jewish identity are removed or relativized. Scriptural warrant is invoked to vindicate the notion of Jesus as living bread (6.31) or as Israel's king (12.15). Most significantly perhaps, 2.17 cites Ps 69.9 in respect of Jesus's prediction of the destruction of the Temple and its restoration as his resurrected body.

Therefore the combination of John's Passion *and* its use of Scripture has the potential to compound the Fourth Gospel's potential anti-Jewish character. The christological hermeneutic that undergirds John's scriptural interpretation can be seen as problematic, particularly if/as it "Christianizes" Scripture, and/or extrapolates it from its Jewish context. This seems to be the position at which Hanson arrives: "By his [i.e., John's] use of Scripture, he presents Jesus as God's decisive revelation of himself to the world. He has taken Jesus out of Judaism and would like to take the Jewish scriptures out of Judaism also, and make them over to the Christian church."[57] Technically, Hanson does not categorize this appraisal in terms of the Fourth Gospel's anti-Judaism, but the implication of his assessment—and the implicit Jewish/Christian separation—remains problematic and ends up presenting the Fourth Gospel's scriptural usage as essentially anti-Jewish. That said, however, we might also query whether it is a fair representation of the Passion Narrative's perspective, in that the term "Christian" is—in itself—an odd one. It implies a distinction from "Jewish/Judaism" that can be easily misunderstood, although is also a term, of course, that the Fourth Gospel itself does not employ. The fact that Scripture is used for adjudicating on Jesus's identity is, of itself, entirely appropriate within contemporary Jewish tradition. Interpretative diversity was already in place within Second Temple exegetical practice, and a christological hermeneutic is not, of itself, anti-Jewish. It is therefore possible that the frequent appeal to their Scriptures is occasioned by intra-Jewish discussion as to Jesus's identity, with the Fourth Gospel attesting an intra-Jewish polemic rather an anti-Jewish one.[58]

Second, and related, is the Fourth Gospel's language of completion or perfection, the notion of "teleiosis" discussed in the previous chapter. Recognizing the volume of fulfillment language is also necessary, bearing in mind how this drives the narrative and its Johannine retelling. It is possible, likely even, that such terminology is heard in negative terms, and, as noted above, as implying an end to Scripture's role now that it has been "completed" in/through Jesus's death. Assessing the notion of completion, Tom Thatcher raises this possibility: "in some sense, Jesus's words on the cross are 'finishing' what the sacred scriptures of Judaism started, a supersessionist claim that inherently challenges the authority of the brokers of the Jewish great tradition who demanded his execution."[59] This isn't so much anti-Judaism *per se*, but is more supersessionist in its aspiration, inferring that the Fourth Gospel assumes absolute priority in terms of its assessment of Scripture.

How might one respond to this? First, a point of clarification. At one level—and whatever significance we draw from 19.16—Israel's Scriptures do not from part of the trial's decision-making process, at least not explicitly so. Indeed, Jesus's trial is absent of any direct appeal to the *scriptural* necessity for his death, surprisingly so perhaps compared to the volume of scriptural/fulfillment language operative in 19.17–37. Although we have noted the significant amount of intertextual allusion operative across the trial scene, its deployment goes beyond the "legal" dimension to the trial's progression. And, as discussed above, both 18.31 and 19.7 appeal to νόμος rather than γραφή as the presenting context for decision-making; the comparative silence (compared to 19.17–37) on matters of scriptural fulfillment remains somewhat loud. Likewise, neither is there any explicit *scriptural* warrant to depict the Jews in negative terms; their Johannine portrayal remains highly problematic, of course, and that is not to deny that such elements feature prominently in the Johannine account. John 19.16 remains an ethical interpretative crux. But Scripture is not a contributory factor to it, at least not primarily so.

At the same time, though, this may be special pleading, and some association with the Scriptures may nonetheless be implied within the Passion's negative portrayal of οἱ Ἰουδαῖοι. For example, if παραδίδωμι, a theme-word of the trial scene (John 19.16; cf. also 19.11), and one that reaches its ultimate outcome/climax at 19.16, does indeed intertextually evoke Isaiah 53 (cf. Isa 53.6, 53.12), and/or forms part of a wider Suffering Servant matrix, then the verse could be said to bear some anti-Jewish sentiment. YHWH's action of handing the Servant over for sins places such sinfulness in the Jewish camp, and, even if indirectly, scriptural warrant is found for Jewish responsibility for Jesus's death. Likewise, there may be some subtle or more indirect scriptural backdrop to 19.15—"we have no king but the emperor." Ford observes that this is in some sense a *scriptural* comment, in that Scripture declares this to be a blasphemy.[60] It is, though, a more deductive claim, and John does not explicitly specify 19.15 in scriptural terms.

One other possible anti-Jewish element of the Passion Narrative, and one which explicitly draws on scriptural warrant, is the contention of 19.37: "they will look upon the one whom they pierced." Sheridan has argued that the Fourth Gospel portrays this as a reference to the Jews' responsibility for Jesus's death, and compares it with 8.28–29 and 8.12–27 in terms of demonstrating the Fourth Gospel's anti-Jewishness. The "seeing" is thus not salvific; their "looking" on Jesus is instead indicative of their sinfulness and non-belief in Jesus.[61] However, as noted previously, it is difficult to make this application; although, with Sheridan, there is intratextual potential to make the connection, it does not seem the most straightforward reading of the narrative. Even though the verbal form changes between 19.34 and 19.37, the soldiers remain the primary agents of piercing in both instances and the most straightforward subject of both 19.37 verbs. And it is harder to see (pun intended) how this extends to the language around non-belief; "seeing is believing" and anticipates some form of salvation hope.

In sum therefore, we might say that John's Passion Narrative itself remains problematic in terms of its presentation of the Jews. It is difficult to get around the 'othering' that the text sets forth. But its use of Scripture is not necessarily an ingredient in that negative portrayal, or at least it remains ambiguous as to whether/how it does so. The christological hermeneutic it brings to the text is prominent of course, but that is not a negative imposition onto Scripture, or at least not in a way that demonstratively presents as anti-Jewish.

Perhaps then, we have a more complex picture than one that merely asserts the anti-Jewish nature of John's Passion Narrative, prominent as that characteristic recognizably continues to be. We might say that what defines "Jewishness," what characterizes it, is reworked by the Passion retelling. It does not speak literally of a *new* Jewishness, but at the very least, it recalibrates that Jewish identity, its festivals and worship for example, and the Scriptures form an integral part of this re-orientation. But their part is outworked differently, to a more limited extent than other concepts or motifs within the Fourth Gospel, and this testifies to the significant role Scripture *continues* to have in its perfected form (and alongside John's own γραφή testimony). As Fuglseth notes: "If the Johannine readers had the same attitude toward the temple as the attitude possibly inherited in the references of the scripture, the temple would neither have been rejected nor neglected."[62] This does not completely exonerate Scripture from anti-Jewish characterization, but it at least relativizes any alleged complicity in it.

CONCLUSION—THE FOURTH GOSPEL AS SCRIPTURE

Reflecting on the self-avowed authority of the Fourth Gospel, Suzanne Luther ponders: "Does the Gospel go beyond the mere claim of telling past events by creating or constructing a new authoritative narrative, a new γραφή?"[63] The answer to Lehne's question, we suggest, is yes. We have ventured that John explicitly invests its narrative with scriptural warrant, whether through ascribing γραφή status to the words of Jesus, whether through its avowed claim to perfect Israel's Scripture, or whether through its internal self-referential, self-fulfilling dimension (as in John 21). We have argued that this impacts then on how "Scripture" operates in John's Passion retelling, particularly after the teleiosis of Israel's Scriptures in 19.28. The evangelist's scriptural lens becomes increasingly bi-focal, drawing on both external and internal γραφή material, both the received Jewish Scriptures and the (new) scriptural witness the Gospel itself attests. The Passion Narrative's use of Scripture thus testifies both to its own sense of what Scripture is and its own sense of being Scripture.

A new γραφή thus emerges. Scripture is redefined as a new entity, one that includes both the texts of Israel's Scriptures and the content of the Fourth Gospel. Scripture continues to be active post- its teleiosis, with even more efficacy, but what Scripture *is* has changed or evolved because of its usage in John's Passion retelling. And in the light of both its christological fulfillment and the determinative Gospel opening (1.1), this new γραφή, this combination of Johannine discourse and scriptural teleiosis, may be better "defined" as Λόγος. The new narrative John elicits is done so under the auspices of the Word, and its perfected status and character is enabled by the action of the enfleshed Word. Israel's Scripture, and that presented by the Fourth Gospel, continue to speak, and do so ultimately in service of Jesus Christ.

We might also invoke the Janus characterization once more. When Hays advocates for the gospel writers "reading backwards," he recognizes that "the intertextual semantic effects can flow in both directions: an earlier text can illuminate a later one, and vice versa."[64] The scriptural exchange is thus dialogical, and fruitfully so. Coupled with this, and complementary to it, Ford advocates for a distinctively Johannine approach of "reading forwards," under the inspiration of the Paraclete, seeking after fresh meaning of the Scriptures and of "the ongoing drama of following the risen Jesus."[65] This enables both a purposeful forward-orientated life for Scripture (whether that of Israel or the Fourth Gospel itself), as the reader explores and develops what it means to be a follower of Jesus. Because the Paraclete is the One who leads into truth, and because the Scriptures are that which reveal the truth about Jesus, scriptural teleiosis and the work/gift of the Paraclete are closely aligned, conceptually and temporally. Just as the Fourth Gospel's first readers were brought into deeper understanding of the Jewish Scriptures, so the modern author is led by the Paraclete into further perception of Scripture's truth. Reading the Scripture that is the Fourth Gospel yields additional insight onto the Scriptures of Israel, and vice versa; once again, the process is mutually informing.

NOTES

1. So Menken, "What Authority," 201: "the Gospel replaces its protagonist, Jesus, so that it has the same impact on people as Jesus had; the Gospel is a new Holy Scripture, fulfilling and exceeding the old Scriptures."

2. Beutler, "Use," 154.

3. Chris Keith, "The Competitive Textualization of the Jesus Tradition in John 20:30–31 and 21:24–25," *CBQ* 78 (2016): 327. Similarly so Senior, *Passion in John*, 53: "the sayings of Jesus already bear the aura of authority the early community attributed to the Old Testament."

4. Keener, *Gospel*, 2.1215.

5. See further D. Moody Smith, "When Did the Gospels Become Scripture?," *JBL* 119 (2000): 3–20.

6. Obermann, *Erfüllung*, 420–21: "eine Art neuer 'heiliger Schrift.'"

7. Obermann, *Erfüllung*, 430: "das Joh als autoritative und in seiner Dignität der Schrift nahekommende Schrift der johanneischen Gemeinde dar."

8. Obermann, *Erfüllung*, 430. He earlier speaks of the Gospel's "nearness" to the circle of scriptural writing (420), thereby perhaps implying some distinction or differentiation.

9. In this regard, Menken moots an allusion to Ezek 48:35 LXX in John 20:31.

10. Menken, "What Authority," 201.

11. Menken, "What Authority," 194.

12. Chennattu, "Scripture," 185.

13. Sheridan, *Retelling*, 32.

14. Julia D. Lindenlaub, "The Beloved Disciple as Interpreter and Author of Scripture in the Gospel of John" (PhD dissertation, University of Edinburgh, 2020), 112.

15. Wolfgang Kraus, "Johannes und das Alte Testament: Überlegungen zum Umgang mit der Schrift im Johannesevangelium im Horizont Biblischer Theologie," *ZNW* 88 (1997), 18: "Mit dem bisher stets für die Schrift geltenden und jetzt auf das eigene Evangelium bezogenen γέγραπται in 20,31 wird dem AT als γραφή das Evangelium *zumindest gleich—wenn nicht gar: übergeordnet.*"

16. Francis J. Moloney, "The Gospel of John as Scripture," *CBQ* 67 (2005): 466. Moloney also draws attention to the programmatic function of the Prologue in this regard: "For the religion of Israel, Scripture (ἡ γραφή) was the definitive revelation of the word (ὁ λόγος) of God" (460).

17. Cf. for example Byrne, "Step," 149–56.

18. The same both/and dimension likely extends to 2.22 and 10.35—so Byrne, "Step," 152. He avers: "the reference [in 20.9] is likely to include Scripture in a holistic sense, that is, to Scripture as the revealed divine 'script' for the mission of the Son" (153).

19. Moloney, "End," 363.

20. Wendy E. S. North, "'The Scripture' in John 17.12," *A Journey Round John: Tradition, Interpretation and Context in the Fourth Gospel* LNTS 534 (London: T&T Clark, 2015), 54–55.

21. Moloney, "The Gospel of John as Scripture," 462.

22. See Ford, *The Gospel of John*, 27–28. The declaration of 1.1, Ford suggests, "is just one of many indications that it [the Fourth Gospel] has been written as Scripture." So also Menken, "What Authority," 196: "The actual form of the allusion [to Gen 1.1] even suggests that John claims for his gospel an authority higher than that of the Scriptures."

23. Chennattu, "Scripture," 183.

24. This is not to offer comment or adjudicate on the historical reality of the event, but merely to stress that, in narrative terms at least, the actuality of the event is fundamental to its purpose and inclusion.

25. Rhonda G. Crutcher, *That He Might Be Revealed: Water Imagery and the Identity of Jesus in the Gospel of John* (Eugene, OR: Pickwick, 2015), 151 characterizes John's depiction of it as "incredibly unusual, perhaps even miraculous."

26. Senior, *Passion in John*, 123.

27. We suggested that it is included within the scope of the 19.37 quotation, but that this is, at best, implicit.

28. Kevin J. Vanhoozer, "Body-Piercing, the Natural Sense, and the Task of Theological Interpretation: A Hermeneutical Homily on John 19:34," *ExAud* 16 (2000): 20–21, emphasis added.

29. So *inter alia* Porter, *Sacred Tradition*, 146; Klink, *John*, 814.

30. Klink, *John*, 814. So also Polinski, *Scriptures*, 137: "The blood flowing forth from the side of the Pierced One attests to the *completed* sacrifice of the Lamb of God who bore the sins of the world as the Suffering Servant."

31. David M. Moffitt, *Atonement and the Logic of Resurrection in the Epistle to the Hebrews*, NovTSup 141 (Leiden: Brill, 2011), 265.

32. Cf. Jacob Milgrom, *Leviticus 1–16: A New Translation and Commentary*, AB 3 (New York: Doubleday, 1991), 711–12: "Blood . . . as life is what purges the sanctuary. It nullifies, overpowers, and absorbs the Israelites' impurities that adhere to the sanctuary, thereby allowing the divine presence to remain and Israel to survive."

33. The rite of purification is sounded at the start of the Cana account (2.6), and the footwashing episode may have some symbolic connection in this regard too. But these are relatively infrequent examples.

34. Lam, "Effusion," 209.

35. Keener, *Gospel*, 1153.

36. Sebastian A. Carnazzo, *Seeing Blood and Water: A Narrative-Critical Study of John 19:34* (Eugene, OR: Pickwick, 2012), 85 avers that the quotation of John 19.37 "was fulfilled by the event in John 19.34." That may be true up to a point, but the scriptural framework for 19.34 is wider than just the scope of 19.37/Zech 12.10. And the significance of 19.34 is more, one suggests, than being merely an "event."

37. So Kerr, *Temple*, 241: "it is difficult . . . to escape the connection of Jn 7.38, 39 with 19.34, where, from the pierced side of the body of Jesus (the eschatological Temple!), water and blood flow."

38. Thus Koester, *Symbolism*, 201 is right to note that the water from Jesus's side cannot "*fully* be identified with the Spirit," if that is meant to disassociate the breathing of the Spirit in 20.22 (emphasis added).

39. 7.38 is classified as a quotation by some (e.g., Freed, *Quotations*; Menken, *Quotations in the Fourth Gospel*) but not by others (Schuchard, *Scripture within Scripture*; Obermann, *Erfüllung*).

40. Moo, *Old Testament*, 220.

41. Crutcher, *That He Might*, 135.

42. The manna of Exodus 16 has just been referred to in the previous chapter so that discourse is already on the Fourth Gospel's radar.

43. Crutcher, *That He Might*, 137: "it is best to view the words 'as Scripture has said'... as directing the hearer's minds to the larger constellation of previous stream/river imagery in the OT rather than a rigid formula signifying the utterance of a direct Scriptural quotation."

44. On the exegetical questions so raised, see for example Lincoln, *Gospel*, 253–57.

45. So Crutcher, *That He Might*, 141.

46. Cf. John 19.37, the final climactic fulfillment of Scripture, offering a (continuous/present) invitation to see the pierced, crucified Jesus. If the recurrent summons of the Fourth Gospel is to "come and see" (1.39, 1.46, 4.29; cf. also 11.34), we might say that Scripture is being used to vindicate and to fulfill the evangelist's own visual invitation.

47. Thus two sets of testimony are juxtaposed—scriptural and eye-witness—both of which are "true" (19.35, 21.24).

48. This is not to suggest that Jesus's testimony was *not* previously "scriptural," but rather that its status as such has been manifestly demonstrated by the Passion narration, and particularly 19.28–30. And the Fourth Gospel reminds the reader that the association between Jesus's words and Scripture was an essentially post-Easter phenomenon (cf. 2.22 or 20.9).

49. Brown, *Gospel According to John*, 951.

50. Lindars, *The Gospel of John*, 587–88.

51. So Lincoln, *Gospel*, 479: "Both the blood and the water, then, point unmistakably to the theme of life, seen here as God's salvific verdict on the death of the one who has been presented as the divine agent in his mission of witnessing and judging."

52. It may also be characterized as anti-Semitic, but that is essentially an ethnic designation. See Ruth B. Edwards, *Discovering John: Content, Interpretation, Reception*, 2nd ed. (London: SPCK, 2014), 131–41.

53. The Fourth Gospel never calls Jesus a Ἰουδαῖος except for 4.9, and the general tenor of the Passion Narrative is to "other" Jesus from οἱ Ἰουδαῖοι—cf. likewise the scripturally resourced notion of 15.25 in that regard.

54. Sheridan, *Retelling*, 48, emphasis original.

55. As is potentially the case for all four Passion accounts—cp., for example Mark Goodacre, "Scripturalization in Mark's Crucifixion Narrative," in *The Trial and Death of Jesus: Essays on the Passion Narrative in Mark*, ed. Geert van Oyen and Tom Shepherd (Leuven: Peeters, 2006), 33–47.

56. Cf. Anton Dauer, *Die Passionsgeschichte im Johannesevangelium; Eine traditionsgeschichtliche und theologische Untersuchung zu Joh. 18,1–19,30* (München: Kösel-Verlag, 1972), 30: "Der Evangelist nimmt die Waffen des Gegners, das Alte Testament, das ihm als Gottes Offenbarung heilig ist, um ihn damit zu widerlegen."

57. Anthony Tyrrell Hanson, *The Living Utterances of God: The New Testament Exegesis of the Old* (London: Darton, Longman & Todd, 1983), 131.

58. So James D. G. Dunn, "The Embarrassment of History: Reflections on the Problem of 'Anti-Judaism' in the Fourth Gospel," in *Anti-Judaism and the Fourth Gospel: Papers of the Leuven Colloquium, 2000*, ed. Reimund Bieringer, et al. (Leiden: Brill, 2001), 57.

59. Tom Thatcher, *Greater Than Caesar: Christology and Empire in the Fourth Gospel* (Minneapolis: Fortress Press, 2009), 115.

60. Ford, *The Gospel of John*, 369.

61. Sheridan, "Pierced," 199–209.

62. Kåre Sigvald Fuglseth, *Johannine Sectarianism in Perspective: A Sociological, Historical, and Comparative Analysis of Temple and Social Relationships in the Gospel of John, Philo and Qumran*, NovTSupp 119 (Leiden: Brill, 2005), 269.

63. Luther, "Authentication," 163. She further suggests this has historical implications too: "Scripture quotations are used to establish a new authority, the authority of the Johannine narrative as an authentic account of history" (164).

64. Hays, *Echoes-Gospels*, 347.

65. Ford, "Reading Backwards," 79.

Conclusion

As noted in our introduction, Jesus's death is the focal theme of the Fourth Gospel and critical to its christological and soteriological claims. The cross is flagged at various points prior to the Johannine Passion, indicative of it being the Gospel's telic goal. Likewise, we recognized John's debt to Israel's Scriptures across its evangelistic terrain, and particularly in the Passion account, where the appeal to scriptural fulfillment in respect of Jesus's death reaches its climax.[1] The question our study has sought to address is the relationship between these two concepts, the extent to which the Jewish Scriptures, and John's engagement with them, informs the evangelist's Passion retelling. What do the Jewish Scriptures contribute to the Passion Narrative, what interpretative significance do they provide for the Johannine portrayal of Jesus's death? To pursue a theatrical motif, are the Scriptures merely a chorus line or supporting cast, or are they integral characters (or even character singular?) driving the narrative and plot?

Our study set forth a three-fold hypothetical proposal in response. First, we conjectured that Israel's Scriptures are fundamental to John's narration of Jesus's death (John 18–19), core to both the content and approach of the Passion retelling. If John's Passion Narrative is indeed, as we suggested in chapter one, the heart of the Fourth Gospel, then Israel's Scriptures provide the metaphorical heartbeat for that Passion heart. Second, we proposed that the status of Israel's Scriptures are impacted by their Passion usage, that they are perfected by the encounter and hence brought to a new stage of maturity. And third, we further ventured that this has ramifications for the Fourth Gospel, too, and that the latter's handling of the Scriptures attests its own γραφή credentials. Through its association with the Jewish Scriptures, the Fourth Gospel's scriptural credentials are espoused, demonstrated, evidenced—fulfilled even. John uses Scripture to perfect Scripture.

These three thesis elements are integrally related, exhibiting a triangular interplay. In the light of the Johannine engagement with Israel's Scriptures, a new Scriptural entity, a new γραφή, is so formed, combining the perfected testimony of the Jewish Scriptures and the witness of the Fourth Evangelist. They corporately testify to the significance of the Christ event.

Scripture—both that of Israel and that of the Fourth Gospel itself—is critical to John's presentation of Jesus's Passion, but the concept is fundamentally changed by the encounter. Quite simply, the combination of the Fourth Gospel's scriptural narration of Jesus's death and the pronounced teleiosis of Israel's Scriptures occasions something genuinely *de nouveau*. A "new" Scripture is born.[2]

Scripture is therefore not just central to John's Passion narration, but it is also integral to *how* the story is told, and *how* the reader is to make sense of the Passion event. Whether through quotation, allusion or narrative echo, Scripture guides the reader on how to interpret the focal significance of Jesus's death. The evangelist keeps certain key elements of its narrative unexplained or undetailed, and leaves its reader to fill in the gaps accordingly. Without the scriptural appeal (and fulfillment), the presenting crux of a crucified Messiah, the tension of how Jesus's death can be κατὰ τὰς γραφὰς, remains unresolved. But with the frequent intertextual and intratextual appeals the evangelist undertakes, the reader is enabled to draw on their scriptural knowledge and come to a view on how the death of John's Jesus is not just according to the Scriptures, but enacts their very purpose and perfection. Whether through John 19.37/Zech 12.10 visualizing the piercing of a divine figure, whether John 19.36 portraying the embodied fulfillment of Israel's Passover, or whether through various narrative reminiscences of the Creation story to illustrate its completion, the Fourth Gospel uses Scripture to spell out how and why Jesus's Passion is the climax of his filial mission. Margaret Davies summarizes the Johannine practice accordingly:

> When Jewish feast are named, their ceremonies are not described, even when they provide the themes of discourses or are pertinent to details in the narrative. For example, of the features which link the sacrifice of the Passover lamb and Jesus's death, its timing (19.14), the presence of hyssop (19.29), the failure to break the bones of his legs (19.31–33) and the removal of the corpse before morning (19.38), only the third is made explicit (19.36) and the others have to be discovered from Exodus 12. These are gaps in the Johannine narrative *which have to be filled from Scripture to provide a full understanding*.[3]

This does not mean that the Passion Narrative deploys Scripture to tidy up every last Johannine ambiguity; Nicodemus's belief, for example, remains unresolved, as does whether Joseph of Arimathea's secret belief is sufficient for John's kerygmatic purpose. But Scripture remains the fundamental lens for making sense of Jesus's death; the *telos* of Jesus's ministry is simultaneously the *telos* of the Scriptures and the *telos* of their combined resolution. John simply cannot talk about Jesus's death without appealing to Scripture. And similarly, the evangelist cannot address Israel's Scriptures without invoking the way in which they impact, and are impacted by, Jesus's death and without transforming the respective γραφή status of both "scriptural" corpuses. The Johannine Jesus's Passion and Israel's Scriptures are inextricably linked; their respective fates and interpretation are interwoven.

Within such discussion, our analysis has drawn out further aspects to this portrayal to which we might draw attention. First, the volume of scriptural appeal varies across the Passion Narrative, or at least the way in which the evangelist appropriates scriptural intertexts differs in each constituent part. The third scene of the Passion triptych is the loudest in terms of scriptural volume, with the crucifixion scene particularly prominent in terms of quotational usage. By contrast, there appears to be comparatively little intertextual appeal in the trial before Pilate; instead, we have suggested, Jesus's own testimony therein likely functions as γραφή, and hence Scripture is resourced differently in this scene. We have also suggested that John's use of allusions function to give a consistent intertextual thread to the Passion Narrative. The Creation theme, in particular, runs throughout the Passion account, serving as a unifying intertextual feature for the whole Narrative.

Second, no one individual scriptural text governs John's Passion account. Some are more prominent than others, of course. The Psalms corpus are clearly significant (and likewise for the Fourth Gospel as a whole),[4] yielding several fulfillment quotations accordingly. Genesis imagery—or creation discourse—features prominently, as does Zechariah 9–14, and Isaiah 53 lurks across several aspects of the Passion retelling. But none dominate in the way that Psalm 22 seemingly dominates the Markan Passion, and/or no one text provides "the" primary interpretive key. On the contrary, it is the complex combination, the jigsaw of scriptural intertexts that necessarily operate in tandem (sometimes explicitly so as composite quotations or allusions) that yields the interpretive value for the Fourth Gospel. The Passion Narrative's scriptural portfolio is diverse and multi-faceted.

Third, and related, *how* Scripture is cited varies across the Passion Narrative. John uses the full variety of the intertextual tool kit available to it. Scripture functions as an indicator both of profound theological significance, critically so in 19.28 and 19.36–37, but equally extends to apparently more mundane matters (cf. 19.24). It can be cited as authoritative in unchanged form (19.24), but also be amended and reworked in composite mode (19.36, 37). Sometimes it is its macro status *qua*-Scripture that matters, sometimes it is the (micro) specificity of the passage that is most noteworthy. Sometimes there is significant intertextual metalepsis, as the 19.37 quotation or the 19.5 allusion both seem to demand, sometimes less so. Sometimes the allusion demands little pre-knowledge from the reader (in terms of the Passover, for instance, only a basic familiarity is really required), sometimes it demands far more detailed awareness of the citation context (of the composite quotation of 19.36, for example). Sometimes John's interpretation is consistent with other contemporary viewpoints (the vindication of the righteous suffer of Psalm 22, perhaps), sometimes it reads the scriptural text quite differently and draws out a somewhat dissimilar or novel interpretation. Isaiah's Servant, for instance, does not suffer in the expected fashion, indeed if at all, and the Passover becomes focused on cruciform rather than exodus imagery. Sometimes Scripture is fulfilled in/by Jesus, sometimes by third parties such as the Roman soldiers, or even by Pilate himself. John's intertextual hermeneutics are multi-dimensional.

Fourth, consistent with the post-Easter interpretive perspective adduced in 2.22 or 20.9, and extending the implications of the Fourth Gospel's γραφή status, attending to scriptural usage in the Passion Narrative deepens the subsequent reading of the *whole* gospel account. Jesus's διψῶ utterance (19.28), referencing Ps 69.3, acts to recall the memory of the Temple incident, and to underscore the relationship of that event to Jesus's death. Passion citation settles earlier "unresolved" scriptural references—whether the unsourced citation of 7.38, the ambiguity of 4.12–14 (a well that surpasses that of Jacob), the later remembrance of 2.17, or the absent quotation of 17.12. As we have seen frequently in our analysis, John's *inter*textuality informs, and is informed by, its *intra*textuality; and vice-versa. Israel's Scripture and John's own scriptural account are mutually informing.

* * *

We began our discussion with Martin Hengel's lament that "the question of John's interpretation of Scripture has been left fully in the shadows of research interests."[5] We noted that a number of recent studies have sought to address Hengel's disquiet, and that the Fourth Gospel's use of Israel's Scriptures has come firmly out of the shadows. It is now a well-resourced, well-examined topic within Johannine studies. We hope that our discussion, the first monograph study focused solely on scriptural usage in the John's Passion Narrative, can offer a further contribution to allaying Hengel's concern.

NOTES

1. So with Köstenberger, "Use of the Old Testament," 41: "There is no doubt that the OT was John's primary source—other than his relationship with Jesus—in composing his Gospel."

2. Working on this basis, or at least on the premise of the Fourth Gospel's own self-conception as Scripture, Ford, "Reading Backwards," 82 reflects: "One implication of this is that when he [i.e., John] teaches us, his readers, how to read his Scriptures he is also teaching us how to read his own writing." The creative, imaginative, intertextual, christological lens the evangelist brings to the Jewish Scriptures may be likewise

extended to the modern reader's engagement with the Fourth Gospel itself. Cf. also Stephen C. Barton, "Memory, Remembrance and Imagination in the Formation of Redemptive Tradition: Reflecting on the Gospel of John with David Brown," in *The Moving Text: Interdisciplinary Perspectives on David Brown and the Bible*, ed. Garrick V. Allen, et al. (London: SCM, 2018), 46: John "takes Scripture and Jesus tradition and reinterprets and develops them for changing circumstances."

3. Davies, *Rhetoric*, 24, emphasis added.

4. See Soards, "fulfillment," 251–67 for an assessment and cataloging of such influence.

5. Hengel, "Old Testament," 24.

Bibliography

Abbreviations are as per *The Society of Biblical Literature Handbook of Style*, 2nd. ed. (Atlanta: SBL Press, 2014).

Adams, Sean A. and Seth Ehorn, eds. *Composite Citations in Antiquity. Volume 1, Jewish, Graeco-Roman, and Early Christian Uses.* LNTS 525. London: T&T Clark, 2016.
———. *Composite Citations in Antiquity. Volume 2, New Testament Uses.* LNTS 593. London: Bloomsbury, 2017.
Ahearne-Kroll, Stephen P. *The Psalms of Lament in Mark's Passion: Jesus' Davidic Suffering.* SNTSMS 142. Cambridge, UK: Cambridge University Press, 2007.
Alkier, Stefan. "Intertextuality and the Semiotics of Biblical Texts." Pages 3–21 in *Reading the Bible Intertextually*. Edited by Richard B. Hays, Stefan Alkier, and Leroy Andrew Huizenga. Waco, TX: Baylor University Press, 2009.
Allen, David. *According to the Scriptures: The Death of Christ in the Old Testament and the New.* London: SCM, 2018.
———. "The Use of Criteria: The State of the Question." Pages 129–41 in *Methodology in the Use of the Old Testament in the New: Context and Criteria*. Edited by David Allen and Steve Smith. LNTS 597. London: T&T Clark, 2019.
Allen, David and Steve Smith, eds. *Methodology in the Use of the Old Testament in the New: Context and Criteria.* Library of New Testament Studies 597. London: T&T Clark, 2019.
Allison, Dale C. *The Intertextual Jesus: Scripture in Q.* Harrisburg, PA: Trinity Press International, 2000.
———. *Constructing Jesus: Memory, Imagination, and History.* London: SPCK, 2010.
Ashton, John. "John and the Johannine Literature: The Woman at the Well." Pages 259–75 in *The Cambridge Companion to Biblical Interpretation*. Edited by John Barton. Cambridge, UK: Cambridge University Press, 1998.
———. *Understanding the Fourth Gospel.* 2nd ed. Oxford: Oxford University Press, 2007.
Attridge, Harold W. "Giving Voice to Jesus: Use of the Psalms in the New Testament." Pages 101–12 in *Psalms in Community: Jewish and Christian Textual, Liturgical,*

and Artistic Traditions. Edited by Harold W. Attridge and Margot E. Fassler. Society of Biblical Literature Symposium Series 25. Atlanta: SBL, 2003.

Auvinen, Ville. "Jesus and the Devout Psalmist of Psalm 22." Pages 132–47 in *Jesus and the Scriptures: Problems, Passages, and Patterns*. Edited by Tobias Hägerland. LNTS 552. London: T&T Clark, 2016.

Bampfylde, G. "John XIX 28: A Case for a Different Translation." *NovT* 11 (1969): 247–60.

Barrett, C. K. *The Gospel According to St John: An Introduction with Commentary and Notes on the Greek Text*. 2nd ed. London: SPCK, 1978.

Barton, Stephen C. "Memory, Remembrance and Imagination in the Formation of Redemptive Tradition: Reflecting on the Gospel of John with David Brown." Pages 37–50 in *The Moving Text: Interdisciplinary Perspectives on David Brown and the Bible*. Edited by Garrick V. Allen, Christopher R. Brewer, and Dennis F. Kinlaw. London: SCM, 2018.

Bauckham, Richard. *Jesus and the Eyewitnesses: The Gospels as Eyewitness Testimony*. Grand Rapids, MI: Eerdmans, 2006.

———. *Jesus and the God of Israel: God Crucified and Other Studies on the New Testament's Christology of Divine Identity*. Grand Rapids, MI: Eerdmans, 2009.

———. *Gospel of Glory: Major Themes in Johannine Theology*. Grand Rapids, MI: Baker Academic, 2015.

Belle, Gilbert van, ed. *The Death of Jesus in the Fourth Gospel*. Leuven: Leuven University Press, 2007.

Beutler, Johannes. "Greeks Come to See Jesus (John 12:20f)." *Bib* 71 (1990): 333–47.

———. "The Use of 'Scripture' in the Gospel of John." Pages 147–58 in *Exploring the Gospel of John: In Honor of D. Moody Smith*. Edited by R. Alan Culpepper and C. Clifton Black. Louisville, KY: Westminster John Knox, 1996.

———. *A Commentary on the Gospel of John*. Grand Rapids, MI: Eerdmans, 2017.

Böhler, Dieter. "'Ecce homo!' (Joh 19,5): ein Zitat aus dem Alten Testament." *BZ* 39 (1995): 104–08.

Bond, Helen K. "Discarding the Seamless Robe the High Priesthood of Jesus in John's Gospel." Pages 183–94 in *Israel's God and Rebecca's Children: Christology and Community in Early Judaism and Christianity*. Edited by David B. Capes, April D. Deconick, Helen K. Bond, and Troy A. Miller. Waco, TX: Baylor University Press, 2007.

———. "The Triumph of the King: John's Trasformation of Mark's Account of the Passion." Pages 251–67 in *John's Transformation of Mark*. Edited by Eve-Marie Becker, Helen K. Bond, and Catrin H. Williams. London: T&T Clark, 2021.

Brant, Jo-Ann A. *John*. Paideia Commentaries on the New Testament. Grand Rapids, MI: Baker Academic, 2011.

Brawley, Robert L. "An Absent Complement and Intertextuality in John 19:28–29." *JBL* 112 (1993): 427–43.

Brodie, Thomas L. *The Gospel According to John: A Literary and Theological Commentary*. OUP, 1993.

Brown, Jeannine K. "Creation's Renewal in the Gospel of John." *CBQ* 72 (2010): 275–90.

———. "Metalepsis." Pages 29–41 in *Exploring Intertextuality: Diverse Strategies for New Testament Interpretation of Texts*. Edited by B. J. Oropeza and Steve Moyise. Eugene, OR: Cascade, 2016.

Brown, Raymond E. *The Gospel According to John*. AB 29. London: Chapman, 1971.

———. *The Death of the Messiah. From Gethsemane to the Grave: A Commentary on the Passion Narratives in the Four Gospels*. 2 vols. The Anchor Yale Bible Reference Library. New Haven, CT: Yale University Press, 2008.

Bultmann, Rudolph. *The Gospel of John: A Commentary*. Oxford: Basil Blackwell, 1971.

Burge, Gary M. *The Anointed Community: The Holy Spirit in the Johannine Tradition*. Grand Rapids, MI: Eerdmans, 1987.

Bynum, William Randolph. *The Fourth Gospel and the Scriptures: Illuminating the Form and Meaning of Scriptural Citation in John 19:37*. NovTSupp 144. Leiden: Brill, 2012.

———. "Quotations of Zechariah in the Fourth Gospel." Pages 47–74 in *Abiding Words: The Use of Scripture in the Gospel of John*. Edited by Alicia D. Myers and Bruce G. Schuchard. SBLRBS 81. Atlanta: SBL, 2015.

Byrne, Brendan. "A Step Too Far: A Critique of Francis Moloney's Understanding of 'the Scripture' in John 20:9." *ITQ* 80 (2015): 149–156.

Carey, Holly J. *Jesus' Cry from the Cross: Towards a First-Century Understanding of the Intertextual Relationship between Psalm 22 and the Narrative of Mark's Gospel*. LNTS 398. London: T&T Clark, 2009.

———. "Psalm 22 in Mark's Gospel: Moving Forward." Pages 121–37 in *New Studies in Textual Interplay*. Edited by Craig A. Evans, B. J. Oropeza, and Paul T. Sloan. LNTS 632. London: T&T Clark, 2021.

Carnazzo, Sebastian A. *Seeing Blood and Water: A Narrative-Critical Study of John 19:34*. Eugene, OR: Pickwick, 2012.

Carroll, John T. and Joel B. Green. *The Death of Jesus in Early Christianity*. Peabody, MA: Hendrickson, 1995.

Carson, D. A. "John and the Johannine Epistles." Pages 245–64 in *It Is Written: Scripture Citing Scripture: Essays in Honour of Barnabas Lindars, SSF*. Edited by D. A. Carson and H. G. M. Williamson. Cambridge, UK: Cambridge University Press, 1988.

———. *The Gospel According to John: An Introduction and Commentary*. The Pillar New Testament Commentary. Leicester, UK: Apollos, 1991.

Chennattu, Rekha M. "Scripture." Pages 171–86 in *How John Works: Storytelling in the Fourth Gospel*. Edited by Douglas Estes and Ruth Sheridan. RBS 86. Atlanta: SBL Press, 2016.

Clark-Soles, Jaime. *Scripture Cannot Be Broken: The Social Function of the Use of Scripture in the Fourth Gospel*. Leiden: Brill, 2003.

———. "Scripture Cannot Be Broken: The Social Function of the Use of Scripture in the Fourth Gospel." Pages 95–117 in *Abiding Words: The Use of Scripture in the Gospel of John*. Edited by Alicia D. Myers and Bruce G. Schuchard. SBLRBS 81. Atlanta: SBL Press, 2015.

Coloe, Mary L. "The Nazarene King: Pilate's Title as the Key to John's Crucifixion." Pages 839–48 in *The Death of Jesus in the Fourth Gospel*. Edited by Gilbert van Belle. Leuven: Leuven University Press, 2007.

———. *John*. Wisdom Commentary 44. Collegeville: Liturgical, 2021.

Coutts, Joshua J. F. "Revelation, Provision and Deliverance: The Reception of Exodus in Johannine Literature." Pages 269–86 in *The Reception of Exodus Motifs in Jewish and Christian Literature*. Edited by Beate Kowalski and Susan Docherty. TBN 30. Leiden: Brill, 2021.

Crutcher, Rhonda G. *That He Might Be Revealed: Water Imagery and the Identity of Jesus in the Gospel of John*. Eugene, OR: Pickwick, 2015.

Culpepper, R. Alan. *Anatomy of the Fourth Gospel: A Study in Literary Design*. Philadelphia: Fortress, 1983.

———. "The Theology of the Johannine Passion Narrative: John 19:16b-30." *Neot* 31 (1997): 21–37.

Daise, Michael A. *Feasts in John: Jewish Festivals and Jesus' "Hour" in the Fourth Gospel*. WUNT 2/229. Tübingen: Mohr Siebeck, 2007.

———. "Quotations with 'Remembrance' Formulae in the Fourth Gospel." Pages 75–91 in *Abiding Words: The Use of Scripture in the Gospel of John*. Edited by Alicia D. Myers and Bruce G. Schuchard. SBLRBS 81. Atlanta: SBL, 2015.

———. *Quotations in John: Studies on Jewish Scripture in the Fourth Gospel*. LNTS 610. London: T&T Clark, 2020.

Daly-Denton, Margaret. *David in the Fourth Gospel: The Johannine Reception of the Psalms*. AGJU 47. Leiden: Brill, 2000.

———. "The Psalms in John's Gospel." Pages 119–37 in *The Psalms in the New Testament*. Edited by Steve Moyise and M. J. J. Menken. London: T&T Clark, 2004.

———. *John: An Earth Bible Commentary: Supposing Him to Be the Gardener*. London: T&T Clark, 2017.

Dauer, Anton. *Die Passionsgeschichte im Johannesevangelium; Eine traditionsgeschichtliche und theologische Untersuchung zu Joh. 18,1–19,30*. München: Kösel-Verlag, 1972.

Davies, Margaret. *Rhetoric and Reference in the Fourth Gospel*. JSNTSupp 69. London: Bloomsbury, 1992.

Dewey, Arthur J. "The Locus for Death: Social Memory and the Passion Narratives." Pages 119–28 in *Memory, Tradition, and Text: Uses of the Past in Early Christianity*. Edited by Alan Kirk and Tom Thatcher. SemeiaSt 52. Atlanta: Society of Biblical Literature, 2005.

Dibelius, Martin. *From Tradition to Gospel*. New York: Charles Scribner, 1934.

Docherty, Susan. "New Testament Scriptural Interpretation in its Early Jewish Context." *NovT* 57 (2015): 1–19.

Dodd, C. H. *According to the Scriptures: The Sub-Structure of New Testament Theology*. London: Nisbet, 1952.

———. *The Interpretation of the Fourth Gospel*. Cambridge, UK: Cambridge University Press, 1953.

Duke, Paul D. *Irony in the Fourth Gospel*. Atlanta: John Knox, 1985.

Dunn, James D. G. "The Embarrassment of History: Reflections on the Problem of 'Anti-Judaism' in the Fourth Gospel." Pages 47–67 in *Anti-Judaism and the Fourth Gospel: Papers of the Leuven Colloquium, 2000*. Edited by Reimund Bieringer, Vanneuville Vandecasteele, and Didier Pollefeyt. Leiden: Brill, 2001.

Edwards, Mark. *John*. Blackwell Bible Commentaries. Oxford: Blackwell, 2004.

Edwards, Ruth B. *Discovering John: Content, Interpretation, Reception*. 2nd ed. London: SPCK, 2014.

Eklund, Rebekah. *Jesus Wept: The Significance of Jesus' Laments in the New Testament*. LNTS 515. London: Bloomsbury, 2015.

Eriksson, Lars Olov. *"Come, Children, Listen to Me!": Psalm 34 in the Hebrew Bible and in Early Christian Writings*. ConBOT 32. Stockholm: Almqvist & Wiksell, 1991.

Evans, Craig A. "On the Quotation Formulas in the Fourth Gospel." *BZ* 26 (1982): 79–83.

———. *Word and Glory: On the Exegetical and Theological Background of John's Prologue*. JSNTSupp 89. Sheffield, UK: JSOT Press, 1993.

Feník, Juraj. "Clothing Symbolism in the Elijah-Elisha Cycle and in the Gospel of John." *Studia Biblica Slovaca* 13 (2021): 49–73.

Fenton, John. *The Passion According to John: With Introduction, Notes, and Meditations*. London: SPCK, 1961.

Fletcher, Michelle. *Reading Revelation as Pastiche: Imitating the Past*. LNTS 571. London: Bloomsbury, 2017.

Ford, David. "Reading Backwards, Reading Forwards, and Abiding: Reading John in the Spirit Now." *JTI* 11 (2017): 69–84.

———. *The Gospel of John: A Theological Commentary*. Grand Rapids, MI: Baker Academic, 2021.

Fortna, Robert T. *The Fourth Gospel and its Predecessor: From Narrative Source to Present Gospel*. Edinburgh: T&T Clark, 1988.

Foster, Paul. "Echoes without Resonance: Critiquing Certain Aspects of Recent Scholarly Trends in the Study of the Jewish Scriptures in the New Testament." *JSNT* 38 (2015): 96–111.

Freed, Edwin D. *Old Testament Quotations in the Gospel of John*. NovTSup XI. Leiden: Brill, 1965.

Frey, Jörg. *The Glory of the Crucified One: Christology and Theology in the Gospel of John*. Waco, TX: Baylor University Press, 2018.

———. *Theology and History in the Fourth Gospel: Tradition and Narration*. Waco, TX: Baylor University Press, 2018.

Fuglseth, Kåre Sigvald. *Johannine Sectarianism in Perspective: A Sociological, Historical, and Comparative Analysis of Temple and Social Relationships in the Gospel of John, Philo and Qumran*. NovTSup 119. Leiden: Brill, 2005.

Garland, David E. "The fulfillment Quotations in John's Account of the Crucifixion." Pages 229–50 in *Perspectives on John: Method and Interpretation in the Fourth Gospel*. Edited by Robert C. Sloan and Mikeal C. Parsons. Lampeter, UK: Edwin Mellen, 1993.

Gerber, Edward H. *The Scriptural Tale in the Fourth Gospel: With Particular Reference to the Prologue and a Syncretic (Oral and Written) Poetics.* BibInt 147. Leiden: Brill, 2017.
Glasson, T. Francis. "Davidic Links with the Betrayal of Jesus." *ExpTim* 85 (1974): 118–19.
Goodacre, Mark. "Scripturalization in Mark's Crucifixion Narrative." Pages 33–47 in *The Trial and Death of Jesus: Essays on the Passion Narrative in Mark.* Edited by Geert van Oyen and Tom Shepherd. Leuven: Peeters, 2006.
Goodwin, Charles. "How Did John Treat His Sources." *JBL* 73 (1954): 61–75.
Gourgues, Michel. "Mort pour nos péchés selon Les Écritures." Pages 181–97 in *The Death of Jesus in the Fourth Gospel.* Edited by Gilbert van Belle. Leuven: Leuven University Press, 2007.
Green, Joel B. *The Death of Jesus: Tradition and Interpretation in the Passion Narrative.* WUNT 2/33. Tübingen: Mohr, 1988.
Hanson, A. T. "John's Use of Scripture." Pages 358–79 in *The Gospels and the Scriptures of Israel.* Edited by Craig A. Evans and W. Richard Stegner. London: T&T Clark, 1994.
Hanson, Anthony Tyrrell. *The Living Utterances of God: The New Testament Exegesis of the Old.* London: Darton, Longman & Todd, 1983.
———. *The Prophetic Gospel: A Study of John and the Old Testament.* Edinburgh: T&T Clark, 1991.
Hays, Richard. *Echoes of Scripture in the Letters of Paul.* New Haven, CT: Yale University Press, 1989.
———. *The Conversion of the Imagination: Paul as Interpreter of Israel's Scripture.* Grand Rapids, MI: Eerdmans, 2005.
———. *Reading Backwards: Figural Christology and the Fourfold Gospel Witness.* London: SPCK, 2015.
———. *Echoes of Scripture in the Gospels.* Waco, TX: Baylor University Press, 2016.
———. "Continuing to Read Scripture with the Evangelists: A Response." *JTI* 11 (2017): 85–99.
Heil, John Paul. *Blood and Water: The Death and Resurrection of Jesus in John 18–21.* CBQMS 27. Washington, DC: Catholic Biblical Association of America, 1995.
Hengel, Martin. *The Atonement: A Study of the Origins of the Doctrine in the New Testament.* London: SCM, 1981.
———. "The Old Testament in the Fourth Gospel." *HBT* 12 (1990): 19–41.
Hera, Marianus Pale. *Christology and Discipleship in John 17.* WUNT 2/342. Tübingen: Mohr Siebeck, 2013.
Hoskins, Paul M. *Jesus as the Fulfillment of the Temple in the Gospel of John.* Paternoster Biblical Monographs. Milton Keynes, UK: Paternoster, 2006.
———. "Deliverance from Death by the True Passover Lamb: A Significant Aspect of the Fulfillment of the Passover in the Gospel of John." *JETS* 52 (2009): 285–99.
Hoskyns, E. C. "Genesis I—III and St John's Gospel." *JTS* 21 (1920): 210–18.
———. *The Fourth Gospel.* London: Faber and Faber, 1947.

Hughes, Graham. *Hebrews and Hermeneutics.* SNTSMS 36. Cambridge, UK: Cambridge University Press, 1979.

Hurtado, Larry W. *Lord Jesus Christ: Devotion to Jesus in Earliest Christianity.* Grand Rapids, MI: Eerdmans, 2003.

———. "Remembering and Revelation the Historic and Glorified Jesus in the Gospel of John." Pages 195–213 in *Israel's God and Rebecca's Children: Christology and Community in Early Judaism and Christianity.* Edited by David B. Capes, April D. Deconick, Helen K. Bond, and Troy A. Miller. Waco, TX: Baylor University Press, 2007.

Jobes, Karen H. *John: Through Old Testament Eyes.* Grand Rapids, MI: Kregel Academic, 2021.

Juel, Donald H. *Messiah and Temple: The Trial of Jesus in the Gospel of Mark.* Society of Biblical Literature Dissertation Series 31. Missoula, MT: Scholars, 1977.

———. *Messianic Exegesis: Christological Interpretation of the Old Testament in Early Christianity.* Philadelphia: Fortress, 1988.

Karakolis, Christos. "'Across the Kidron Brook, Where There Was a Garden' (John 18,1): Two Old Testament Allusions and the Theme of the Heavenly King in the Johannine Passion Narrative." Pages 751–60 in *The Death of Jesus in the Fourth Gospel.* Edited by Gilbert van Belle. Leuven: Leuven University Press, 2007.

Keefer, Arthur. "The Meaning and Place of Old Testament Context in OT/NT Methodology." Pages 75–85 in *Methodology in the Use of the Old Testament in the New: Context and Criteria.* Edited by David Allen and Steve Smith. LNTS 597. London: T&T Clark, 2019.

Keener, Craig S. *The Gospel of John: A Commentary.* 2 vols. Peabody, MA: Hendrickson, 2003.

Keith, Chris. "The Competitive Textualization of the Jesus Tradition in John 20:30–31 and 21:24–25." *CBQ* 78 (2016): 321–337.

Kerr, Alan. *The Temple of Jesus' Body: The Temple Theme in the Gospel of John.* JSNTSup 220. London: Bloomsbury, 2002.

Klink, Edward W. *John.* Zondervan Exegetical Commentary on the New Testament 4. Grand Rapids, MI: Zondervan Academic, 2016.

Koester, Craig R. *Symbolism in the Fourth Gospel: Meaning, Mystery, Community.* 2nd ed. Minneapolis: Fortress Press, 2003.

——— "Why Was the Messiah Crucified? A Study of God, Jesus, Satan and Human Agency in Johannine Theology." Pages 163–80 in *The Death of Jesus in the Fourth Gospel.* Edited by Gilbert van Belle. Leuven: Leuven University Press, 2007.

———. "Narrative-Critical Interpretation of John 20." Pages 141–54 in *Come and Read: Interpretive Approaches to the Gospel of John.* Edited by Alicia D. Myers and Lindsey S. Jodrey. Lanham, MD: Fortress Academic, 2019.

Köstenberger, Andreas J. "John." Pages 415–512 in *Commentary on the New Testament Use of the Old Testament.* Edited by G. K. Beale and D. A. Carson. Grand Rapids, MI: Apollos, 2007.

———. "The Use of the Old Testament in the Gospel of John and the Johannine Epistles." *SwJT* 64 (2021): 41–55.

———. "Exodus in John." Pages 88–108 in *Exodus in the New Testament*. Edited by Seth M. Ehorn. LNTS 663. London: T&T Clark, 2022.

Kraus, Wolfgang. "Johannes und das Alte Testament: Überlegungen zum Umgang mit der Schrift im Johannesevangelium im Horizont Biblischer Theologie." *ZNW* 88 (1997): 1–23.

Kubiś, Adam. *The Book of Zechariah in the Gospel of John*. EBib 64. Pendé: J. Gabalda, 2012.

———. "The Old Testament Background of 'Ecce Homo' in John 19:5." *Biblica et Patristica Thoruniensia* 11 (2018): 495–519.

Labahn, Michael. "Scripture Talks Because Jesus Talks: The Narrative Rhetoric of Persuading and Creativity in John's Use of Scripture." Pages 133–54 in *The Fourth Gospel in First-Century Media Culture*. Edited by Anthony Le Donne and Tom Thatcher. LNTS 426. London: T&T Clark, 2011.

Lam, Tat Yu. "The Effusion of Blood and Water for Purity and Sanctity: Jesus's Body, the Passover Lamb, and the Red Heifer in Johannine Temple Christology." Pages 203–22 in *Johannine Christology*. Edited by Stanley E. Porter and Andrew W. Pitts. Leiden: Brill, 2020.

Lappenga, Benjamin J. "Whose Zeal Is It Anyway? The Citation of Psalm 69.9 in John 2.17 as a Double Entendre." Pages 141–59 in *Abiding Words: The Use of Scripture in the Gospel of John*. Edited by Alicia D. Myers and Bruce G. Schuchard. SBLRBS 81. Atlanta, 2015.

Lee, Dorothy. "Creation, Ethics, and the Gospel of John." Pages 241–59 in *Johannine Ethics: The Moral World of the Gospel and Epistles of John*. Edited by Sherri Brown and Christopher W. Skinner. Minneapolis: Fortress, 2017.

Lett, Jonathan. "The Divine Identity of Jesus as the Reason for Israel's Unbelief in John 12:36–43." *JBL* 135 (2016): 159–73.

Licona, Michael R. *Why Are There Differences in the Gospels? What We Can Learn from Ancient Biography*. New York: Oxford University Press, 2017.

Lieu, Judith. "Scripture and Feminine in John." Pages 225–40 in *Feminist Companion to the Hebrew Bible in the New Testament*. Edited by Athalya Brenner. London: Bloomsbury, 1996.

———. "Narrative Analysis and Scripture in John." Pages 144–63 in *Old Testament in the New Testament: Essays in Honour of J.L. North*. Edited by Steve Moyise. Sheffield, UK: Sheffield Academic Press, 2000.

———. "Text and Authority in John and Apocalyptic." in *John's Gospel and Intimations of Apocalyptic*. Edited by Christopher Rowland and Catrin H. Williams. London: Bloomsbury, 2013.

Lieu, Judith and Martinus C. de Boer. *The Oxford Handbook of Johannine Studies*. Oxford Handbooks. Oxford: Oxford University Press, 2018.

Lim, Timothy H. *Pesharim*. London: Sheffield Academic Press, 2002.

———. *The Formation of the Jewish Canon*. The Anchor Yale Bible Reference Library. New Haven, CT: Yale University Press, 2013.

Lincoln, Andrew T. *Truth on Trial: The Lawsuit Motif in the Fourth Gospel*. Peabody, MA: Hendrickson, 2000.

———. *The Gospel According to Saint John*. Black's New Testament Commentaries. Peabody, MA: Hendrickson, 2005.

———. "The Lazarus Story: A Literary Perspective." Pages 211–32 in *The Gospel of John and Christian Theology*. Edited by Richard Bauckham and Carl Mosser. Grand Rapids, MI: Eerdmans 2008.

Lindars, Barnabas, *New Testament Apologetic*. London: SCM, 1961.

———, *The Gospel of John*. New Century Bible. London: Marshall, Morgan & Scott, 1972.

Lindenlaub, Julia D. "The Beloved Disciple as Interpreter and Author of Scripture in the Gospel of John." PhD diss., University of Edinburgh, 2020.

Litwa, M. David. "Behold Adam: A Reading of John 19:5." *HBT* 32 (2010): 129–43.

Loader, W. R. G. "Revisiting Tensions in Johannine Christology." Pages 457–67 in *The Death of Jesus in the Fourth Gospel*. Edited by Gilbert van Belle. Leuven: Leuven University Press, 2007.

Luther, Susanne. "The Authentication of the Narrative: The Function of Scripture Quotations in John 19." Pages 155–66 in *Biblical Interpretation in Early Christian Gospels. Volume 4: The Gospel of John*. Edited by Thomas R. Hatina. LNTS 613. London: T&T Clark, 2020.

McCasland, S. Vernon. "Matthew Twists the Scriptures." *JBL* 80 (1961): 143–48.

McWhirter, Jocelyn. "Messianic Exegesis in the Fourth Gospel." Pages 124–48 in *Reading the Gospel of John's Christology as Jewish Messianism: Royal, Prophetic, and Divine Messiahs*. Edited by Benjamin Reynolds and Gabriele Boccaccini. Ancient Judaism and Early Christianity 106. Leiden: Brill, 2018.

Meeks, Wayne A., *The Prophet-King: Moses Traditions and the Johannine Christology*. NovTSup 14. Leiden: Brill, 1967.

Menken, Maarten J. J. "The Minor Prophets in John's Gospel." Pages 79–96 in *The Minor Prophets in the New Testament*. Edited by M. J. J. Menken and Steve Moyise. LNTS 377. London: T&T Clark, 2009.

———. "Genesis in John's Gospel and 1 John." Pages 83–98 in *Genesis in the New Testament*. Edited by Steve Moyise and Maarten Menken. LNTS 466. London: T&T Clark, 2012.

———. "What Authority Does the Fourth Evangelist Claim for His Book?" Pages 186–202 in *Paul, John, and Apocalyptic Eschatology: Studies in Honour of Martinus C. de Boer*. Edited by Jan Krans, L. J. Lietaert Peerbolte, Peter–Ben Smit, and Arie W. Zwiep. Leiden: Brill, 2013.

———. "Old Testament Quotations in the Gospel of John." Pages 29–45 in *New Testament Writers and the Old Testament: An Introduction*. Edited by John Court. London: SPCK, 2002.

———. *Old Testament Quotations in the Fourth Gospel: Studies in Textual Form*. Kampen, Netherlands: Kok Pharos, 1996.

———. "Observations on the Significance of the Old Testament in the Fourth Gospel." *Neot* 33 (1999): 125–43.

Michaels, J. Ramsey, *The Gospel of John*. Grand Rapids, MI: Eerdmans, 2010.

Milgrom, Jacob, *Leviticus 1–16: A New Translation and Commentary*. AB 3. New York: Doubleday, 1991.

Miller, Geoffrey D. "Intertextuality in Old Testament Research." *CurBR* 9 (2010): 283–309.

Miller, Paul. "'They Saw His Glory and Spoke of Him': The Gospel of John and the Old Testament." Pages 127–51 in *Hearing the Old Testament in the New Testament*. Edited by Stanley E. Porter. Grand Rapids, MI: Eerdmans, 2006.

Moffitt, David M. "'If Another Priest Arises': Jesus' Resurrection and the High Priestly Christology of Hebrews." Pages 68–79 in *A Cloud of Witnesses: The Theology of Hebrews in Its Ancient Contexts*. Edited by Richard Bauckham, Daniel Driver, Trevor Hart, and Nathan MacDonald. London: Bloomsbury, 2008.

———. *Atonement and the Logic of Resurrection in the Epistle to the Hebrews*. NovTSup 141. Leiden: Brill, 2011.

Moloney, Francis J., *The Gospel of John*. SP4. Collegeville, MN: Liturgical, 1998.

———. "The Gospel of John as Scripture." *CBQ* 67 (2005): 454–68.

———. "The Gospel of John: The 'End' of Scripture." *Int* 63 (2009): 356–66.

———. "'For as yet They Did Not Know the Scripture' (John 20:9): A Study in Narrative Time." *ITQ* 79 (2014): 97–111.

Montanaro, Andrew. "The Use of Memory in the Old Testament Quotations in John's Gospel." *NovT* 59 (2017): 147–170.

Moo, Douglas J., *The Old Testament in the Gospel Passion Narratives*. Sheffield, UK: Almond Press, 1983.

Moo, Douglas J. and Andrew David Naselli. "The Problem of the New Testament's Use of the Old Testament." Pages 702–46 in *The Enduring Authority of the Christian Scriptures*. Edited by D. A. Carson. Grand Rapids, MI: Eerdmans, 2016.

Moore, Anthony M., *Signs of Salvation: The Theme of Creation in John's Gospel*. Cambridge, UK: James Clarke, 2013.

Moore, Stephen D., *Poststructural-Ism and the New Testament: Derrida and Foucault at the Foot of the Cross*. Minneapolis: Augsburg Fortress, 1994.

Moyise, Steve. "Intertextuality and Historical Approaches to the Use of Scripture in the New Testament." Pages 23–32 in *Reading the Bible Intertextually*. Edited by Richard B. Hays, Stefan Alkier, and Leroy Andrew Huizenga. Waco, TX: Baylor University Press, 2009.

———. *Was the Birth of Jesus According to Scripture?* London: SPCK, 2013.

———. *The Old Testament in the New: An Introduction*. 2nd ed. London: Bloomsbury, 2015.

———. "Dialogical Intertextuality." Pages 3–15 in *Exploring Intertextuality: Diverse Strategies for New Testament Interpretation of Texts*. Edited by B. J. Oropeza and Steve Moyise. Eugene, OR: Cascade, 2016.

Myers, Alicia D. *Characterizing Jesus: A Rhetorical Analysis on the Fourth Gospel's Use of Scripture in its Presentation of Jesus*. LNTS 458. London: T&T Clark, 2012.

———. "Abiding Words: An Introduction to Perspectives on John's Use of Scripture." Pages 1–20 in *Abiding Words: The Use of Scripture in the Gospel of John*. Edited by Alicia D. Myers and Bruce G. Schuchard. SBLRBS 81. Atlanta, 2015.

Myers, Alicia D. and Bruce G. Schuchard. *Abiding Words: The Use of Scripture in the Gospel of John*. Society of Biblical Literature Resources for Biblical Study 81. Atlanta, 2015.

Nielsen, Jesper Tang. "The Lamb of God: The Cognitive Structure of a Johannine Metaphor." Pages 217–56 in *Imagery in the Gospel of John: Terms, Forms, Themes, and Theology of Johannine Figurative Language*. Edited by Jörg Frey, Ruben Zimmermann, and J. G. Van der Watt. WUNT 200. Tubingen: Mohr Siebeck, 2006.

North, Wendy E. S. *A Journey Round John: Tradition, Interpretation and Context in the Fourth Gospel*. LNTS 534. London: T&T Clark, 2015.

———. "'The Scripture' in John 17.12." Pages 45–56 in *A Journey Round John: Tradition, Interpretation and Context in the Fourth Gospel*. LNTS 534. London: T&T Clark, 2015.

———. *What John Knew and What John Wrote: A Study in John and the Synoptics*. Lanham, MD: Fortress Academic, 2020.

Novakovic, Lidija. *Raised from the Dead According to Scripture: The Role of Israel's Scripture in the Early Christian Interpretations of Jesus' Resurrection*. T&T Clark Jewish and Christian Texts Series 12. London: Bloomsbury T&T Clark, 2012.

Obermann, Andreas. *Die Christologische Erfüllung der Schrift im Johannesevangelium: Eine Untersuchung zur Johanneischen Hermeneutik anhand der Schriftzitate*. WUNT 2/83. Tübingen: Mohr Siebeck, 1996.

Omanson, Roger L. *A Textual Guide to the Greek New Testament: An Adaptation of Bruce M. Metzger's Textual Commentary for the Needs of Translators*. Stuttgart: Deutsche Bibelgesellschaft, 2006.

Oropeza, B. J. and Steve Moyise. *Exploring Intertextuality: Diverse Strategies for New Testament Interpretation of Texts*. Eugene, OR: Cascade, 2016.

Parker, Thomas J. "Jesus and Scripture: A Comparative Study of Hebrews, James, 1 and 2 Peter and Their Use of the Old Testament and Jesus Traditions." PhD diss., Vrije Universiteit Amsterdam, 2022.

Parsons, Kyle R. L. "Search the Scriptures: A Survey of Approaches to the Use of Scripture in the Fourth Gospel." Pages 1–28 in *Biblical Interpretation in Early Christian Gospels. Volume 4: The Gospel of John*. Edited by Thomas R. Hatina. LNTS 613. London: T&T Clark, 2020.

Patterson, Richard Duane. "Psalm 22: From Trial to Triumph." *JETS* 47 (2004): 213–33.

Perry, Peter S. "Relevance Theory and Intertextuality." Pages 207–21 in *Exploring Intertextuality: Diverse Strategies for New Testament Interpretation of Texts*. Edited by B. J. Oropeza and Steve Moyise. Eugene, OR: Cascade, 2016.

Peterson, David. *Hebrews and Perfection*. SNTSMS 47. Cambridge, UK: Cambridge University Press, 1982.

Polinski, Nathanael R. *That the Sciptures Might Be Fulfilled through Perfect Christian Worship*. Eugene, OR: Pickwick, 2019.

Porter, Stanley E. "Can Traditional Exegesis Enlighten Literary Analysis of the Fourth Gospel? An Examination of the Old Testament fulfillment Motif." Pages 396–428 in *The Gospels and the Scriptures of Israel*. Edited by Craig A. Evans and W. Richard Stegner. London: T&T Clark, 1994.

———. *John, His Gospel and Jesus: In Pursuit of the Johannine Voice*. Grand Rapids, MI: Eerdmans, 2015.

———. *Sacred Tradition in the New Testament: Tracing Old Testament Themes in the Gospels and Epistles.* Grand Rapids, MI: Baker Academic, 2016.

———. "The Linguistic Function of Biblical Citations in John's Gospel." Pages 121–36 in *Biblical Interpretation in Early Christian Gospels. Volume 4: The Gospel of John.* Edited by Thomas R. Hatina. LNTS 613. London: T&T Clark, 2020.

Puskas, Charles B. and C. Michael Robbins. *The Conceptual Worlds of the Fourth Gospel: Intertextuality and Early Reception.* Eugene, OR: Cascade Books, 2021.

Reim, Günter. *Studien zum alttestamentlichen Hintergrund des Johannesevangeliums.* SNTSMS 22. Cambridge, UK: Cambridge University Press, 1974.

Reinhartz, Adele. *Cast out of the Covenant: Jews and Anti-Judaism in the Gospel of John.* Lanham, MD: Fortress Academic, 2018.

Ridderbos, Herman N. *The Gospel According to John: A Theological Commentary.* Grand Rapids, MI: Eerdmans, 1997.

Rogers, Bret A. *Jesus as the Pierced One: The Use of Zechariah 12.10 in John's Gospel and Revelation.* Eugene, OR: Pickwick, 2020.

Rosik, Mariusz. "Discovering the Secrets of God's Gardens. Resurrection as New Creation (Gen 2:4b-3:24; Jn 20:1–18)." *Liber Annuus* 58 (2008): 81–98.

Schaser, Nicholas J. "Inverting Eden: The Reversal of Genesis 1–3 in John's Passion." *WW* 40 (2020): 263–70.

Schlund, Christine. *"Kein Knochen soll gebrochen werden": Studien zu Bedeutung und Funktion des Pesachfests in Texten des frühen Judentums und im Johannesevangelium.* Neukirchen-Vluyn: Neukirchener Verlag, 2005.

Schnackenburg, Rudolf. *The Gospel According to St John.* 3 Vols. Tunbridge Wells, UK: Burns & Oates, 1968.

Schuchard, Bruce G. *Scripture within Scripture: The Interrelationship of Form and Function in the Explicit Old Testament Citations in the Gospel of John.* SBLDS 133. Atlanta: Scholars Press, 1992.

———. "Form Versus Function: Citation Technique and Authorial Intention in the Gospel of John." Pages 23–45 in *Abiding Words: The Use of Scripture in the Gospel of John.* Edited by Alicia D. Myers and Bruce G. Schuchard. SBLRBS 81. Atlanta: SBL, 2015.

———. "Temple, Festivals and Scripture in the Gospel of John." Pages 381–95 in *The Oxford Handbook of Johannine Studies.* Edited by Judith Lieu and Martinus C. de Boer. Oxford: Oxford University Press, 2018.

Scott, Matthew. *The Hermeneutics of Christological Psalmody in Paul: An Intertextual Enquiry.* SNTSMS 158. New York: Cambridge University Press, 2014.

Senior, Donald. *The Passion of Jesus in the Gospel of John.* The Passion Series 4. Collegeville, MN: Liturgical Press, 1991.

Sheridan, Ruth, *Retelling Scripture: "The Jews" and the Scriptural Citations in John 1:19–12:15.* BibInt 110. Leiden: Brill, 2012.

———. "They shall look upon the One they have pierced: Intertextuality, Intra-Textuality and Anti-Judaism in John 19.37." Pages 191–209 in *Searching the Scriptures: Studies in Context and Intertextuality.* Edited by Craig A. Evans and Jeremiah Johnston. LNTS 543. London: T&T Clark, 2015.

———. *The Figure of Abraham in John 8: Text and Intertext.* First ed., Library of New Testament Studies 619. London: T&T Clark, 2020.

Shin, W. Gil. "Internarrativity and *ecce homo*: A Masterplot Underlying Zechariah 6.9–15 and 1 Samuel 9.1–11.15 and its Function in John 19.1–16." *JSNT* 43 (2020): 194–213.

Smith, D. Moody. "When Did the Gospels Become Scripture?" *JBL* 119 (2000): 3–20.

Smith, Steve. "The Use of Criteria: A Proposal from Relevance Theory." Pages 142–54 in *Methodology in the Use of the Old Testament in the New: Context and Criteria.* Edited by David Allen and Steve Smith. LNTS 597. London: T&T Clark, 2019.

Soards, Marion L. "The Psalter in the Text and Thought of the Fourth Gospel." Pages 251–67 in *Perspectives on John: Method and Interpretation in the Fourth Gospel.* Edited by Robert C. Sloan and Mikeal C. Parsons. Lampeter UK,: Edwin Mellen, 1993.

Sosa Siliezar, Carlos Raúl. *Creation Imagery in the Gospel of John.* LNTS 546. London: Bloomsbury, 2015.

———. *The Savior of the World: A Theology of the Universal Gospel.* Waco, TX: Baylor University Press, 2019.

Stanley, Christopher D. "Composite Citations: Retrospect and Prospect." Pages 203–09 in *Composite Citations in Antiquity. Volume One, Jewish, Graeco-Roman, and Early Christian Uses.* Edited by Sean A. Adams and Seth Ehorn. LNTS 525. London: T&T Clark, 2016.

Stibbe, Mark W. G. *John as Storyteller: Narrative Criticism and the Fourth Gospel.* SNTSMS 73. Cambridge, UK: Cambridge University Press, 1992.

———. *John.* Sheffield, UK: JSOT Press, 1993.

Stovell, Beth M. *Mapping Metaphorical Discourse in the Fourth Gospel: John's Eternal King.* Linguistic Biblical Studies 5. Leiden: Brill, 2012.

Suggit, John. "Jesus the Gardener: The Atonement in the Fourth Gospel as Re-Creation." *Neot* 33 (1999): 161–68.

Syreeni, Kari. *Becoming John: The Making of a Passion Gospel.* LNTS 590. London: T&T Clark, 2019.

Tabb, Brian. "Jesus's Thirst at the Cross: Irony and Intertextuality in John 19:28." *EvQ* 85 (2013): 338–51.

———. "Johannine Fulfillment of Scripture: Continuity and Escalation." *BBR* 21 (2011): 495–505.

Talbert, Charles H. *Reading John: A Literary and Theological Commentary on the Fourth Gospel and the Johannine Epistles.* Rev. ed. London: Smith & Helwys, 2005.

Thatcher, Tom. *Greater Than Caesar: Christology and Empire in the Fourth Gospel.* Minneapolis: Fortress Press, 2009.

Thompson, Marianne Meye. "'They Bear Witness to Me': The Psalms in the Passion Narrative in the Gospel of John." Pages 267–83 in *The Word Leaps the Gap: Essays on Scripture and Theology in Honor of Richard B. Hays.* Edited by J. Ross Wagner, Christopher Kavin Rowe, and A. Katherine Grieb. Grand Rapids, MI: Eerdmans, 2008.

———. *John: A Commentary.* New Testament Library. Louisville, KY: Westminster John Knox, 2015.

———. "Hearing Voices: Reading the Gospels in the Echo Chamber of Scripture." *JTI* 11 (2017): 37–48.

Vanhoozer, Kevin J. "Body-Piercing, the Natural Sense, and the Task of Theological Interpretation: A Hermeneutical Homily on John 19:34." *ExAud* 16 (2000): 1–29.

Vistar Jr, Deolito V. *The Cross-and-Resurrection: The Supreme Sign in John's Gospel.* WUNT 2/508. Tübingen: Mohr Siebeck, 2020.

Watson, Duane Frederick, *The Intertexture of Apocalyptic Discourse in the New Testament.* Atlanta: Society of Biblical Literature, 2002.

Wedderburn, A. J. M., *The Death of Jesus: Some Reflections on Jesus-Traditions and Paul.* WUNT 299. Tübingen: Mohr Siebeck, 2013.

Wheaton, Gerry. *The Role of Jewish Feasts in John's Gospel.* SNTSMS 162. Cambridge, UK: Cambridge University Press, 2015.

Whitenton, Michael R. *Configuring Nicodemus: An Interdisciplinary Approach to Complex Characterization.* LNTS 549. London: T&T Clark, 2019.

Wilk, Florian. "Paul as User, Interpreter, and Reader of the Book of Isaiah." Pages 83–99 in *Reading the Bible Intertextually.* Edited by Richard B. Hays, Stefan Alkier, and Leroy Andrew Huizenga. Waco, TX: Baylor University Press, 2009.

Williams, Catrin H. "Isaiah in John's Gospel." Pages 159–173 in *Isaiah in the New Testament.* Edited by Steve Moyise and M. J. J. Menken. London: T&T Clark, 2005.

———. "Composite Citations in the Gospel of John." in *Composite Citations in Antiquity. Volume 2, New Testament Uses.* Edited by Sean A. Adams and Seth Ehorn. LNTS 593. London: Bloomsbury, 2018.

———. "Persuasion through Allusion: Evocations of 'Shepherd(s)'and their Rhetorical Impact in John 10." Pages 111–24 in *Come and Read: Interpretive Approaches to the Gospel of John.* Edited by Alicia D. Myers and Lindsey S. Jodrey. Lanham, MD: Fortress Academic, 2019.

———. "'Seeing,' Salvation and the Use of Scripture in the Gospel of John." Pages 131–54 in *Atonement: Jewish and Christian Origins.* Edited by Max Botner, Justin Harrison Duff, and Simon Durr. Grand Rapids, MO: Eerdmans, 2020.

Windal, Martine. "«J'ai Soif » L'accomplissement de l'Écriture en Jn 19, 28." *Revue des sciences religieuses* 89 (2015): 25–46.

Witherington, Ben. *John's Wisdom: A Commentary on the Fourth Gospel.* Cambridge, UK: Lutterworth, 1995.

Witkamp, Leonard Theodor. "Jesus' Thirst in John 19:28–30: Literal or Figurative?' *JBL* 115 (1996): 489–510.

Wright, Arthur M. "The King on the Cross: Johannine Christology in the Roman Imperial Context." Pages 127–51 in *Johannine Christology.* Edited by Stanley E. Porter and Andrew W. Pitts. Leiden: Brill, 2020.

Wright, N. T. "Pictures, Stories, and the Cross: Where Do the Echoes Lead?" *Journal of Theological Interpretation* 11 (2017): 49–68.

Zimmermann, Ruben. "Symbolic Communication between John and his Reader: The Garden Symbolism in John 19–20." Pages 221–35 in *Anatomies of Narrative Criticism: The Past, Present, and Futures of the Fourth Gospel as Literature.*

Edited by Tom Thatcher and Stephen D. Moore. Atlanta: Society of Biblical Literature, 2008.

Zumstein, Jean. "Intratextuality and Intertextuality in the Gospel of John." Pages 121–35 in *Anatomies of Narrative Criticism: The Past, Present, and Futures of the Fourth Gospel as Literature*. Edited by Tom Thatcher and Stephen D. Moore. Atlanta: Society of Biblical Literature, 2008.

———. "The Purpose of the Ministry and Death of Jesus in the Gospel of John." Pages 331–46 in *The Oxford Handbook of Johannine Studies*. Edited by Judith Lieu and Martinus C. de Boer. Oxford: Oxford University Press, 2018.

Index

Abraham, 1, 134
Absalom, 113
Adam, 6, 112–13, 131, 136; allusions to, 115–21
Ajijah, 54
Akedah, 82, 134
Alkier, Stefan, 20, 25
Allison, Dale, 15
allusions, 107–36; adjudication, 24–27; function, 108–9; to Scripture 6, 23–24; thematic usage, 23–24, 108–9, 124
Annas, 134
Ashton, John, 95n82
Auvinen, Ville, 95n74

Balaam, 118–19
Bampfylde, G., 97n107, 167n22
Barrett, C. K., 45, 104n228
Barton, Stephen C., 200n2
Bauckham, Richard, 100n153, 141n96
Beloved Disciple, 2, 14, 29n18, 48–49, 79–81, 119–21, 124, 185; community founder, 120–21; and Scripture, 80, 174–75, 177–78; testimonial function, 80–81, 124, 146, 173–75, 178–80
Ben-Porat, Ziva, 136

Beutler, Johannes, 3, 9n27, 23, 33n72, 62, 92n31, 96n90, 115, 142n106, 172
blind man, 110
Bond, Helen K., 30n32, 93n55
Brant, Jo-Ann A., 104n227
Brawley, Robert L., 62, 74, 98n119, 101n174
Brodie, Thomas L., 55, 93n48, 95n87
Brown, Jeannine K., 101n175, 137n21
Brown, Raymond E., 62, 83, 92n38, 93n50, 96n99, 98n115, 101n173, 101n183, 102n196, 103n204, 103n214, 137n13, 151, 168n23, 186
Bultmann, Rudolph, 93n47, 128, 167n6
Burge, Gary M., 168n34
Bynum, William Randolph, 32n49, 75, 103n203, 103n215
Byrne, Brendan, 32n53, 193n18

Caiaphas, 92n32, 116, 134
Cana, sign, 120
Carnazzo, Sebastian A., 194
Carson, D. A., 45, 50, 67, 101n171
Chennattu, Rekha M., 149, 152, 173, 178
Clark-Soles, Jaime, 161, 164, 170n62
Coloe, Mary L., 56, 126, 137n22
Coutts, Joshua J. F., 108, 167n5

creation, 6, 13, 57, 110, 123, 132, 136, 145, 159, 199; completion of, 57, 110, 120–21; thematic allusion, 109–21
crucifixion, 14, 17–20, 99n149; cursedness, 17–19; of Jesus, 12, 14–15, 17–19, 44, 54, 79–80, 107–8, 118, 120; and lifting up, 11, 51, 55, 79, 88, 128–29; and scripture, 15, 55, 89, 105n252
crurifragium, 71, 79, 87
Crutcher, Rhonda G., 194n25, 195n43
Culpepper, Alan, 12, 34n84, 94n60, 97n111

Daise, Michael A., 38, 104n245, 123
Daly-Denton, Margaret, 28n9, 52–54, 88, 92n35, 94n70, 95n80, 99n145, 110, 138n31
Dauer, Anton, 195n56
David, 31n45, 52–56, 67, 87, 100n156, 113, 116, 176, 183; tomb of, 113–14
Davies, Margaret, 198
devil, 112–13, 118
Dibelius, Martin, 15
Docherty, Susan, 93n42
Dodd, C. H., 18, 29n15, 31n41, 123, 140n74
Duke, Paul D., 31n36

echoes of Scripture, 6, 24, 108–9, 130
Edwards, Mark, 101n170
Elijah, 58
Evans, Craig A., 19, 39, 96n100, 142n108
Eve, 6, 112, 118–21, 136
exodus, 124–25, 127; book of, 72, 181
Ezekiel, book of, 184

Feník, Juraj, 50–51
Fenton, John, 49, 92n32, 93n53
Fletcher, Michelle, 100n165
foot-washing, 48

Ford, David F., 64, 86, 99n135, 143n114, 177, 190, 192, 194n22, 200n2
Fortna, Robert, 12, 28n4
Foster, Paul, 34n76
Freed, Edwin D., 38, 93n51, 101n170
Frey, Jörg, 12, 93n51, 99n149, 128–29, 169n49
fulfillment: and audience, 154; christological nature, 154–59, 161; as event, 47–48; of Jesus's ministry, 4, 156–58, 181; and Jesus's words, 90, 175–77; micro/macro, 4, 151–53, 158, 175, 199; and quotations 6, 13, 19, 37, 44–50, 52–53, 57–61, 67–68, 78–84, 86–88; of Scripture 3–5, 11, 18–19, 49–50, 58–61, 74, 78, 116–17, 147, 150–59, 163–64
Fuglseth, Kåre Sigvald, 191

garden, 13, 109, 119, 123, 135–36; allusive image, 110–15, 117, 120–21; bookending function, 110; of Eden, 111–13, 118–19; of Gethsemane, 16, 114–15, 138n32, 138n36
Garland, David E., 32n51, 72, 104n239
Genesis, book of, 13, 101n175, 109–12, 114, 117–18, 123, 199; creation stories, 111–13, 115–21
glory: book of, 12–13; glorification, 17, 20, 32n53, 51, 66, 77, 114, 128–29; and revelation, 12, 84; and visualization, 2, 53, 77, 80, 84
Golgotha, 43, 54, 110, 116, 119
good shepherd, 14, 82, 113–14
Gospel of John: and atonement, 17, 66, 126–28; audience, 19, 78; and belief, 2, 25, 77, 80, 112, 129, 175; birth imagery, 121, 182, 187; characterization of Jesus, 8nn12–13; christological lens, 42, 45, 54, 83, 85–86, 93n42, 136n2, 146, 151–53, 185–86, 189; conception of Scripture, 89, 146–47, 157–58; eucharistic aspects, 182; eyewitness

testimony, 16, 50, 79–80; and feasts, 122–23, 127; fulfillment of Scripture, 3–5, 42, 58, 147–59, 174, 177–78; impact on Scripture, 147–64; intratextual character, 22, 178; intratextual reading as Scripture, 179–87; kerygma, 21; purpose, 2, 21, 25, 27, 79, 84; retrospective lens, 19–20, 29n17, 132, 137n23, 160, 173; scriptural self-identity, 4–6, 22, 172–79; scriptural usage, 1–5, 17–20, 22, 146–66; signs discourse, 12, 148; sources of, 16, 21; Synoptic relationship, 16, 30n31, 69; trial motif, 16

Gospel of Luke, 51; Passion Narrative, 97n104

Gospel of Mark, 95n74; Gethsemane discourse, 114; Passion Narrative, 58; scriptural usage, 51

Gospel of Matthew: and scriptural fulfillment, 40, 148–49

Gourgues, Michel, 142

Green, Joel B., 30n26, 93n46, 138n34

Hanson, A. T., 146, 170n60, 189

Hays, Richard, 8n12, 21, 24, 33n63, 34n79, 52, 55–56, 67, 85, 99n151, 103n200, 105n249, 108, 128, 156, 164, 169n46, 192

Hebrews, epistle to, 11, 160–61; and new covenant, 165

Hengel, Martin, 1, 96n100, 99n150, 137n11, 158, 167n18, 170n59, 200

high priest, 14, 93n55, 117

Hoskins, Paul M., 101n176, 141n88, 141n90

Hoskyns, E. C., 137n18

Hurtado, Larry W., 29n17, 84

hyssop, 65, 93n43, 97n103, 109, 125, 141n84, 141n85

Intertextuality, 6, 20–28; methodological considerations, 11, 20–28; role of reader, 22, 25–27, 109, 134; intertextual sources, 16

Intratextuality, 6, 22, 50, 59, 67, 74, 80, 89–90, 123, 178

irony, 44, 46, 49, 51–53, 55, 57, 61, 67, 88–89, 98n122, 115, 126

Isaac, 134, 136

Isaiah, 2, 87, 129–30, 165, 167n12

Jacob's well, 61

Jeroboam, 54

Jerusalem, 19, 81–82, 129, 183

Jesus: betrayal of, 112, 153; binding of, 134; blood of, 82, 124, 126, 181–83; blood/water outflow, 62, 80, 82, 89, 104n226, 121, 126, 179–87; body of, 50, 68, 126; bones of, 52, 69, 102n197, 122, 126; burial of, 14, 125, 131; clothing of, 44–48, 53–54, 74, 88, 117–18, 120, 162; controlling fulfillment, 46, 58–59, 62, 64–65, 68, 71, 79, 93n43, 96n95, 128, 143n120, 146, 150–54, 165; crowning of, 53; crucified messiah, 17–20, 31n40, 56, 129; divine creator, 111, 155; divine identity, 83–84, 119; enthronement of, 17, 53, 95n82, 116; exaltation of, 17, 31n36, 60, 128–29, 141n96; Historical Jesus, 15–16; humanity of, 115–18; innocence of, 14, 130; kingship of, 14, 17, 46, 53–56, 67, 100n155, 113–17, 125, 129, 131, 143n119, 176; and living water, 61, 82, 98n114, 181, 183–85; of Nazareth, 56; perfection of, 160–61; piercing of, 69, 77–84, 88, 102n197, 124, 131, 154, 179–87; priestly characterization, 49, 93n55; prologue, 2, 18, 193n16; public ministry, 2–3, 39, 70, 114, 123, 148; resurrection of, 1, 13, 81, 160; as righteous sufferer, 51–53, 61, 63, 65–67, 72–74, 158; sabbath working, 110; Son of God, 117; Son of Man, 19, 117; suffering of, 17, 66–67,

128, 131, 154; thirst of, 52, 58–61, 53–69, 97n107, 97n111, 152, 154, 183; trial before Pilate, 14–15, 115, 125, 139n56, 145, 176, 190; unbroken body, 50, 69–74, 158, 162; verbalizing psalms, 46, 60, 62, 68, 155; Word of God, 119, 122, 176–77; words as Scripture, 5, 39, 41–42, 68, 155–56, 175–77, 186
Jews, the, 92n32, 100n161; and Jesus's death, 15, 156, 164, 187–91; and piercing of Jesus, 79
Jobes, Karen H., 67, 87, 102n189, 137n25
Johannine Community, 49–50, 57, 80, 120, 162, 178
John the Baptist, 11, 124, 129
Joseph of Arimathea, 14, 82, 198
Judas, 45, 47, 112–13, 134, 143n122, 153, 156
Juel, Donald, 18, 31n45, 132
Justin Martyr, 18

Kähler, Martin, 12
Karakolis, Christos, 113, 138n32
Keefer, Arthur, 42
Keener, Craig, S., 94n58, 95n87, 137n17, 138n27, 143n124, 172
Keith, Chris, 172
Kerr, Alan, 141n95, 169n51, 194n37
Kidron valley, 110, 113–14, 126, 138n32
king, 14, 17; of the Jews, 53–55; kingly attire, 53
Klink, Edward W., 117, 181
Koester, Craig, R., 31n40, 98n122, 194n38
Köstenberger, Andreas J., 50, 52, 65, 82, 91n15, 92n40, 96n95, 98n120, 131, 200n1
Kraus, Wolfgang, 174
Kubiś, Adam, 60, 82–83, 104n238, 143n113

Labahn, Michael, 166

Lam, Tat Yu, 123, 141n82
lamb of God, 26, 34n86, 115, 123–24, 127, 140n70; slaughtered lamb, 131
Lappenga, Benjamin J., 100n161
Lee, Dorothy, 136n7
Lett, Jonathan, 88, 130, 142n108, 142n110
Lieu, Judith, 24, 29n13, 97n101, 103n217, 105n252, 105n257, 110, 146–47, 167n4
Lim, Timothy H., 169n40
Lincoln, Andrew, 93n47, 195n51
Lincona, Michael, 69
Lindars, Barnabas, 18, 31n43, 92n39, 102n197, 186
Lindenlaub, Julia, 174
Litwa, M. David, 118, 139n56
Loader, W. R. G., 140n75
Luther, Susanne, 105n264, 156, 191, 196n63

Malchus, 111, 133
Mary Magdalene, 82, 110–11, 121
Masoretic Text: as quotation source, 41, 76–78, 82–83
McWhirter, Jocelyn, 31n45, 102n190, 129
Meeks, Wayne, 117, 139n58
Menken, Maarten J. J., 2, 30n23, 32n59, 38, 41, 72–73, 81, 90n8, 91n14, 91nn19–20, 92n28, 100n160, 101n172, 102n186, 102n193, 103n212, 173, 193n1, 193n9, 194n22
metalepsis, 23, 51–52, 63, 199
Michaels, J. Ramsay, 94n62, 99n140
Milgrom, Jacob, 194n32
Miller, Geoffrey D., 35n88
Miller, Paul, 104n246, 169n36, 169n47
Moffitt, David M., 181
Moloney, Francis J., 29n18, 137n17, 143n120, 161, 166n1, 168n23, 174, 193n16
Montanaro, Andrew, 71
Moo, Douglas J., 42, 50, 94n62, 101n177, 164, 184

Moore, Anthony M., 110
Moore, Stephen D., 98
Moses, 2–3, 124, 167n12, 186
mother of Jesus, 49–50, 119–21, 168n35; community founder, 120–21
Moyise, Steve, 21–22, 25–26
Myers, Alicia D., 7n3, 33n60, 38, 92n33, 99n141, 169n50

Naselli, Andrew David, 164
Nathanael, 178
Nicodemus, 14, 82, 198
Nielsen, Jesper Tang, 34n86, 140n70
North, Wendy E. S., 30n31
Numbers, book of, 72, 183

Obermann, Andreas, 22, 51–52, 91n14, 97n102, 99n128, 148, 153, 166n1, 167n20, 173–74, 193nn6–8
Olives, Mount of, 113
Omanson, Roger L., 92n30

Paraclete, 13, 29n15, 110, 178, 192; handover of, 131, 155–56, 183–84; scriptural reference, 155, 183–84
Parsons, Kyle R. L., 7n3
Passion Narrative, 3–7, 11–21; anti-Jewish character, 188–91; book of the Passion, 12–13; centrality of, 12, 29, 60, 197; concept of, 15–16; fulfillment character, 153, 167n10; Janus function, 60–61, 152; Johannine form, 5, 11–17; Markan form, 12, 30n32; pre-Markan form, 15–16, 30n26; scope, 5, 11–13; Synoptic forms, 11, 13, 15–17, 45, 51, 70, 75; triptych structure, 14, 29n19, 86, 108
Passover, 6, 70–74, 101n169, 101n176, 109, 122–28, 132, 135–36, 145, 159, 181–82, 187, 199–200; day of Preparation, 125; meal, 125, 127; narrative of, 122–23; paschal lamb, 14, 34n86, 70–71, 73–74, 89, 101n169, 101n171, 101n176, 102n184, 122–28, 140n70, 158, 181; sacrifice of, 101n176, 126; slaughter of lambs, 125–26; thematic allusion, 122–28; timing, 125
Paul, 11, 17; Pauline epistles, 15
Perry, Peter S., 34n80
Peter, 14, 111–12, 133–34, 178
Peterson, David, 169n52
Philip, 2
Pilate, 113–17, 119, 156, 188, 200; and fulfillment, 92n32, 116–17; handwashing, 40; headquarters, 125, 127, 182; and Jesus's trial, 14, 113–17, 119, 130–31, 188; and titulus, 46, 54–55, 95n87
Polinski, Nathanael R., 77, 102n184, 194n30
Porter, Stanley, 93n46, 123, 126, 140n73, 140n76, 140n80
Psalms, book of, 23, 73, 199; numbering, 31n42; parallelism, 45–46
Puskas, Charles B., 22

Qumran: pesher, 42, 54, 57, 70, 91n23
Quotations, 6, 23; christological lens, 85; composite form, 23, 41, 44, 57, 72–73, 77, 85, 122, 136n3; definition, 23, 40–41, 61; and Fourth Gospel, 38–40, 84–90; identification of, 40–43, 184; introductory formula, 39–40, 58–61, 74, 176; limits, 107; and memory, 41, 71–72; and oral tradition, 41; *sensus plenior*, 42, 165; source, 41–42, 44, 85, 92n28; textual form, 8n9. *See also* fulfillment

Rahab, 181
reader, 8n9; interpretative responsibility, 24–27, 62, 79, 86, 109, 113, 116, 128, 134–35, 154; reading community, 16
Reim, Günter, 32n59, 71
Reinhartz, Adele, 139
relevance theory, 24, 34n80

resurrection narrative, 13, 39
resurrection of Jesus, 13; scriptural warrant, 1, 13–14, 39, 160–61, 174
Rewritten Bible, 42
Ridderbos, Herman N., 63, 77, 101n169, 143n117
Robbins, C. Michael, 22
Rogers, Bret A., 83, 104n239

Samaritan woman, 89
Samuel, 54
Saul, 54, 116
Schaser, Nicholas J., 118–19, 121
Schlund, Christine, 127
Schnackenburg, Rudolph, 2, 92n36
Schuchard, Bruce G., 7n3, 90n8, 94n60, 104n246, 169n42
Scott, Matthew, 68, 95n86
Scripture: concept of, 4, 6, 155, 159; and divine identity, 162; fulfillment modes, 48, 86–87, 158; fulfillment of, 18–19, 39–40, 42, 46–47, 55–60, 62–64, 74–75, 78, 80–81, 83, 86–87, 122, 128, 145, 148, 153, 180; as γραφή, 7n2, 21–22, 54–56, 95n87, 96n90, 104n226, 157–58, 172–73, 177; and Law, 163–64; oral usage, 71; perfection of, 4–6, 22, 46, 96n99, 160–62; *sensus occultus*, 164–65; *sensus praegnans*, 164–65; status of, 147–53, 159–64; *testimonia*, 18, 76–77; unbrokenness of, 162–63
Scriptures of Israel: and Jesus's death, 3–4, 11, 15, 17–20, 57, 149, 197–200; and Jesus's resurrection, 1, 5, 81; testimonial function, 2–3, 16–20, 38, 80–81, 148, 161; within the Fourth Gospel, 1–4, 146–64
seeing, theme of, 69–70, 77, 79–83, 89, 103n218, 112, 118–19, 124
Senior, Donald, 29n29, 96n97, 168n34, 193n3
Septuagint, 9n19, 41, 53, 61–62; and Old Greek, 9n19
serpent imagery, 112, 136

Sheridan, Ruth, 9n26, 33n60, 33n68, 38, 40, 82, 104n223, 161, 167n9, 174, 188, 190–91
Shin, W. Gil, 108, 116, 139n50
Simon of Cyrene, 143n125
Smith, Steve, 24, 34n82
Soards, Marion L., 201n4
soldiers, Roman, 121, 188; breaking Jesus's legs, 71; division of clothing, 44–46, 48–50, 55, 71, 86, 94n59; fulfillment of Scripture, 44–45, 50, 55, 60, 63, 71, 92n32, 93n43, 117, 154, 200; mockery of Jesus, 17, 116; piercing Jesus, 78–79, 81, 126, 191; wine offering, 58, 63, 67, 93n43, 97nn103–4, 124–25
Sosa Siliezar, Carlos Raúl, 52
Stanley, Christopher D., 33n74
Stibbe, Mark, 13–14, 93n52, 138n27
Stovell, Beth M., 28n2
Strauss, David, 49
Suffering Servant, 6, 34n86, 77–78, 109, 122, 128–32, 135–36, 158, 190
Synoptic Gospels, 16–17; passion accounts 16, 111; resurrection accounts, 111; scriptural usage, 2, 11, 13, 15–17, 21, 39, 49, 89, 158
Syreeni, Kari, 28n10

Tabb, Brian, 67, 99n128, 99n143, 100n154, 153, 168n27, 168n30
Tabernacles, feast of, 183
teleiosis, 3–5, 39, 60, 65, 78, 87, 96n100, 148, 150–66, 172–74, 183, 189, 192
temple, 152, 191; and body of Jesus, 126, 132, 187, 189; and death of Jesus, 49, 182; rebuilding of, 175; and resurrection of Jesus, 160, 189; temple incident, 67–68, 132, 200
Thatcher, Tom, 189
Theodotion, 77, 103n214
Thompson, Marianne Meye, 53, 90n11, 98n123, 100n155, 154, 169n37
titulus, 44, 46, 53–56, 116, 132

Tree of Life, 111, 118, 120
Trypho, 18

unity, 49–50

Vanhoozer, Kevin J., 180
vine, 113, 152
Vistar Jr, Deolito V., 58, 167n10

wine, 58, 64, 67–68, 88, 93n43, 97nn103–4, 125, 149, 152, 183
water, 61, 82, 88, 183–87
Watson, Duane Frederick, 20

Wheaton, Gerry, 122, 127, 169n48
Wilk, Florian, 32n58
Williams, Catrin H., 72–73, 77, 85, 109, 142n104
Windal, Martine, 98n115
Witkamp, Leonard, 65–66
Wright, N. T., 110

Zechariah, book of, 13, 23, 74–75, 80, 83, 100n168, 103, 117, 154, 184
Zimmermann, Reuben, 25, 35n89
Zumstein, Jean, 9n19, 22, 33n65, 34n85, 125, 128

About the Author

David M. Allen is academic dean at the Queen's Foundation for Ecumenical Theological Education, Birmingham. He has a particular interest in the way in which the New Testament uses the Hebrew Scriptures and the intertextual reading strategies this generates. He is the author of *According to the Scriptures: The Death of Christ in the Old Testament and the New* and *Deuteronomy and Exhortation in Hebrews: An Exercise in Narrative Re-Presentation*.